California in the American System

Fifth Edition

Craig M. Scarpelli

Mc
Graw
Hill
Education

5 6 7 8 9 LKV 24 23 22

ISBN-13: 978-1-260-93227-0
ISBN-10: 1-260-93227-3

Solutions Program Manager: Donna Debenedict
Project Manager: Jennifer Bartell
Cover Photo Credits: IS09AM1FT.jpg; 172798892.jpg

ABOUT THE AUTHOR

Craig M. Scarpelli is a member of the Department of Political Science at California State University, Chico. Professor Scarpelli received his BA in Sociology from the University of San Francisco in 1983 and his MA in Political Science from California State University, Chico in 1988. He has spent 32 years as a college instructor teaching up and down California at six community colleges, Chapman University, and the past 22 years at CSU, Chico. In addition, Professor Scarpelli was a District Chief of Staff in the California State Assembly in the early 1990's and also worked on two State Assembly campaigns, a Congressional campaign, and a state initiative campaign. In 2008, Professor Scarpelli was granted honorary faculty membership into the California State University, Chico Chapter of the Phi Eta Sigma National Honor Society. He currently lives in Chico with his wife Julie and their two daughters Jessica and Melissa.

CONTENTS

CHAPTER TWO

CALIFORNIA POLITICAL HISTORY   47

CHAPTER THREE

CALIFORNIA ELECTIONS

CHAPTER FOUR

THE EXECUTIVE BRANCH

CHAPTER FIVE

THE LEGISLATURE 113

ever increasing **population** (39.5 million), **water** (the state enduring drought conditions once again after two consecutive dry winters in 2020 and 2021), **agriculture**, **energy**, **transportation**, the **environment**, **health care**, and the rising costs of **education** are all challenges confronting the state. In this first chapter, we will examine these important California issues. How California addresses such problems involves the ongoing debate about the role of government at the federal, state, and local levels. This book is a comparative study of how California's government operates under our system of Federalism created by the United States Constitution. **Federalism can be described as two or more governments exercising power and authority over the same people and the same territory.**

In discussing California issues throughout this first chapter, we will provide examples of how federal and state government laws and policies developed, and the **Politics** associated in the crafting of the laws and policies. **Politics involves the process by which decisions are made.** It should be noted that when government makes laws, rulings, or policy decisions there will always be some groups satisfied with the government while other groups remain deeply unsatisfied. Government at any level is about making choices, and those choices come with political consequences. Elections occur every two years, and California voters are asked to make decisions not just on who should govern them, but on proposed laws and state constitutional amendments.

Subsequent chapters will detail California's admission as a state, the state's two constitutions, the Progressives legacy, the evolvement of democracy and the electoral process, the three branches of California government, the state budget, and local government. In examining these areas, the book will continually reinforce the comparisons and contrasts between California government and the federal government. We begin by examining key issues California is facing.

THE ECONOMY

California's economy is enormous, churning out a gross domestic product (GDP) of $3.1 trillion annually. **The Gross Domestic Product reflects the total output of goods and services produced inside of a nation's borders.** Based on GDP, if California were a separate nation, the state would rank as the fifth largest economy in the world.[1] Major areas of the state's economy include agriculture ($51 billion), construction ($89 billion), manufacturing ($319 billion), transportation ($75 billion), leisure and hospitality ($112 billion) information ($326 billion), wholesale and retail trade ($300 billion), finance, real estate and insurance ($558 billion), professional and business services ($391 billion), and government ($292 billion)[2].

CHAPTER

CALIFORNIA ISSUES

Former Beatle Paul McCartney was performing in Sacramento several years ago. During a break in the show, McCartney told the packed house at Arco Arena that he recorded his latest album in Los Angeles, and on a day off from recording took a drive up California's scenic Highway 1. "It was one of the most beautiful places I have been", he said and was the inspiration for one of the songs he wrote for his new album. McCartney was extolling the geographic virtues of California, a place of dense forests, towering mountains, rich agricultural valleys, sweeping deserts, and spectacular coastlines. The state is home to the entertainment capital of the world, has a diversity of agricultural crops unmatched, is a leader in the electronics and computer industry, conducts massive trade given its location on the Pacific Rim, and is a prime destination for tourists. California's population is as diverse as its geography and steadily increasing. Given the Mediterranean climate, coupled with the economic opportunities the state offers, it is not surprising that so many have sought to fulfill their dreams by settling here.

However, despite California's history of being a desired destination since it became the 31st state back in 1850, problems continue to plague the Golden State, some that have been long term (like water allocation) and some that are the result of a changing economic and demographic environment. And in the wake of the catastrophic fires of 2018 and 2020, coupled with the Covid-19 pandemic sweeping the planet, California faces some steep challenges in the future. The **economy** (though rapidly improving since the Great Recession of 2008) fell back into a tailspin when the pandemic forced the closure of thousands of businesses throughout the state, **housing** (a lack of affordable units) a

With the nation's largest population (39.5 million) California has lots of consumers, making the state a place companies want to do business in. However, California's taxation and regulatory policies on small and large businesses have elicited complaints from business interest groups, anti-tax organizations, Republican lawmakers, and conservative media argue that the state does not promote a pro business environment. These critics cite California's personal income tax, set at 9.3% for individuals making over $40,000 and couples earning over $80,000, as amongst the highest income tax rates in the country.[3] With the passage of Proposition 30 in 2012, state income tax has gone up dramatically for those making over $250,000. Proposition 30 created four new high income tax brackets, imposing tax rates of 10.3% on taxable income between $250,000 and $300,000, 11.3% on taxable income between $300,000 and $500,000, 12.3% on taxable income between $500,000 and $1 million, and 13.3% on taxable income over $1 million, infuriating conservatives.[4] In 2016, California voters extended the increased taxes from Proposition 30 by twelve years. Business interests and conservatives alike have also bitterly complained about a 2006 law that requires greenhouse gas emissions in the state be reduced to 1990 levels by 2020, dubbing the Global Warming Solutions Act a jobs killer.

Prior to the pandemic hitting the state in March of 2020, the unemployment rate in California fell to 3.9%, but with COVID-19 surging, Governor Gavin Newsom ordered a lockdown of the state, forcing schools and businesses to close and unemployment rose to 9% in January 2021.[5] With Governor Newsom's administration working to accelerate the availability of vaccines to blunt the spread of the virus, there is optimism a loosening of restrictions on businesses can allow them to re-open. However, even if many of the estimated 1.5 million lost jobs return, most of these jobs do not pay enough to cover the high cost of living in places like Los Angeles and the Bay Area. Prior to the pandemic, 17 million Californians were employed, some 2 million of them earning minimum wage, which, as of January 1, 2021 is set at $13 per hour for employers with 25 employees or less and $14 per hour for employers with 26 employees or more.[6]

The reality is that California workers find themselves in a stratified system consisting of a more dramatic divide in wages as compared to past generations. Upper tier employees (many of them college educated) are in the fields of technology, education, medicine, law, communications, finance, real estate, transportation, and government. Lower tier employees languish economically in retail, tourism, food service, agriculture, construction, and manufacturing, and it was these lower tier workers the pandemic hit the hardest because the lions share of the 1.5 million lost jobs in 2020 have come from the service sector industry. Many top tier employees were able to transition through zoom to work at home, an opportunity not available to lower tier employees. In addition, upper tier employees have seen their wages increase over the past few decades while low tier workers have endured a decline in income during the same period of time. Since 1995, incomes for the poorest 10 percent of California families have dropped 20 percent. In contrast, incomes for the wealthiest 10 percent of California families have increased 60 percent over the past thirty years.[7] Given this wide income chasm, obtaining a college degree is necessary for most upper tier employment and the economic benefits accrued from working in such professions.

The growing income gap, coupled with inflation (including housing, which we will address next), prompted the Democratic controlled State Legislature to approve a rolling increase of the minimum wage in 2017, which will plateau at $15 per hour in 2022, much to the chagrin of Republicans and business interests who believe increasing the minimum wage will result in a loss of jobs due to businesses leaving the state, and automation (in the form of robots) replacing employees.

HOUSING

Go to a California city public park during the day and chances are good of finding homeless people using the facility. Some homeless in California take advantage of shelters, but many do not. In 2017, it was estimated that over 78,000 of the 118,000 homeless people in the Golden State were unsheltered, a staggering number given New York, with some 86,000 homeless, had only 3,500 unsheltered in 2017.[8] Why the huge disparity in the unsheltered homeless populations of California and New York? The answer in part is due to a lack of affordable housing in California.

In 2017, the U.S. Census Bureau estimated California's population was growing by 300,000 annually. To provide adequate housing for the increased population, some 180,000 housing units need to be constructed, but based on data collected by state housing officials through the Legislative Analyst's Office, California is building on average each year only 80,000 housing units.[9] Not only is there a shortage of housing units being constructed, but of the ones going up, affordable housing projects are anything but a priority for local governments and developers.

There are several reasons affordable housing projects are shunned by communities across the Golden State. First, in 2011, Governor Jerry Brown, facing a $25 billion hole in the state budget, gutted over 400 city and county redevelopment agencies. These redevelopment agencies (funded through a share of property tax revenue) were the vehicles for local government to use when building affordable housing. However, that funding dried up when Governor Brown convinced the Legislature to eliminate redevelopment agencies.

Second, local governments, strapped for funds, have increased permit and development impact fees on builders, which has driven up the expense of housing projects. Combine these fees with a government requirement that developers using taxpayer funds pay a **prevailing wage (a mandated wage for construction workers that keeps pace with the cost of living)** and developers are motivated to construct higher end housing units catering to the affluent instead of affordable housing, something building consultant Richard Lyon noted, *"Because the costs have risen so much, a luxury product is the only thing that will pencil out."*[10]

Third, many local government elected officials are reluctant to support affordable housing units when community NIMBY's (Not In My Back Yard groups) organize opposition to such housing projects. NIMBY groups often fear a growth of low-income populations in the community will increase crime and lower property values. Ray Pearl, executive director of the California Housing Consortium sums up the problem, *"We've seen strong (Not In My Back Yard) opposition from those who view housing as an evil. That leads elected officials to making a political calculation to not cross those loud voices, and they just throw up their arms."*[11]

The lack of affordable housing not only is linked to homelessness but impacts millions of Californians struggling to make a living. For example, California's Department of Housing and Community Development has determined that over 1.5 million California households pay more than half of their income toward rent.[12] In 2019, median monthly rent in California was $1,657.[13] Some local governments have attempted to revive **rent control (laws that freeze the amount a landlord can charge per unit the date local ordinances are adopted)**, but interest groups representing landlords have opposed such laws, maintaining that rent control is counterproductive by diminishing the incentive to construct new housing.

At the state level, several proposed laws were introduced in 2017 to address affordable housing shortages. Senate Bill 2 by state Senator Toni Atkins imposes a $75 to $225 fee on real estate transactions, raising an estimated $250 million that would be used to finance the construction of affordable housing. State Senator Jim Beal's Senate Bill 3 would ask California voters to approve a $4 billion bond for housing construction, and another proposal calls for eliminating state income tax deductions of interest on a second home mortgage, calculated to bring in $600 million annually to augment funding of affordable housing.[14] However, even if all three of these measures pass, they represent a drop in the bucket of the $60 billion required to finance the construction of

180,000 housing units per year that will be needed to keep pace with California's growing population.[15]

The pandemic only accelerated the problem of affordable housing with the hemorrhaging of jobs in 2020. In response, Governor Newsom enacted a statewide eviction moratorium that was extended to June 30, 2021. Under the proposal, tenants who pay at a minimum 25% of their rent will not face eviction. The law also offers landlords rent subsidies (paid from a $2.61 billion federal fund) covering up to 80% of owed rent conditioned on the landlord not initiating eviction proceedings against the tenant.[16]

COVID-19 and the wildfires of 2018 and 2020 have only grown the estimated number of homeless people in California (determined to be 151,000). One of the policies Governor Newsom has enacted to mitigate the swelling number of homeless is using available federal funds to acquire $600 million in hotel properties. Governor Newsom wants to turn the purchased hotel and motel properties into permanent housing through a program called Project Homekey. By June of 2020, it was estimated that 14, 200 California homeless people were permanently living in these converted hotel and motel properties.[17] However, the NIMBY naysayers opposed Project Homekey; the cities of Bell Gardens, Lynwood, and Norwalk passing ordinances prohibiting hotels in their cities from housing the homeless.[18]

POPULATION AND POLITICS

California is a majority/minority state, meaning that non-white residents outnumber white residents in the sate. Diversity best describes California's people. Ethnic groups from virtually every corner of the planet are represented in the state's population. Latinos are the largest ethnic group (14 million), and the California Department of Finance estimates that Hispanics will comprise a majority of the state's population by 2042.[19]

Asians comprise the second largest non-white group (5 million), while some 2.5 million African Americans live in California. Concentrations of various ethnic groups can be found in communities all around the state. Hispanics reside in Southern California, Northern California, and the Central Valley. Arabs, Persians, Filipinos, Indians, Laotians, Hmong, Chinese, Japanese, Europeans, and Ethiopians (to name a few) are examples of the diverse number of ethnic groups that have settled in communities throughout the state.

Undocumented immigrants have been a portion of California's population for several years, prompting voters to approve Proposition 187 in 1994, a law that required California officials in such areas as education and health care to report to the federal government's Immigration and Naturalization Service suspected illegal immigrants utilizing state services. The law was struck down by a federal judge, but it highlighted Californian's frustration with illegal immigration in the state. But times have changed. It is currently estimated that 2.7 million undocumented immigrants reside in California.[20] With the growing Hispanic population impacting the political landscape, state lawmakers passed, and Governor Jerry Brown signed legislation that would grant drivers licenses to undocumented immigrants, legislation that took effect in 2015.

With the 2016 election of Donald Trump as President, a candidate promising tough policies against illegal immigration, California became one of the key states fully invested in resisting the Trump administration's immigration actions. The heavily Democratic state, which Hillary Clinton in 2016 and President Joe Biden in 2020 won overwhelmingly, opposed Trump's plan of constructing a border wall between Mexico and the United States. California's Legislature approved a **'Sanctuary State' bill that limited cooperation between state and local government law enforcement and federal immigration authorities in identifying undocumented immigrants for possible deportation.** In addition, the state engaged in a lawsuit against the Trump administration over federal executive orders signed by the President authorizing a travel ban from predominately Muslim nations. Another lawsuit challenged the President's authority to end the **Deferred Action for Childhood Arrivals (DACA) program, an Obama administration policy protecting some 800,000 unauthorized young immigrants from deportation**. The Trump administration threatened to cut federal funding to California in select areas in response to the state's defiance, but in June 2020 the U.S. Supreme Court upheld the DACA program, and with the election of Joe Biden as President in November 2020, threats of federal funding cuts evaporated.

While California's population (currently 39.5 million) continues to increase, it is changing. The change is not just attributable to a rising number of Latinos and Asians, which account for 80 percent of California's population growth.[21] California's shifting population also reflects an exodus of non-Hispanic whites from the state over the past two decades. According to the U.S. Census Bureau, between 2000 and 2010, the number of non-Hispanic whites residing in the state has decreased by 850,000. In 2000, 15.8 million Caucasians called California home, but by 2010 white residency in the Golden State dropped slightly below 15 million.[22] And it appears that a significant number of those fleeing California are heading to Texas. Between 2010 and 2019, the U.S. Census Bureau estimates that 687, 000 departed California for the Lone Star State.[23] But race is not the only demographic explaining the departure of people from the Golden State. Based on data provided by the Internal Revenue Service, those leaving

California are younger and comprise working class families making less than $50,000, something to be expected given the high cost of living in California.[24]

These population changes are significantly altering the politics of the Golden State. As California Field Poll director Mark DiCamillo points out, Latinos and Asians are inclined to vote for Democrats, and even though non-Hispanic whites continue to comprise 64 % of registered voters, they split their voter registration (40% Republican, 37% Democrat, and 23% non-partisan).[25] Overall, based on data by the California Secretary of State's Office 46% of California voters are registered as Democrats, compared to 24% registered as Republicans. The tangible results can be found in California's elections. In 2020, Democrat Joe Biden defeated Donald Trump by 4 million votes in California. Californians also elected a slew of Democrats to Congress and the State Legislature in the 2020 election. In 2021, 42 of the 53 seats California is granted in the U.S. House of Representatives are held by Democrats and both U.S. Senate seats have been Democrat since 1992. In the California Legislature (2021), Democrats hold two-thirds of the seats in both the State Assembly and State Senate, allowing them to approve measures that would otherwise require Republican votes. Similar results occurred in the 2018 election as Gavin Newsom easily won the election for Governor and Democrats continued their dominance in holding all of the statewide executive offices. It is also worth noting that California has voted Democrat in each presidential election since 1992.

Another key population demographic to consider is age. Based on projections from the California Department of Finance, by 2030 for every senior there will be three working age adults. Back in 1950, there were seven working age adults per senior citizen in California. An explanation for the diminishing ratio can be found in life expectancy for Californians increasing to 81 years, while the birth rate of 13.1 births per 1000 residents in 2013 was the lowest birth rate in the Golden State since 1933, when the nation endured the Great Depression.[26]

Estimates suggest that only 40% of Californians have a private retirement plan, and of those that do many of them do not have an adequate reserve built up for their retirement. As previously mentioned, California's two tiered economy consists of millions of lower tiered workers in agriculture, service sector, and other low paying industries with no private retirement plans available. A reduced working age population coupled with an increasing senior age population will place a tremendous burden on government run retirement programs that are partially funded by current employee contributions (like Social Security at the federal level and California pension programs CALPERS and CALSTRS for state workers).

WATER

On April 1, 2015 Governor Jerry Brown stood in a Sierra Nevada mountain meadow that should have been covered in snow. Instead, Governor Brown looked out on a dry strip of land as a water surveyor searched in vain for a place to take a measurement of the snowpack. When actual snow was found to measure, the results were bleak, a scant 5% of average snowpack for the year, shattering the previous record of 25%, which was recorded in 2014 and back in 1977. *"We're in an historic drought, and that demands unprecedented action"*, Governor Brown stated, emphasizing the seriousness California faced entering a fourth year of drought, *"People should realize we're in a new era. The idea of your nice little green grass getting lots of water every day, that's going to be a thing of the past."*[27] Using his executive authority, Governor Brown ordered mandatory water curtailment for local governments, cities, and residents; the first ever mandatory water cuts in California history. Governor Brown's Executive Order required **The State Water Resources Board** to do the following:

- Grant the State Water Resources Board the power to enforce 25% cuts in urban water use compared to 2013
- Require urban water agencies to set rates, fees, and penalties that compel residents to conserve water
- Mandate all newly constructed homes and buildings to incorporate drip irrigation or micro-spray systems to water landscapes
- Create incentives for state residents to replace 50 million acres of lawns with drought resistant landscape
- Compel agricultural water suppliers to file detailed drought management plans

Governor Brown's actions were historic in granting the **State Water Resources Board (a five member board appointed by the Governor and confirmed by the Senate to four year terms that regulates water allocation and enforces water quality standards)** such sweeping authority over water curtailment for California residents.

But what a difference two years can make. The winter of 2016/2017 was the wettest winter in California history, with statewide snowpack at an astonishing 196% of normal, ending the drought at the time. The record precipitation prompted Governor Brown to rescind his drought related executive orders of 2015, but he kept in place drought emergency water assistance for Fresno, Kings, Tulare, and Tuolumne counties due to depleted groundwater supplies, ensuring the continuance of emergency drinking water programs for those counties. The governor also allowed the State Water Resources Board to continue enforcing urban water use controls stating, *"This drought emergency is over, but the next drought could be around the corner. Conservation must remain a way of life."*[28]

Governor Brown was most prescient in his assessment of California's inconsistent weather patterns. After months of dry weather in 2018, wildfires scorched California in early November of that year, literally burning down the Northern California town of Paradise and forcing the evacuation of 28,000 people, many of whom never returned to the town. With cruel irony, rains came to Northern California about a week after Paradise burned in 2018. If the rains had arrived a week earlier, the town would have been spared, along with the 86 who perished in the Camp Fire, making it the deadliest fire in California history.

Two years later, in 2020, after another dry winter, California and the entire western portion of the United States were enveloped in smoke from an array of wildfires, many of them sparked by lightning that set dry brush on fire and resulted in a series of fires that torched a record 4 million acres in California, led by the August Complex Fire in Northern California that burned over 1 million acres.

In 2018, after the Camp Fire ravaged Paradise, President Donald Trump gave his reasoning for the pattern of devastating fires in California, *"There is no reason for these massive, deadly and costly forest fires in California except that forest management is so poor."*[29] But University of Alberta fire scientist Mike Flanigan, in explaining the rash of wildfires that have developed in places like Australia and California, said, *"The hotter and drier the weather, the easier it is for fires to start, spread, and burn more intensely."* Flanigan went on to note that for every 1.8 degrees Fahrenheit that the air warms, it needs 15 percent more rain to make up for the drying of the fuel.[30] Drier brush, whipping winds, and hotter summers make for a toxic mixture of conditions that are driving the flurry of wildfires California has experienced over the past several years.

California's persistent drought conditions have been attributed to cold Pacific Ocean surface temperatures scientists believe have caused the lack of precipitation in California over the past two decades. Once again, California is facing drought; the past two winters of 2020 and 2021 being extremely dry. Snow surveyors for the California Department of Water Resources, in April of 2021, measured the Sierra Nevada snowpack, discovering it held only 59% of its historical average of snow for this time of year. A reduction of the snowpack in California's vast 400-mile Sierra Nevada mountain range is significant given it provides about one-third of California's water supply to cities and farms.[31]

Historic drought notwithstanding, California's expanding population and industrial development over the years has created a never-ending fight over arguably the state's most precious resource. While the bulk of the snow and rainfall occurs in the northern third of the state, demands for water are greatest in the agricultural rich Central Valley and the heavily populated communities of Southern California. Since the Central Valley and Southern California depend on Northern California water, the persistent drought brought about large reductions in water delivery to those regions in 2015 and will most likely repeat itself again in 2021. The California Department of Water Resources, which operates the **State Water Project**, informed cities and Central Valley farms in the Spring of 2021 they can expect a mere 5% of contracted water supplies due to the drought.[32]

Diverting water from Northern California to the Central Valley and Southern California became a necessity as the agricultural industry expanded in the vast Central Valley and the population exploded in Southern California between the 1930's and 1950's. Two massive water projects of the twentieth century were undertaken to meet the demands of farmers and urbanites. **The Central Valley Project (CVP)** was developed by the federal government in the late 1930's after the state failed to finance the $793 million project. The CVP is a combination of rivers, dams, aqueducts, and power plants that traverse some 500 miles from the Shasta Dam in Redding down to Bakersfield. Water from the CVP is primarily supplied to farmers in the Sacramento and San Joaquin valleys, but the project also provides water for hydroelectricity and can be a vehicle to control flooding.[33]

In 1960, California voters approved a $1.75 billion bond authorizing construction of the **State Water Project (SWP)**. The 750-mile network of dams and aqueducts is the largest state-built water delivery and power generating system in the nation.[34] Anchored by the Oroville Dam, the SWP moves water through 19 reservoirs, 17 pumping stations, 8 hydroelectric power plants, and some 660 miles of open canals and pipelines. Based on contractual agreements, 70 percent of SWP water goes to cities and 30 percent is allocated to farmers.[35]

Despite these impressive water delivery systems, California, because of its industrial development and growing population, needs to enhance its water infrastructure. An average year of rainfall in California produces 71 million acre-feet of water, but only 37 million acre-feet of water is captured by the state's existing water infrastructure.[36] The current water capturing capacity is not sufficient to meet the state's demands. In times of drought, as the state has recently endured, California's deficiency in water infrastructure becomes magnified.

In response to this, California voters approved in 2014 a $7.5 billion water infrastructure **bond** package that will include water storage projects, drought relief projects, groundwater protection, and environmental preservation of the Sacramento San Joaquin Delta. **A bond is a tool used by governments to borrow money. In California, if the state wants to issue bonds (borrow money) to finance parks, schools, water infrastructure, or other capital-intensive projects, the bond must be approved by the voters. If the voters approve the bond, the state will borrow the money, but must pay off the bond, plus interest.**

But capturing and diverting water through the use of dams can have its pratfalls as the near collapse of the Oroville Dam on February 12, 2017 prompted the evacuation of 200,000 people from three Northern California counties (Butte, Yuba, and Sutter). A hole in the Dam's main concrete spillway developed and grew larger. As torrential rains caused Lake Oroville to rise beyond 900 feet and breach the dam's top, water began running down the emergency spillway that was not lined with concrete. Erosion developed in the hillside below the emergency spillway, compromising the integrity of the dam and raising the risk of a quarter million acre feet of water flooding communities in its path.[37] Fortunately the dam held, but the near catastrophe highlighted the need to improve California's water infrastructure not only to conserve water in drought years, but to ensure massive dams (the Oroville Dam is the tallest in the United States) do not fail.

Governor Brown's Water Tunnels Cut in Half by Governor Newsom

Another water infrastructure project was unveiled by Governor Jerry Brown and U.S. Interior Secretary Ken Salazar in 2012 involving the construction of two giant underground tunnels that would ship Sacramento River water south under the Delta to Central Valley farmers and Southern California cities.[38] The 40-foot wide and 30- mile-long tunnels were estimated to cost $17 billion and would be paid by agricultural districts and municipal water agencies representing 25 million residents and overseeing 3 million acres of farmland.[39]

However, conflict developed over the project as Northern California farmers and environmentalists opposed the tunnels; the farmers concerned about less water being available to them and the environmentalists worried about the damage to the Delta if too much fresh water from the Sacramento River is removed from the estuary. A group of Northern California cities and counties filed lawsuits in 2017 attempting to stop the project. The federal government's Environmental Protection Agency weighed in on the tunnels as well, highlighting concerns that diverting more freshwater from the Sacramento River under this plan would increase concentrations of salinity, mercury, bromide, chloride, selenium, and pesticides into the Delta.[40]

Compounding the problem of securing funds for the $17 billion water tunnels, some water districts, who were supposed to pay for the construction, are getting cold feet, threatening the entire project. In September 2017, Westlands Water District, representing Central Valley farmers, voted against helping to finance the water tunnels after concluding the cost of water delivery to the farmers would climb from $160 per acre-foot to $600 per acre-foot.

When Governor Gavin Newsom came to office, he put on hold the water tunnels plan in 2019, but in 2020 he renewed the project, only now there will be one water tunnel, not two. The revised plan will carry less water, but if completed would augment the **State Water Project**, which sends water to over 27 million Californians and 3 million acres of farmland.[41]

Other Water Measures

California's enduring drought problems compelled the state to take additional steps in efforts to preserve water. A state law passed in 2009 mandates any improvements to most California homes, apartments, and commercial buildings include the installation of low-flow fixtures (like toilets, faucets, and showerheads).[42] The state has also set aside some of the 2014 voter approved water bond money (over $1 billion) for **Desalination, a process to desalt seawater**, and a large San Diego county desalination plant opened in 2015.[43]

In 2014, the State Legislature passed and Governor Brown signed legislation allowing the state to regulate the use of groundwater, a source of water many California farmers turned to as a result of the state curtailing water deliveries from the Central Valley Project and the State Water Project during the drought. Agricultural interests in the state opposed government regulation of the groundwater and threatened legal action. We examine California's agricultural industry in the following section.

AGRICULTURE

California agriculture is a $51 billion juggernaut comprised primarily of giant corporate farms. Known as agribusiness, these corporate farms (along with the ever-shrinking small farmer) produce over 250 crops, making California the undisputed leader in agricultural production in the nation. The state supplies 45 percent of the fruits and vegetables and 25 percent of the table food consumed by the country.[44]

Providing such a large variety and volume of crops, California agribusiness has successfully locked in contracts with the government guaranteeing them a seemingly unlimited supply of cheap water. Governor Brown's 2015 order mandating water reductions of 25% did not apply to farms, and they continue to be exempt from paying more for the water they use (which in part explains why the Westland Water District voted against funding the water tunnels in 2017). A 2004 report on agribusiness water fees found that the average price farmers paid for Central Valley Project water was less than 2 percent of what Southern Californians pay for drinking water.[45] California agriculture utilizes a whopping 80 percent of the state's water supply, and the industry makes no apologies, arguing the water use is justified given the economic benefits the state reaps from being the nation's top crop producer.

Yet all has not been roses for agribusiness. Constant battles over water allocation with environmentalists and urban communities have endured over the years, and the aforementioned 2014 law allowing the state to regulate groundwater use has been vehemently opposed by the state's agriculture industry, especially given farmers received a fraction of the water they had been annually allotted through the Central Valley Project and the State Water Project during the 2015 drought and will be significant reductions in water once again in 2021.

But the drought is not the sole reason California farmers complain about water allocation. Central Valley farmer Larry Starrh, testifying at a 2014 House Natural Resources Committee field hearing in Fresno, told members of Congress he had to let 1000 acres of his land go dry due to water curtailment, blaming government environmental policies that protect fish like the Delta Smelt under the **Endangered Species Act (a 1973 federal law that protects species of animals and plant life that are in danger of extinction in their natural habitat)** as the reason he lost his water, not the drought, *"These water shortages were created and controlled by regulations that have been imposed and brandished like weapons,"* Starrh lamented, *"Sadly, in the real world, water is about power. Water is a weapon."*[46] The Trump Administration attempted to have more water pumped out of the Sacramento-San Joaquin Delta, rewriting federal government environmental rules that would allow more Northern California water from the Delta to be diverted down to Central Valley farmers. However, California sued the Trump Administration over the rule change, and with the election of Joe Biden as President in 2020, Central Valley farmers, like Larry Starrh, may not receive as much water from the Delta, even if drought conditions improve in the future.

But one farmer's problem can be another farmer's opportunity. As previously mentioned, farmers fortunate enough to own land with ample supplies of groundwater have not only used the resource to irrigate their crops, but have, in some cases, sold the water for a huge profit. In 2014, two Merced County landowners agreed to sell their water to the Del Puerto Water District in Stanislaus County. The deal involved the two landowners providing Del Puerto with 23,000 acre-feet of their well water a year for two years at a cost estimated to be $500 an acre-foot, equating to a multi-million-dollar pact for the two land-owners. Frustrated Merced County farmers showed up at a County Board of Supervisors meeting to oppose the deal, but the county could do little to prevent the two landowners from selling their groundwater because no Merced County ordinance existed to restrict the transfer of water out of the county.[47] The lack of groundwater regulation by the state allowed the Merced County landowners to negotiate such a deal. A few months later, the State Legislature passed and Governor Brown signed legislation granting the state the authority to regulate groundwater extraction.

Farm Labor

California's giant agriculture industry requires a steady labor force, and despite the criticism of illegal immigrants by President Trump during the 2016 presidential campaign, the reality is that many of the 400,000 plus agriculture workers toiling in the fields of California have worked under difficult conditions. Beginning in the 1960's, spurred by the efforts of Cesar Chavez and Dolores Huerta, farm workers began organizing in the state, culminating with the formation of the **United Farm Workers Union (UFW). The United Farm Workers was a union created in 1966 to represent farm workers and negotiate on their behalf with the growers for fair pay and better working conditions.** Much to the chagrin of the growers, who were not supportive of the UFW union, Governor Jerry Brown, during his first term as Governor, created the **Agricultural Labor Relations Board in 1975, a five-member board which guarantees stability in agricultural labor relations by mediating disputes between the growers and workers, and providing the means for field workers to vote in secret ballot elections for or against unionizing.**

Working conditions for farm laborers have improved, but the UFW has pressed the state to do more in providing a safer working environment after 13 workers died due to heat exposure in 2005. The state responded by issuing new regulations through **Cal-OSHA (the Occupational Safety Health Administration which protects workers from health and safety hazards on the job in most California workplaces).** The Cal-OSHA regulations mandated all outdoor employment sites make shade available and provide at least one quart of water per employee per hour.[48] However, those regulations did not require breaks be given to the employees, and since so many of the farm laborers are undocumented, many of them were reluctant to ask for breaks. Claiming 28 more workers died from heat exposure between 2005 and 2013, the UFW filed lawsuits against Cal OSHA, and in 2015 a settlement of the lawsuits was reached between the two parties. Terms of the settlement require Cal-OSHA to conduct more inspections, go after repeat offenders, and enforce a 2012 state law that water be assessable within 10 feet and shade be available within 200 feet. In addition, the settlement also provides that workers should not be punished for taking water breaks.[49]

Like other essential laborers who needed to continue working through the pandemic, farmworkers in California have been impacted by COVID-19. A 2020 joint study on California farmworkers conducted by the Clinica de Salud del Valle de Salinas and the University of California, Berkeley School of Public Health found one in five farmworkers tested positive for COVID-19 antibodies.[50] The study also revealed 7% of the surveyed farmworkers indicated they knew of a loved one who perished from the virus.[51] What has been a consistent problem for California farmworkers long before COVID-19 hit is adequate housing for them. Crowded housing conditions for those working in agriculture during the pandemic is a factor that can be attributed to the virus spreading through the estimated 800,000 California farmworkers.

In response to the dangers associated with working in California agriculture during COVID-19, the city of Coachella in Southern California passed an ordinance on February 10, 2021 requiring various industries (including agriculture) to pay their workers an additional $4 an hour for at least 120 days.[52] Coachella was the first city nationwide to make farmworkers and packinghouse laborers eligible for **"Hero Pay",** additional compensation for essential workers who have remained working during the pandemic. The Western Growers Association, the California Fresh Fruit Association, and Growing Coachella Valley, groups representing the agriculture industry that hire farmworkers in Coachella, filed a suit in Riverside County Superior Court in March 2021, asking the court to rule the city of Coachella "Hero Pay" ordinance unconstitutional.[53]

While the United Farm Workers laud the efforts of Coachella to augment the pay of fieldworkers during the pandemic, what the UFW believes would improve working conditions for farm laborers are more union members. In 2012, Governor Brown vetoed a bill that would have made it easier for farm laborers to become union members. Accordingly, the UFW felt betrayed by the Governor's veto given his past record; but in 2016, Governor Brown sided with the UFW, signing legislation raising overtime wages for agricultural workers incrementally over a four-year period that will require time-and-a-half pay for someone working in excess of 8 hours a day or 40 hours a week.[54]

Farm Subsidies

A constant refrain from farmers when agribusiness is criticized for government **subsidies** is "Farmers feed America!" That may be true, but American agribusiness is global, and a number of the crops grown in the United States are exported overseas. Spurred by the huge national debt ($28 trillion in 2021) the federal government has amassed, Congress approved significant changes to agricultural **subsidies** with the 2014 Farm Bill. **A Subsidy is a financial or other form of aid bestowed by government upon private individuals, companies, or groups to improve their economic position and accomplish some public objective.** The subsidy changes Congress **approved** targeted direct payments that farmers were given regardless of what they grew, crop insurance to protect from losses, and conservation money, which pays farmers to protect environmentally sensitive land.[55] While the changes eliminated guaranteed payments farmers received despite their crop yield or crop prices, farmers will continue to benefit from government subsidies. Based on a report by FAPRI (the Food and Agriculture Policy Research Institute), "Payments under the 2014 Farm Bill programs increase when crop prices fall." Because crop prices fell in 2015, FAPRI estimated that crop subsidies for farmers in 2015 would be $6.5 billion and crop insurance offered by the government will average over $8 billion a year for the next ten years.[56] Critics of agribusiness have called the subsidies 'corporate welfare' and are quick to point out that 10 percent of the nation's farms get 74 percent of the subsidies.[57]

ENERGY

With California being the 5th largest economy worldwide and boasting a population of 40 million, the state's energy consumption is significant. Climate change concerns have impacted the Golden State's energy use over the past several decades, especially when it comes to how electricity is generated and the amount of oil remaining in demand for transportation purposes.

California's main energy sources for generating electricity include natural gas (44%), and renewable energy in the forms of solar, wind, hydropower and geothermal technologies (47%). Nuclear energy provides 9% of electricity, but the state only has one remaining nuclear power plant operating near San Luis Obispo.[58]

Natural gas is a leading source of energy in California, and a majority of the natural gas California uses comes from Canada, the Rocky Mountain States, and the Southwest. It is delivered through a complexity of long-range pipelines. Burning natural gas provides heat, and the energy source is utilized in homes, businesses, industries and power plants.[59]

California has been scaling up the use of renewable energy sources to power the state's electrical grid. In 2019, California's use of renewable energy topped the nation. Concerning solar, the southeastern deserts of California are where the largest solar plants exist, and by 2019 14% of the state's electricity was produced through solar energy.[60] Wind accounted for 7% of California's electricity in 2019, and one of the major wind power areas is also located in the southeastern desert region of the San Gorgonio Pass. Hydroelectric power provided 19% of California electricity in 2019, but hydropower can fluctuate, being less reliable as an energy source during years of weak precipitation as demonstrated during the drought in 2015 when hydropower only supplied 7% of the state's electricity.[61] Currently, geothermal power fuels 6% of California's electrical grid, and the largest cluster of geothermal power plants in the world can be found in the Mayacamas Mountains north of San Francisco.[62]

With one of the state's two nuclear facilities shut down (the San Onofre power plant in San Clemente) and the other (Diablo Canyon near San Luis Obispo) set to close in 2024, the state is moving toward a greater reliance of renewable energy options, but California remains dependent on southwestern and northwestern states to provide 28% of electricity used, importing it via a network of interstate transmission lines. However, as the electricity crisis between 2001 and 2003 demonstrated, dependence on electricity from outside entities can be dicey.

Energy Crisis

In 2001, the price of electricity suddenly spiked as out of state companies that delivered electricity to California began drastic rate increases, threatening bankruptcy for two of the state's largest utility companies (Pacific Gas and Electric and Southern California Edison). Pacific Gas and Electric did file for bankruptcy in April of 2001, but Southern California Edison avoided it. Faced with financial insolvency, the utility companies were able to convince the state's **Public Utilities Commission (PUC)** to approve 40% rate increases on customers. **The Public Utilities Commission is a five seat commission whose members are appointed by the governor. The commission is charged with regulating utility rates (natural gas, water, and electricity) that utility companies can charge their customers.**

Not only were prices rising, but electricity supplies the state depended on from the Northwest were declining as a result of water powered plants providing less electricity due to a sustained drought.[63] Rolling blackouts occurred across the state in the summer of 2001, and in places of intense heat, seniors were given information on where to go if their air conditioning units failed. In response to the crisis, Governor Gray Davis entered into secret negotiations with the out of state power companies, securing long term contracts that locked in prices these companies could charge for electricity. However, as the crisis abetted, Governor Davis was criticized for signing contracts with these companies when prices were at their highest. This episode proved to be Governor Davis's Waterloo. He was recalled by the voters in a special election in 2003, the first Governor ever recalled in the state's history. **Recall is a tool voters can use to remove an elected official from office before their term is complete.**

While Governor Davis became the scapegoat for the crisis, the real culprits were the state's utility companies (PG&E and Southern California Edison), who successfully convinced state lawmakers to pass and Governor Pete Wilson to sign Assembly Bill 1890 in 1996, a bill that partially deregulated the power industry. The 100-page bill had many flaws, but the most egregious part of the legislation allowed wholesale energy prices (those prices charged by the out of state power companies) to be set by the free market while the state (through the Public Utilities Commission) regulated the retail price California customers would pay. Investigations of the crisis revealed that out of state companies providing electricity to California (Enron, Reliant Energy, Duke Energy, Dynegy Corporation, and The Williams Company) "rigged" the system by withholding supplies to artificially inflate short term prices.[64] Details also became public from the 2002 investigation that some power plants deliberately shut down to enhance power shortages and drive prices higher.[65]

Oil

Despite California's attempt to transition to renewable energy options when powering the electrical grid, oil remains a significant energy source when it comes to transportation in the Golden State. In state production accounts for 30 % of the oil Californians use. While Alaska still provides some oil, the bulk of petroleum imports comes from foreign nations (primarily Saudi Arabia, Iraq, and Ecuador).[66] California's love affair with the gas fueled automobile and constant population growth will make reducing consumption of this fossil fuel a challenge in the future. In an attempt to wean Californians off of gas fueled automobiles, Governor Newsom in 2020 signed an **Executive Order (a rule or regulation issued by the President, a Governor, or some administrative authority that has the effect of law)** ending sales of new gas-powered cars in the state by 2035. Governor Newsom's office claims the executive order will result in a 35% reduction in greenhouse gas emissions.[67] Under the executive order, used gas-powered vehicles can still be bought or sold in California, and new gas-powered cars can be purchased outside of the state and brought into California. Even with Governor Newsom's executive order, transitioning to electric powered automobiles may prove difficult to achieve. In 2019, for every passenger vehicle powered by electricity there were 70 fueled by gasoline.[68]

Going Green

The early 2000's electricity crisis, environmental concerns of greenhouse gas emissions, and a growing demand for energy have prompted the state's transition to the alternative energy sources previously discussed. After replacing Gray Davis, Governor Arnold Schwarzenegger called for more in state energy production and was a big advocate for alternative energy sources, issuing a 2008 executive order requiring that "All retail sellers of electricity shall serve 33% of their load with renewable energy by 2020."[69] Governor Schwarzenegger, as previously noted in this chapter, also signed the landmark carbon emission reduction law (AB 32 in 2006), hich set California on a path to reduce greenhouse gas emissions to 1990 levels by 2020.

Enter Governor Jerry Brown, who after being elected in 2010, fully embraced the concept of California expanding its use of clean, green energy. Under Brown's leadership, California invested $120 billion on renewable energy projects designed to make the Golden State less dependent on carbon emitting fossil fuels like oil and coal. Part of the money has been spent on alternative transportation (construction of a high-speed bullet train allowing passengers to get from San Francisco to Los Angeles in a few hours), the addition of 1.5 million green automobiles on California roads within the next decade, and making solar and other renewable energy sources provide more than one third of the state's electricity by 2020, which has been achieved. In 2016, Governor Brown signed SB 32, doubling down on reducing carbon emissions even more. Under the law, the state will set a goal of reducing greenhouse gas emissions 40% below 1990 levels by 2030, and 80% below 1990 levels by 2050.[70] To achieve such reductions, the state's electrical power grid will gradually increase its use of renewable energy with a target of being powered 100% by renewables come 2045.

However, business and industry are critical of these policies, claiming the cost of doing business in California is becoming too expensive due to green energy mandates the state is attempting to achieve over the next 25 years. In addition, it has been argued California's green energy movement hurts low income earners in the Golden State. A CNN study found that someone living in Sacramento has to pay 22% more for basic living needs like groceries, housing, health care, transportation, and utilities compared to someone living in Austin, Texas.

Transitioning to 100% renewable energy is costly given the state currently depends on natural gas sources to provide nearly half of its electrical energy generation. Reconfiguring the electrical grid to run on 100% renewable energy will be a massive and expensive energy infrastructure project. The majority of California electricity is generated at large, centralized power plants that transmit power throughout the state via a network of transmission lines. This is high end energy infrastructure. But as Craig Lewis, executive director of the Clean Coalition (a non-profit clean energy group) points out, *"Renewable energy projects are sprouting up on rooftops and parking lots across the state."* Lewis argues *"that local renewable energy projects generate electricity close to where it is used, reducing the need for new transmission investments."*[71] Lewis could be right that local renewable energy projects will be more cost effective, but as long as utility corporate giants Southern California Edison, Pacific Gas and Electric, and San Diego Gas and Electric continue providing electricity to millions of Californians through the state power grid, converting that grid to 100% renewable energy will be expensive. A bill requiring utility companies transition to 100% renewable energy by 2045 for all retail electricity sold in the state was signed by Governor Jerry Brown in 2018.

It is also worth noting that the oil and gas industry produces some 456,000 jobs in California, responsible for 3.4% of the states' Gross Domestic Product.[72] California is the third largest oil and gas producing state in the nation (cranking out on average 500,000 barrels of oil a day primarily from the Central Valley), and while going green is the directive from the current Newsom Administration and the Democratically controlled legislature, the transition away from fossil fuels in a state that extracts them in large quantities is somewhat of an enigma. With that said, these green energy policies appear to be working. According to the California Air Resources Board, greenhouse gas emissions dropped from 493 million metric tons in 2004 to 424 million metric tons in 2017, and the state exceeded the mark set by AB 32 of achieving annual emissions of 431 million metric tons by 2020, the same amount of carbon pollution recorded back in 1990.[73]

However, challenges remain to cut greenhouse gas emissions even more. In March 2021, California State Auditor Elaine Howle, in a report reviewing the state's intent on curtailing greenhouse gas emissions some 40% by 2030, believes the California Air Resources Board, the state agency tasked with enacting policies to cut greenhouse gas emissions, will fail to meet the 40% goal. Howle has concluded that the current ratio of one electric powered passenger vehicle for every 70 gas fueled cars in California will not be good enough to meet the desired reduction in greenhouse gas emissions by 2030.

TRANSPORTATION

With 30 million cars cruising around the state, California, generation after generation, has clung to a paradigm that equates the automobile to freedom, autonomy, and happiness. Well, maybe Californians have not been as happy in their cars as they used to be. A Goggle of "road rage California" reveals one million hits, and is no doubt linked to the average time we spend stuck in traffic, esti-mated in 2017 to be 54 extra hours a year nationally. In California that annual amount of time stuck in traffic ballooned in 2017 to 119 hours in Los Angeles and 103 hours in the San Francisco Bay Area.[74]

If there is anything positive to come from the pandemic, it may be the signif-icant reduction in traffic congestion in 2020 when COVID-19 hit. However, in the Spring of 2021, with many California regions re-opening their economies, traffic congestion has returned to the populated urban centers of the Golden State. Even if some employees are working from home, a Caltrans study sug-gests only 30% of those employed work in a vocation that allows them to be at home.[75]

Traffic congestion remains a lingering problem for California, and the gov-ernment's attempt to mitigate the problem has been rife with political disputes. When Californians approved a 1990 proposition to raise the state gas tax, the political debate on how to spend the money was waged between advocates for mass transit and pro highway construction groups. However, the state may never be able to meet highway capacity for California's growing population. In the 1980's and 1990's, Golden State highway capacity increased 4 percent while the population grew by 50 percent.[76] During that time period, San Jose built two highways (Highway 87 and Highway 85). Upon completion, both of them joined the city's other clogged freeways during rush hour, doing little to relieve the congestion of a city whose population is larger than the city of San Francisco. Gridlock in San Jose is not limited to the weekday commute. As the weekend approaches, attempting to leave San Jose on a Friday or return on a Sunday can lead to long hours in traffic. This problem is even more exaggerated during three day weekends. Similar scenarios can be found in Los Angeles, San Francisco, and San Diego.

In attempts to relieve the congestion, carpool lanes were added across the state. In the 1990's, car pool miles increased from 149 miles to 1,011. Unfortu-nately, the percentage of California drivers going to work alone slightly edged up during that same time period, from 71.6 to 71.8 %. Instead of making an effort to carpool, some commuters went to such lengths as placing mannequins in the passenger seat to trick police.[77]

When Highway's 85 and 87 were built in San Jose, it was the first time in the state that local residents voted to tax themselves to pay for the freeways, which cost some $785 million. Measure A, approved by Santa Clara County voters in 1984, increased local sales tax by a half-cent for ten years, providing the funds needed to construct the new freeways.[78] In 1988, San Jose opened a light rail line, and Santa Clara County voters approved taxes to expand light rail in 2000 and 2008.[79] San Francisco's Bay Area Rapid Transit (BART) has been operating trains from San Francisco to Freemont since 1974, and as a result of Santa Clara County voters approving taxes for light rail expansion in 2000 and 2008, BART has been extended to South Bay cities Milpitas, San Jose, and Santa Clara. Phase 1 of the BART Silicon Valley project was completed in June 2020 with the opening of the Berryessa BART station in North San Jose. Phase 2 of the project, underway in 2020, will move through downtown San Jose and reach the city of Santa Clara.[80] Light rail systems have also been constructed in Los Angeles and San Diego, yet California remains lacking when it comes to a statewide mass transit system, something supporters of mass transit hope to change.

The Bullet Train

In 2008, California voters approved Proposition 1A, a $9 billion bond that would finance construction of a high-speed bullet train system, allowing passengers to travel from San Francisco to Los Angeles in three hours. The project was also infused with an additional $4 billion in federal funding and is estimated to create 100,000 jobs. Sounds great, but politics always makes things more complicated. The initial construction was set to begin in the Central Valley, but opposition developed quickly from anti-railroad groups (like the libertarian Reason Foundation) who claimed beginning the project in the Central Valley would create a "train to nowhere." Even the non-partisan **Legislative Analyst's Office** believed funds should first be used to upgrade light rail systems in Orange County and the Bay Area before constructing the rail line through the Central Valley.[81] **The Legislative Analyst's Office is a non-partisan office that provides objective analysis of all California legislation, the budget, and public works projects.** The high-speed rail project was also challenged by Bay Area Peninsula communities concerned about bullet trains barreling through their cities.

Overall projected costs for the railroad, currently tagged at $80 billion, have triggered more skepticism and opposition, highlighted by an attempt of the Republican controlled Congress in 2014 to gut all federal funding for the bullet train. Leading the opposition in Congress was a California Republican, Jeff Denham, who represents a congressional district the train would run through in the Central Valley, *"This is a project that is going out of control,"* Denham claimed while speaking on the floor of the House, *"It's a project that has no end in sight. We've got to stop this train wreck."*[82] As it turned out, approving the high-speed bullet train was the easy part, getting the project off the ground proved to be much more difficult.

Despite the political opposition to the bullet train, the State Legislature, in July 2012, approved financing for the initial construction of the project's first phase that will run 130 miles from Merced south to Bakersfield. Federal funds of $3.8 billion for the railroad had already been secured by California before the attempt in Congress to halt funding in 2014. In 2017, President Trump's Transportation Secretary, Elaine Chao, froze a $637 million federal grant to connect Northern California light rail to the Bullet Train line.[83] The Trump Administration also attempted to axe a $929 million federal grant for the project, arguing California was not making enough progress in completing the first 119 miles of construction between Bakersfield and Madera in the Central Valley. Predictably, the state sued the Trump Administration for withholding the funds.[84]

With federal support waning in 2017, Governor Brown sought revenue streams elsewhere, using funds for the railroad from a **cap-and-trade program, which exacts revenue from polluting industries that buy credits in order to continue emitting greenhouse gasses above state limits.** The cap-and-trade program diverts 25% of its annual revenues to the bullet train.

But fortunes have improved for the bullet train in 2021 now that Joe Biden is President, and Biden's Transportation Secretary Pete Buttigieg indicated he supports high speed rail infrastructure projects like the bullet train. That is music to the ears of California's High Speed Rail Authority, the state agency tasked with overseeing construction of the bullet train. In February 2021 California requested the Biden Administration grant the state another year (until 2023) to complete the Central Valley portion of the project.[85] Construction of the bullet train began in 2013, and while the project remains controversial, it would not be the first time a railroad impacted California politics as will be discussed in Chapter 2.

Financing Road Maintenance

Other transportation challenges are on the horizon. As mentioned already, Californians love their cars, but with an estimated 300 billion miles of travel on the state's highways each year, maintaining them is expensive. Financing for road maintenance in California comes from the taxes levied on fuel, and the gas tax had not changed in twenty years.[86] Since the gas tax is based on fuel purchases, more fuel-efficient automobiles has equated to revenues for road maintenance remaining flat. In Governor Brown's 2015 **State of the State Address (a speech by California's Governor to the State Legislature each year highlighting the Governor's legislative priorities for the upcoming year)** he asked the Legislature to develop funding for $59 billion in "needed upkeep and maintenance" on the state's highways. Increasing fuel taxes on California motorists was one of the ideas floated to pay for road repairs.

In April 2017, the State Legislature passed, and Governor Brown signed a $52 billion tax and fee package to fund highway infrastructure. The law, known as Senate Bill 1 (SB 1), increased the base gas tax 12 cents per gallon, imposed a transportation improvement fee based on the value of vehicles, and raised diesel fuel taxes.[87] However, Republican George Runner, a member of the **State Board of Equalization (a five member elected board that administers the state's sales tax and oversees the assessment of property tax statewide)**, noted that prior to SB 1's passage *"Californians already paid about 64 cents per gallon in taxes and fees – the second-highest rate in the nation."* Runner also pointed out that lawmakers raided the transportation fund during lean budget years in the past.[88] Financing transportation infrastructure projects become quite the political conundrum as lawmakers attempt to ensure adequate roads, highways, and public transportation are available to the state's 40 million people.

THE ENVIRONMENT

In 1542, Portuguese navigator Juan Rodriguez Cabrillo sailed into what is today Los Angeles Harbor. He described the harbor as "the bay of smokes", alluding to the Indian campfires which hung in the air. Native Americans called the Los Angeles basin "the land of a thousand smokes" before the settlers arrived. Present day Los Angeles (and surrounding communities), on bad smog days, are engulfed in a perpetual thick blanket of muck which stretches one hundred miles from Pasadena to the San Gorgonio Pass. When visible, the Los Angeles basin is quite scenic, surrounded on three sides by mountains. Unfortunately, its' geography, coupled with a persistent inversion layer that traps the smog, makes Los Angeles the most polluted city not only in the state, but also in the nation.[89] Besides wasted time, wasted gasoline, and the potential of developing road rage, California drivers stuck in endless miles of traffic emit more smog when their vehicles are idling, and no city has more drivers clogged in traffic each day than Los Angeles, an urban area with a population of 10 million.

Air pollution in the Golden State is by no means limited to Los Angeles. The **California Air Resources Board** has concluded that over 90 percent of Californians breathe unhealthy levels of at least one air pollutant during some part of the year.[90] **The California Air Resources Board (ARB) consists of 11 board members appointed by the Governor. The ARB has the authority to set air quality standards for California and regulate industries to ensure air quality standards are being met. The ARB also oversees the activities of 35 local and regional air pollution control districts.** "Smog alert" days have been around since the 1970's, and on such days public alert notices issued by local governments will lead to youth sporting events being cancelled, and children and the elderly (the people most susceptible to respiratory ailments) being advised to remain indoors. However, the California Air Resources Board points out that due to innovative air pollution control strategies over the years, smoggy days in Los Angeles where air quality was unhealthy have been cut in half from over 200 per year in the 1970's, but smog continues to be a problem in the City of Angels.[91]

The emitting of carbon dioxide, sulfur dioxide and other compounds into the atmosphere by humans primarily through transportation, the production of electricity, and industrial activities has led to the conclusion by scientists world-wide that global warming is occurring through what is known as the "greenhouse effect." **The Greenhouse Effect suggests that the buildup of gases in the atmosphere is preventing the sun's heat from escaping and, as a result, is warming the planet.** Scientists have determined that long term warming would be disastrous for California, leading to rising ocean levels, crop losses in agriculture, higher cases of skin cancer, and a diminished water supply stemming from a lighter snowpack in the Sierra Nevada Mountains. The devastating wildfires California suffered in 2018 and 2020 have also contributed to the state's air pollution problems. Government monitoring stations during the 2020 wildfires found that some 38 million people in five western states, including California, were exposed to unhealthy amounts of wildfire smoke for a minimum of five days.[92]

Cap-And-Trade

As has been discussed in this chapter, AB 32 in 2006 and SB 32 ten years later, are laws designed to significantly reduce greenhouse gas emissions, and the cap-and-trade program, administered by the California Air Resources Board, is the centerpiece of the two laws. Under this approach, companies can amass credits by reducing their greenhouse gas emissions then sell those credits to polluting companies. Each year, the number of credits available shrinks, and are available for sale either by companies holding credits or through state run auctions held every three months. The goal of cap and trade is to provide a financial incentive for companies to pollute less. However, cap and trade has not been embraced by all in the environmental community, as demonstrated by Bill Gallegos, executive director of Communities for a Better Environment: *Trading gives polluters allowances or the "right" to pollute. Industries will be given free allowances (to pollute) for years. The best thing would be for the California Air Resources Board to acknowledge cap and trade's failure, abandon its pollution trading plan, and replace that plan with pollution controls that will ensure verifiable emission reductions.*[93]

AB 32, SB 32, and other California Air Resource Board rulings that place restrictions on emissions have not been well received by some in the state's business community. Delta Construction President Skip Brown of Sacramento voiced his frustration with the California Air Resource Board. According to Brown, the mandates placed on his company required him to retrofit or replace all of his diesel-emitting equipment by 2014 at a cost of $5 million. "We're pretty much done under the particulate matter regulations", he said, "They've destroyed my ability to finance, operate, and bond my business."[94] As Bill Gallegos and Skip Brown point out, proposed methods for curbing greenhouse gas emissions create different concerns for various interest groups. Both also highlight the tremendous influence the California Air Resource Board has when it comes to the regulation of emissions in California.

Despite their criticism, though, cap-and-trade has been extended to 2030 by legislation enacted in 2017, Governor Brown securing a two-thirds vote from lawmakers in both the State Assembly and State Senate on Assembly Bill 398.[95] Achieving the two-thirds majority was significant because opponents of cap-and-trade sued in court, arguing that compelling companies to purchase the credits was akin to a tax, and under California law tax increases can only be approved by the State Legislature with a two-thirds vote.

California Auto Emission Standards and the Battle with the Trump Administration

During Barack Obama's presidency the Obama Administration and the California Air Resources Board developed auto emission standards that would mandate automakers reduce emissions and improve fuel milage by 30% by 2025. Under the agreement, California was allowed to adopt these emission standards, requiring automakers to comply. With the election of President Donald Trump in 2016, the Trump Administration proposed a less restrictive auto emissions standard nationwide. When California resisted the Trump Administration's easing of carbon emission and milage standards, President Trump attempted to strip California of its unique power of setting its own air-pollution rules for automakers. This led to yet another court battle between the state and the Trump Administration. But it also put the auto industry in a difficult position as automakers were forced to choose sides, some agreeing to manufacture their vehicles based on the less restrictive carbon emission and milage standards called for by the Trump Administration. But five automobile companies (Ford, Volkswagen, Honda, BMW, and Volvo) sided with California and cut a deal with Governor Newsom and the Air Resources Board to accept more stringent emission and milage standards than those proposed by the Trump

Administration. After the election of Joe Biden as President in November 2020, the automakers who were willing to go with President Trump's less restrictive rules dropped out of the lawsuit initiated by the Trump Administration against California. This episode is a good example of how election outcomes have real world consequences.

Water Pollution and the Delta

Concerning water pollution issues, environmentalists and the agriculture industry have squared off over water preservation in California. Pesticide use by farmers can lead to toxins entering rivers, creeks, and lakes. When it rains, chemicals from insecticides sprayed on the crops mix into the runoff and have been responsible for polluting water systems. Over 40 wells had to be closed in Fresno when it was discovered that the agricultural pesticide DBCP had seeped into the water supply.[96]

Environmental concerns have also developed over the **740,000 acres known as the Sacramento San Joaquin Delta, the largest estuary in the Western United States** where the Sacramento and San Joaquin rivers meet before emptying into San Francisco Bay. Since completion of the State Water Project, environmentalists have been worried about the diversion of freshwater from the Delta. If more water from the Sacramento and San Joaquin rivers is diverted, saltwater content from the San Francisco Bay will increase, threatening the Delta's fragile ecosystem whose species depend on freshwater. Too much saltwater would also be devastating to Northern California farmland that relies on the Delta for irrigation. An unusual coalition of environmental groups and Delta area farmers joined forces in 1982 to help defeat the Peripheral Canal, a proposed canal project put before the voters that would have diverted more freshwater from the Delta. This same coalition reunited again to oppose Governor Brown's water tunnels project that would send more Delta freshwater to the Central Valley and Southern California communities. Even though Governor Newsom halved the water tunnels project down to one tunnel, Northern California farmers and environmentalists continue to oppose diverting more fresh water out of the Delta.

Ground Waste and Recycling

With a population of 40 million, California's environmental concerns are not limited to clean air and water, but also encompass the consumption of goods that generate millions of tons of waste annually. As the state's population increased 50% between 1980 and 2000, large California urban areas struggled to find solutions to their waste disposal problems as existing landfills began to reach capacity. Los Angeles, faced with diminishing landfill space, turned to neighboring Riverside County for help. The result was the Eagle Mountain Landfill project, a proposed landfill in the Riverside County desert that would accept Los Angeles trash for one hundred years. The Riverside County Board of Supervisors (The governing board of the county) approved the project in 1992, and over a decade of legal battles ensued between environmentalists and Riverside county residents opposed to the landfill and Mine Reclamation (the company that wanted to build the landfill). In 2013, the Los Angeles County Sanitation Districts gave up on the Eagle Mountain site, and the proposed landfill project died.[97] Up north, San Francisco reached an agreement with Yuba County that will send 500,000 tons of its trash each year to the town of Wheatland.[98]

Not only is California confronted with finding adequate landfill sites for its garbage, but the state's recycling program is being severely strained with the closing of some 560 recycling centers statewide, which represented a 25% decline of the centers in 2017. In 2019, California's largest recycler of beverage containers (rePlanet) shuttered all 284 of its recycling centers and terminated 750 employees. A key reason for the closures was the price of oil remaining below $50 a barrel the past few years, though in April 2021 oil has ticked up to $60 per barrel. As oil prices dropped, so did the costs of new manufactured materials, resulting in falling prices for recycled items and rendering many of these recycling centers financially inoperable. This has also impacted the grocery industry given state law requires supermarkets have a recycling center located a half mile from their location or pay the cost of the recycled item or a fine. It is estimated that in 2017 over 300 recycling centers near supermarkets closed.[99]

As a result of this, the California Department of Resources Recycling and Recovery (CalRecycle) reported that 2017 beverage container recycling rates dipped under 80% for the first time since 2008. CalRecycle has a $250 million fund that is supposed to subsidize recycling centers, but according to Jared Blumenfeld, a former federal Environmental Protection Agency official, CalRecycle froze those payments in 2016 as prices fell for recycled goods. Attempts by the Legislature and Governor Brown to stabilize funding for the program was not addressed in the 2016/2017 state budget, and CalRecycle did not renew subsidies to recycling centers in 2017. Blumenfeld claims the state's inaction is adding 2 million beverage containers per day in the form of litter or garbage sent to landfills.[100]

In 2018, the State Legislature approved SB 452, a recycling bill that would have increased recycling center subsidies and appropriated $3 million in surplus funds to encourage recycling in underserved areas of the state. However,

Governor Jerry Brown vetoed the bill.[101] In 2019, Governor Gavin Newsom's budget provided $5 million in temporary aid for low-volume recyclers, and the money was parsed out to some 416 recycling centers at $1000 a month over a 12-month period.[102] But more needs to be done to prop up the California recycling industry and prevent greater amounts of waste from accumulating. While it is estimated that the state now has enough landfill space for the next fifty years, that space will fill up more quickly if recycling infrastructure continues to wane.

HEALTH CARE

The Affordable Care Act (dubbed "Obamacare" by political pundits) was signed into law by President Barack Obama in March of 2010. The sweeping health care reform law was designed to lower health care costs, make health insurance available to the 30 million Americans lacking it, and prevent the health insurance industry from denying coverage to any American with a pre-existing condition. Controversial aspects of the law included mandating Americans with no coverage to purchase health insurance or be subject to a monetary penalty, requiring businesses with fifty or more employees to offer health insurance to their workers, and increasing taxes on wealthier Americans and levying taxes on insurance providers, pharmaceutical companies, and manufacturers of medical equipment to help finance the program. The complex, 1000-page bill became a deeply partisan exercise in Congress. No Republicans voted for the law in the House of Representatives or the Senate.

The ink had scarcely dried from President Obama's signing of the Affordable Care Act (ACA) when 28 states initiated lawsuits to overturn the law, claiming the mandate requiring Americans purchase health insurance unconstitutional overreach by the government. In June of 2012, the U.S. Supreme Court, in a 5-4 ruling, upheld the Affordable Care Act, determining the federal government under its constitutional authority to tax could impose a financial penalty on those who failed to purchase health insurance. Despite the U.S. Supreme Court's ruling, 29 state legislatures pursued legislative action to nullify portions of Obamacare, and in August 2010, Missouri voters convincingly approved a ballot measure that would exempt the state from the law.

However, California moved in the opposite direction regarding the ACA, something that should come as no surprise given the state's political makeup which has given control of governing to the Democrats.

California lawmakers have passed legislation to enforce and implement significant portions of the Affordable Care Act. In 2010, the California Legislature approved such measures as allowing young adults up to the age of 26 to remain on their parent's health insurance plan and prohibiting health insurers from denying coverage to children with a pre-existing condition.

California was also the first state in the country to pass legislation creating a health benefit exchange.[103] These health insurance exchanges are a centerpiece of the federal law. Each state would operate a health insurance exchange, offering a marketplace where individuals and small businesses can shop policies and premiums, then purchase insurance that best suits their needs. **The California Health Benefit Exchange administers the program and consists of a five-person board, whose members are appointed by the Governor and the Legislature.**[104]

Many Republican controlled states refused to set up their own health insurance exchanges, and under the law citizens in those states could enroll in a federal government run health insurance exchange. Some six million enrolled, but a legal challenge ensued claiming the Affordable Care Act only allowed government **subsidies (government assistance in purchasing health insurance)** be provided to those that enrolled in a state government run exchange, not a federal government run exchange. In 2015, the United States Supreme Court ruled 6-3 that citizens could receive the government backed subsidy if enrolled in the federal government exchange. With the U.S. Supreme Court upholding Obamacare for the second time in three years, the law was maintained, despite Republican efforts to end it.

According to analysis by the State Senate Health Committee, health insurance premiums in California have increased 134 percent since 2002. Yearly health care premiums in the Golden State averaged over $14,000 for families and around $5,400 for individuals in 2010.[105] In response to these escalating health insurance premiums, the Legislature attempted, but failed to pass a law in 2011 that would have granted the **State Insurance Commissioner** the authority to approve, reject, or alter proposed rate hikes by health insurers operating in the state.[106] The proposed law, known as AB52, like other laws and policies already discussed in this chapter, had its supporters and detractors.

An editorial by the Sacramento Bee advocating passage of AB52 cited the ability of health insurers to raise premiums on consumers with impunity: *Anthem Blue Cross announced a proposed May 1 rate increase for 120,000 members. State officials reviewed the increase and announced in April that it was unreasonable. Yet Anthem went ahead with the increase anyway.* According to the Bee, the rate increase averaged out to a 16 percent hike on the 120,000.

California Medical Association President, Dr. James G. Hinsdale, opposed AB52, concerned that the proposed law would only make access to doctors and medical providers deteriorate even more, *"If regulators set rates at a level that doesn't meet the cost of providing care, insurers will be forced to lower reimbursements to physicians like me, hospitals, and other providers. Lower reimbursements will result in reduced access to physicians and hospitals, substandard facilities and lower quality of care."* Dr. Hinsdale also points out that **Medi-Cal, the state's health care program for the poor,** ranks 49th in the nation in **Medicaid** reimbursement to physicians.[107] **Medicaid is the federal health system for the poor, aged, blind, and disabled which provides medical, hospital, and long-term care. Medicaid is jointly financed by the federal government and state governments.**

Rising Health Insurance Premiums

After the defeat of AB 52 by the Legislature in 2011, Proposition 45, an **Initiative** that would have granted the **Insurance Commissioner** authority to approve changes in health insurance rates, qualified for the 2014 ballot. Proponents of Proposition 45 claimed that five health insurance companies controlling 88% of California's insurance market contributed $25 million to defeat the initiative, while opponents of the measure suggested Proposition 45 exempted big corporations from the law and encouraged frivolous lawsuits by greedy lawyers.[108] In the end, voters soundly defeated Proposition 45 as 60% rejected the measure.

The Affordable Care Act has made significant progress in enrolling Californians in a health care insurance plan. By 2016, 3.7 million Californians enrolled in Medi-Cal under the ACA and another 1.4 million purchased insurance through the state's health exchange (Covered California). The law lowered the rate of uninsured Californians to 8.5%, and nationwide 90% of Americans had health insurance in 2016.[109]

Despite the ACA's success in reducing the uninsured rate both in California and nationwide, health insurance premiums have continued to rise. In California, the average costs of family premium have spiked 45% since 2010[110]. And, as noted, the state's Insurance Commissioner was not given authority to regulate the cost of health insurance coverage. Other factors related to the premium hikes involve inflationary pressures associated with the health care system (such as new medical technologies and doctors' wages). It also should be noted that while the Affordable Care Act has expanded health care access for millions of Americans, those purchasing health care were required to buy more robust plans that offered extensive coverage, and those plans were more expensive.

Repeal ACA, Fix it, or Single Payer

Rising premiums, mandates placed on businesses to provide health care for their employees, and requirements that individuals purchase health insurance if they don't have it are the keys reasons Republicans disliked the Affordable Care

Act. Many Republicans in Congress believe health care policies should be left to the states and the ACA repealed. With the election of President Trump and a Republican Congress, the repeal of Obamacare was assumed to be a foregone conclusion. But politics has a nasty habit of getting in the way of foregone conclusions sometimes. Turns out it was much easier for Republicans in Congress to vote for repealing the ACA when President Obama still occupied the White House and he could veto it. Things became more complicated for Republicans in Congress when President Trump came to office in 2017 and urged them to repeal and replace Obamacare. Repeal and Replace bills reviewed by the **Congressional Budget Office (a non-partisan body that studies and analyzes proposed budget related legislation)** determined the Republican proposals would result in some 20 million losing health care coverage, and public opinion soured on repealing Obamacare. The House passed a repeal and replace bill, but in the Senate, even with a parliamentary provision that required only 50 of 52 Senate Republican votes, the GOP could not muster the votes to repeal Obamacare. But they came close. On July 27, 2017, Republican Senator John McCain joined Senate GOP colleagues Susan Collins and Lisa Murkowski in voting against the repeal of the Affordable Care Act. However, in December 2017 President Trump and congressional Republicans were able to muscle through a massive tax cut bill that eliminated the federal penalty on individuals who failed to purchase health insurance. California, though, went in a different direction, the State Legislature in 2019 passing a measure to tax people who refuse to purchase health insurance; legislation signed by Governor Newsom.

Frustrated with the rising costs of health care, some California lawmakers are advocating the state move to a **single payer system in which health insurance companies are eliminated, and health care coverage is provided to everyone by the government**. Such a bill was proposed in 2017 by Democrat State Senators Ricardo Lara and Toni Atkins. The problem was the bill included no funding methods for covering 39.5 million people at an estimated cost of $400 billion, more than double what the entire state budget encompasses each year, and though it passed in the State Senate, it died in the State Assembly when Assembly Speaker Anthony Rendon prevented it from reaching the Assembly floor for a vote.[111]

A national single payer health care law has been introduced by progressive U.S. Senator Bernie Sanders, and in the 2020 Democratic primary presidential candidate Kamala Harris (a California U.S. Senator at the time, and now the first woman to ever hold the office of Vice President) initially supported a single payer system before backtracking, stating she was for a government run health care program that would allow private health insurance to still be available. Senator Sanders, also a candidate for President in 2020, continues to support having the government provide health care for everyone. But Joe Biden did not support a single payer health care system, arguing it would be better to improve on the Affordable Care Act by increasing federal subsidies so people can afford premiums.

COVID-19 has only exacerbated the debate about affordable health care, and with so many people hospitalized and over a half-million dead due to the virus as of April 2021, the Biden Administration will face even more pressure from Progressive Democrats like Bernie Sanders and Alexandria Ocasio Cortez to expand health care access for all. However, the immediate health care access President Biden wants to see implemented in 2021 is centered on getting as many Americans as possible vaccinated.

The Pandemic Fosters a Mental Health Crisis

It would be disingenuous to say mental health problems have been exaggerated when political debates erupt over the closing of schools and businesses on account of the pandemic. The collective effect of being bereft of social interaction (be it seeing family or friends, or simply not being able to interact with others in public places) can't be ignored. Over a year of lockdowns has been mentally taxing on everyone. A Brookings Institution study ("America's Crisis of Despair") cites that annually 70,000 Americans die each year from "deaths of despair" that include not just suicides, but drug overdoses as well. But that number may have nearly doubled to 130,000 suicides and drug overdoses from March 2020 to March 2021 due to the pandemic.[112] We will consider the mental health implications for our children, many of whom have been learning from home via zoom throughout the pandemic as we discuss public education in the next section.

EDUCATION K-12

California's 1000 K-12 school districts are the basic unit governing public education from kindergarten through high school. Voters in each school district elect a local school board that establishes school district policies, authorizes the district's budget, and appoints a Superintendent to oversee and implement the School Board's policies. All K-12 public school districts adhere to state curriculum, testing standards, and minimum graduation requirements set by the **California State Board of Education, a 10-member Board appointed by the Governor.**

Shrinking budgets created the necessity by school administrators to collect every dollar of funding available. When Congress passed and President George W. Bush signed the No Child Left Behind Act in 2001, schools across the country were charged with increasing the proficiency of their students in English and Math. The law required schools administer standardized exams to third through eighth graders in English and Math. Financial incentives for districts whose students met the proficiency standards prompted school administrators to impose strict curriculum requirements on their teachers. "Teaching to the test" became the curriculum. A common refrain from teachers was that all of their creative teaching methods were taken from them as a result of No Child Left Behind. Sacramento County schools Superintendent David Gordon noted that teachers focused their lessons on the "relatively narrow measures" they were held accountable for on the state achievement test. "We're not teaching writing much anymore, or history, social science, and physics", Gordon said in 2011.[113]

In California, the results of No Child Left Behind were mixed. Despite the state cutting education funding to K-12 schools by 14 percent between 2008 and 2010, the percentage of second to seventh grade students scoring proficient on the state's standardized English test improved from 48 percent to 55 percent. Such results were encouraging, but enthusiasm was tempered given that California students regularly scored under the U.S. average on major categories of the national exams.[114]

A new approach to strengthen students' academic performance not just in California, but across the nation, was the introduction in 2013 of **Common Core, a program embraced by 45 states, including California, that created new standardized tests and encouraged these 45 states to accept common academic goals for students and compel teachers to create more rigorous lesson plans that require problem solving and critical thinking by their students. (97)**[115]

Student to Teacher Ratio and Remedial Education

According to data from the California Department of Education, statewide high school dropout rates in the 2019/2020 school year remained steady at 8.9% compared to 9% the previous year. While it would be fantastic to lower the number of high school dropouts, it was encouraging the number did not increase in a school year where most California high schools transitioned midway through the spring semester to distance learning due to COVID-19. However, prior to the pandemic, graduating high schoolers entering college the following year faced some challenges. A California State University (CSU) study found that 57 percent of incoming freshman required remedial instruction either in English or Math. California ranks in the bottom tier among the states in its K-12 student to teacher ratio (47th in 2014 and 50th in 2020) and this certainly can be a contributing factor when considering why so many students are not prepared for college or the work force.[116]

In 2017, only 19% of incoming freshman at CSU campuses graduated in four years. Given increasing tuition costs (which we will presently address), CSU, in 2018, attempting to increase four-year graduation rates, implemented a program in which remedial Math and English courses (once non-credit courses) become for-credit classes and accepted as course units for graduation. The CSU is aware of concerns that such a policy change could degrade an undergraduate degree, and CSU spokesman Mike Uhlenkamp, responding to such concerns said, *"We will only do this if we can do it without dumbing down the degree."*[117]

The state attempted to address the student to teacher ratio problem in 1996 by limiting class sizes to 20 students in kindergarten through third grade. There were hopes the class size reduction program could be expanded to higher grades, but severe budget cuts to K-12 as a result of the Great Recession of 2008 torpedoed the program. Class sizes for kindergarten through third grade are no longer limited to 20 students, and some elementary schools combined grades (1st and 2nd graders as an example) into one class with up to 30 students in response to the budget cuts.

Governor Jerry Brown's Administration confronted classroom overcrowding in 2014 by mandating schools reduce their kindergarten through third grade class sizes or lose 10 % of their state funding, but a caveat in the funding plan allowed school districts to maintain the larger sized classes if the union representing the school districts' teachers agreed.[118] Why would teachers' unions accept maintaining the larger sized classes? Given teachers in many school districts saw their pay frozen or in some cases cut during the Great Recession, the priority of improving teacher pay trumped reducing classroom sizes.

English as a Second Language

Another factor associated with California's education troubles involves the number of students attending Golden State schools in which English is not their language of origin. Based on California Department of Education numbers, nearly a quarter of the state's K-12 students are not sufficiently proficient in English to be instructed in the language. Such students are referred to as English Learners (EL), and nearly one half of all Hispanic K-12 students are English Learners. These EL students were enrolled in bi-lingual classes, and many of them remained in these courses provided by the school district for multiple years. That changed in 1998 when California voters approved **Proposition 227, a measure that limited bi-lingual education for English Learner students to one year in public schools.** However, language in Proposition 227 allowed parents to request their children remain in bi-lingual education.

COVID-19 Impacts on K-12 Schools

As previously mentioned, the pandemic is having detrimental impacts on the mental health of people, and that includes children. With many of California's school districts remaining closed to in person instruction, teachers are conducting their classes with students via zoom. Students have been struggling with the zoom format for a variety of reasons, but child development specialist Patricia Perez, an associate professor of Psychology in Chicago, may have put it best, *"Young people like to make plans for the future, and it's difficult to do that when they don't know low long this new way of life will last."*[119] And this new way of life concerning education involves children being expected to learn in isolation, something not natural to them. School is just not about learning the three r's (reading, writing, and arithmetic), but it also encompasses children acquiring social skills through their daily interactions with peers and educators. Zoom cannot replicate that, regardless of how innovative a teacher may be in delivering online instruction.

The politics in California over educating the state's 6 million K-12 students in the midst of the worst pandemic in 100 years pits various groups against one another. Labor unions across California, especially those representing teachers in the larger urban area school districts, remained skeptical of re-opening the schools, fearing the school districts would not do enough to mitigate the potential spread of the virus if schools were opened back up for live instruction. However, even in the union friendly city of San Francisco, the city government took the unusual step of suing their own school district in hopes of forcing the district to reopen the schools.[120] K-12 students in San Francisco have been denied in person instruction for over a year as of April 2021.

But in some parts of the state, even if school districts partially re-opened the schools, that was not good enough for some frustrated parents. In the city of Chico, the group Chico Parents for In-Person Learning attempted to **Recall (a process of removing an elected official from office before their term is up)** four Chico Unified School Board members because the Board refused to fully re-open the schools, opting to finish the 2020/2021 school year in a hybrid am/pm model in which students are only on campus half of the day.[121]

In 2021, Governor Gavin Newsom is looking at the real prospect of facing his own Recall election to remove him from office. Part of the angst being generated against Governor Newsom involve the lockdown policies he has pursued to reduce the spread of COVID-19, and that includes school closures. In response to so many California K-12 schools educating children solely online, Governor Newsom has developed a plan to get students back into classrooms, signing a bill in March 2021 that provides $6.6 billion to help schools reopen by mid-April 2021.[122]

EDUCATION FUNDING

Education funding represents the largest chunk of the state budget in California. The 1000 K-12 school districts (6 million students), the 109 community college campuses (2.6 million students), the 23 California State University campuses (450,000 students), and the 9 University of California campuses (216,000 students) comprise nearly 50 percent of budget expenditures annually. The Great Recession California found itself mired in for several years created dire circumstances for these education institutions in terms of funding cuts, overcrowded classrooms, hyper inflated tuition increases, and quality of education.

In 1978, Californians approved **Proposition 13, a ballot initiative that cut property taxes and required a two- thirds vote of the State Legislature to increase taxes.** Proposition 13 immediately lowered property taxes 57 percent and was seen as a tremendous victory for California taxpayers. However, for the state's K-12 public schools, which derive a significant portion of their revenues from local property tax, Proposition 13 eroded a vital funding source. In the 1950's and 1960's, California ranked near the top in education funding amongst the states. In the wake of Proposition 13, California's per pupil funding dropped significantly. In 2011, the Golden State ranked near the bottom (47th) in per pupil spending, allocating $7,700 per student. Things have improved, though, and in the 2020/2021 state budget, per pupil spending rose to over $17,000 per student.[123]

In the 2020/2021 state general fund budget, K-12 and higher education spending totaled $77 billion, but given the state has amassed a $15 billion surplus due to unanticipated tax revenue collections from high-income earners who did not lose their jobs during the pandemic, spending for K-12 and community colleges is set to reach $85.8 billion in the 2021/2022 budget.[124]

The reason such huge budget allotments are carved out for public education is because K-12 and community colleges are guaranteed funding through **Proposition 98 (a voter approved initiative in 1988 that mandates 40% of the State Budget goes to K-12 schools and community colleges)** Sounds great for the schools, but not everybody has been happy with education gobbling up so much of the windfall. Advocates for the poor and disabled argued that poverty programs for the needy took large budget cuts during the Great Recession of 2008 and have not seen those cuts replaced by the Legislature and the Governor. *"Among human service advocates there is mounting frustration with a lack of investment in the state's safety net, post-recession, in general"*, noted Chris Hoene, executive director of the California Budget and Policy Center, an organization that studies the budget's impact on impoverished Californians.[125] **Proposition 98** benefits and protects funding for California public education, but nothing like it exists to guarantee poverty related monies in the budget, prompting some lawmakers to suggest poverty programs should be covered by Proposition 98 as well.

However, with Congress approving the COVID-19 relief package in March 2021, the child tax credit was significantly expanded, and low-income families eligible for the entire credit will receive payments of up to $300 per child per month until the end of 2021. In addition, Governor Newsom and the State Legislature are using some of the $15 billion surplus to provide $600 payments to low-income Californians. While expanding the child tax credit at the federal level and giving poor Californians additional money at the state level will help in 2021, advocates for the impoverished, like Chris Hoene, would prefer making permanent guaranteed funding for the poor akin to the mandated spending on public education Proposition 98 provides.

HIGHER EDUCATION

As already mentioned, California has three institutions of higher learning, the California Community College System, the California State University, and the University of California. All three are covered under the Master Plan For Higher Education. **The Master Plan For Higher Education was created from the Donahoe Higher Education Act passed by the State Legislature in 1960. Under the Master Plan, California's three higher education institutions would have distinct missions, enrollment requirements, and governing structures.**

The California Community Colleges offer General Education courses students must complete to be eligible for a Bachelors Degree. These General Education courses are transferrable to California State University and University of California colleges as called for by the Master Plan. The state's community colleges also provide vocational training courses in such areas as law enforcement, fire fighting, auto mechanics, and agriculture. Admission to a community college is open to all students applying. The 112 California Community Colleges currently serve some 2.6 million students, the largest college system in the nation. Governance of this immense system is shared between a 17 seat Board of Governors whose members are appointed by the Governor and a locally elected Board of Trustees charged with operating the local colleges within their district. There are 72 community college districts dispersed throughout the state, and each district has a Board of Trustees.[126]

The California State University (CSU) offers Bachelors and Masters Degrees in such fields as Business, Computer Science, Liberal Studies, Nursing, Science, Social Science, and Education. Following the Master Plan, California State University considers admission of the top one third of high school graduates. The 23 California State University campuses currently enroll 450,000 students. A 25-member Board of Trustees governs the CSU and is responsible for broad curricular development of academic course content and the management of funds, property, facilities, and investments by the system and the campuses. The Governor appoints 16 of the 25 Board of Trustees, the balance of seats consists of the Governor, Lieutenant Governor, State Superintendent of Public Instruction, Speaker of the Assembly, and the Board Chancellor. Alumni, faculty, and student appointees round out the Board membership.[127]

The University of California (UC) consists of the state's major research campuses, and while they provide Bachelors and Masters Degrees, UC campuses are the only public universities in California where students can obtain Doctoral Degrees. The State Legislature in 2006 authorized CSU to offer a Doctorate in Education Leadership, but obtaining a Doctorate from a public university in California remains the province of the UC.[128] Admission to the University of California, as described by the Master Plan, is designed for the top 12.5 percent of high school seniors. The 9 UC's across the state annually enroll 216,000 students. Article IX, section 9 of the California Constitution created the UC Board of Regents to govern the UC system. The board consists of 26 members, 18 of which are appointed by the Governor. Other Regents include the Governor, Lieutenant Governor, State Superintendent of Public Instruction, Speaker of the Assembly, and the UC President. Alumni, faculty, and student members fill the remaining seats.

The Master Plan For Higher Education encompassed a system of affordable, high quality education for Californians through these three institutions. Under the Master Plan of 1960, students would not be charged tuition, only modest fees. One of the cruel ironies of California's two-tier economy is that many of today's upper tier workers in the state benefited from the low-cost education the Master Plan provided them. Today, students enrolled in a state community college or state university are being confronted with spiraling tuition increases and reduced course offerings never envisioned in the Master Plan.

Tuition Increases and Largesse

In the 2011/2012 budget, the State Legislature imposed devastating cuts on California's three institutions of higher education; $400 million for the California Community College System and $650 million apiece for the state's two university systems (California State University and University of California). The Legislature also approved in 2012 a $10 per unit fee increase on community college students, raising the cost to $46 a unit. That set the cost of a three-unit community college course to $138. In 2000, a three-unit community college course would have cost the student $33.[129]

Fee increases have been equally dramatic at the state's two university systems. Students attending CSU in 2002 were paying $1,507 a year. By 2011, CSU students were paying $5,472 a year, a 263 percent hike over the ten-year period. UC fees in 2002 were $3,564 annually. Students attending a UC began shelling out $12, 192 a year in 2011, a 242 percent jump since 2002.[130] In 2017, both CSU and UC approved tuition hikes on their students, the first in six years, CSU adding $270 and UC imposing an additional $280.

CSU and UC officials were quick to cite that financial aid absorbs tuition costs for California's low-income students. At CSU, students from families earning up to $70,000 qualify for grants that pay the tuition. UC grants covering tuition are available for students whose families earn up to $80,000. However, that leaves a wide gap of middle-class families that don't qualify for the grants, and struggle to afford the tuition hikes CSU and UC have approved. According to a UC report, the share of UC students from middle class families has declined (the very group these tuition hikes hit the hardest), while the portion of UC students from low income and upper income families has increased over the past ten years.[131]

In the summer of 2011, both the CSU Board of Trustees and the UC Board of Regents approved 20 percent fee increases from the previous year on their students. After the CSU Board of Trustees voted to increase the fees, California State University, Chico President Paul Zingg said, *"No trustee is happy to authorize another fee increase. Yet, they are keenly aware what the implications are for reduced access and diminished quality if the loss of at least another $650 million this year is not addressed with student fee revenues and ongoing cost reductions on all campuses."*[132]

Chico State President Zingg acknowledged the severity of the $650 million hit the CSU endured from the state in the 2011/2012 budget. However, at the same meeting in which the CSU Board of Trustees approved the 20 percent fee hike, the Trustees also approved raising the salary of the new incoming San Diego State President by $100,000, prompting the following scathing response from the Chico Enterprise Record newspaper, *The CSU system claims it has no money, and therefore students must pay more, but the truth is, administrators always seem to find money to take care of themselves.* Similar complaints about the salary spike were echoed in other newspapers across the state.

A less noticed, but more significant action undertaken by the University of California and California State University in 2011 was the loaning of large chunks of money to the state. Senate Bill 79 allowed the state to borrow cash reserve funds held by the UC and CSU systems. UC loaned the state **$1 billion** and CSU sent the state **$700 million**. SB 79 was passed as part of the

2011/2012 budget deal, shortly before both the CSU Board of Trustees and the UC Board of Regents approved the 20 percent fee increases on the students.

Robert Turnage, CSU Assistant Vice Chancellor For Budget, acknowledged that the CSU is sitting on **$2 billion** in reserve funds. When asked why some of that money could not be used to prevent the student fee hikes, Turnage replied, *"The budget cut just delivered by the Legislature is a permanent cut in our base funding from the state...if we were to draw down our short-term investment pool to avoid other steps like a fee increase, then we would have another hole next year."* Turnage estimated CSU would garner a 1.5 percent return on the loan.[133]

In 2017, as UC officials voted to increase tuition, a state audit revealed UC secretly held a $175 million slush fund that it reportedly spent on administrator bonuses and home renovations of campus chancellors, eliciting a fierce response from Assemblyman Dante Acosta, *"California students were hit with a tuition increase shortly before the slush fund was made public. Calls to give the UC benefit of the doubt do students and parents a disservice. We've seen bloated administrator salaries, budget trickery and resistance to oversight. If the Legislature won't look out for students and demand accountability, who will?"*[134]

Determining how much money these higher education institutions hold may not be known. In 2019, California State Auditor Elaine Howle unearthed **$1.5 billion** in surplus funds held by the California State University System. The money was stashed away in outside accounts.[135] And, while all this money was hidden, CSU raised tuition on students and asked the California State Legislature for more funding. CSU Chancellor Timothy P. White attempted to rationalize CSU's holding back such a massive amount of money, *"Reserve funds are like a family savings account or the much-acclaimed state of California Rainy Day Fund which is built up gradually over time and used to pay for one-time necessary expenses or protect against uncertainties."* But the Sacramento Bee Editorial Board pointed out, *"Few families have an extra **$1.5 billion** lying around, and families generally don't raise tuition on their own children."*[136]

Both the CSU and UC pursue other avenues to enhance their revenue streams. In 2011, California State University developed **Student Success Fees, additional fees a CSU campus levies on students for such things as the hiring of more faculty, the addition of more class sections, and upgrades in technological equipment.** By 2014, 12 of CSU's campuses included Student Success Fees from $162 per year at CSU, San Bernardino to $630 per year at San Jose State and Cal Poly San Luis Obispo. While some CSU campuses had these fees approved by a student vote, the fees have not been well received by all. Sonoma State backed off on plans to introduce Student Success Fees after angry students drew up and distributed petitions encouraging a moratorium of donations to the college. San Jose State reduced their Student Success Fees by $40 after a budget review of the university's expenditures revealed that the college spent 40% of the Student Success Fees on athletics (San Jose State had intended to increase their Student Success Fees $160 before the budget review became public).[137]

In 2021, with the virus prompting the conversion to online instruction, students attending CSU and UC continue being levied fees for on campus services (such as gyms, health centers, and student centers) they can't access due to the pandemic. In 2020, this resulted in class action lawsuits being filed in federal court against the CSU and UC systems on behalf of some 700,000 students.[138] The lawsuits, if successful, would compel CSU and UC to refund millions of dollars in fees, something neither university system is keen on doing given both have already lost hundreds of millions of dollars in housing and dining expenses students chose to forgo on account of COVID-19.[139] Perhaps CSU and UC could settle and refund the service fees to the students. After all, both the CSU and UC have that "family savings account" for uncertainties CSU Chancellor Timothy P. White was talking about.

Another revenue generating strategy employed by both the CSU and UC is increasing the number of out-of-state and international applicants admitted to both institutions because those students can be charged additional tuition (which generates hundreds of millions of dollars) state residential students do not pay. In 2015, out-of-state applicants (31,651) and international applicants (29,839) for the University Of California's nine campuses resulted in one-third of UC students statewide not being California residents.[140]

Student Debt

The 1960 Master Plan For Higher Education in California was the product of UC President Emeritus Clark Kerr and former Governor Edmund G. Brown, the father of current California Governor Jerry Brown. These visionaries designed the plan to provide quality college and university educational opportunities for all Californians. Not only is the Master Plan being compromised by rising costs, but students shelling out more in fees are being confronted with a higher amount of debt when leaving college.

Based on a report by the Federal Reserve Bank of New York, college student loan debt across the nation has tripled in a decade. In 2021, some 45 million Americans collectively are on the hook for $1.7 trillion in student debt.[141] The California Legislative Analyst's Office concluded in 2017 that 53% of UC and CSU students graduate with an average debt of $19,500. Such staggering student loan debt is creating structural shifts in both education and the economy.

Between 2008 and 2013, California experienced a 40% reduction of teachers with less than 6 years of experience. A college graduate confronted with extensive student loan debt may opt to seek more lucrative employment other than teaching, especially given the hyper inflated cost of California housing covered earlier in the chapter. In addition, college student loan debt is lowering the number of college graduates entering the real estate market. In 2018, first time home buyers represented 33% of real estate purchases in California, according to the California Association of Realtors.

Free College?

With college students confronted with soaring tuition, larger amounts of student debt, and higher living expenses ($25,000 the average annual cost of attending a CSU and $35,000 the average annual cost of attending a UC), a movement is afoot nationwide to make public higher education, like K-12 public schools, free. At the national level, U.S. Senator Bernie Sanders has introduced legislation that would cover college tuition at all public universities for students whose annual family income is below $125,000 and make community college free for everyone. Sanders would finance all this by taxing stock transactions.[142] In January 2021, newly elected President Joe Biden has indicated he supports Senator Sanders' plan.

In 2017, the California Legislature approved $46 million for the state's 114 community colleges in a special fund that gave the higher education institutions flexibility in how to spend the money to help students cover some of their costs, and many of the colleges have used the funds to provide free first year tuition for all of their students, not just the ones who qualify for financial aid.[143]

California lawmakers in 2017 also considered a number of approaches to eliminate higher education costs. One idea would levy a 1% tax on annual California household incomes in excess of $1 million that could be coupled with federal and state financial aid to end tuition and fees for all public colleges and universities in the Golden State. Another measure would develop a 'debt free' college plan that would expand financial aid to cover living expenses for some 400,000 CSU and UC students whose families earn under $150,000 per year. A third idea developed by a consortium of California faculty associations, unions, and advocacy groups would level a $48 per household tax, generating $9.4 billion annually, cancelling student tuition and increasing funding for all state colleges and universities.[144] It is worth noting though, as mentioned earlier in the chapter, that taxes have been imposed and extended on those earning over $250,000 already, and, as we will examine in the next chapter, proposals like these would most likely need to be approved by the voters.

CALIFORNIA IN THE AMERICAN SYSTEM

As defined, politics is the process by which decisions are made and we have examined several of California's most pressing issues in this first chapter. Solutions for these problems are anything but simple given the various interests competing to obtain government policies beneficial to their needs. With California's **economy** growing more stratified between top tier and lower tier income earners, do we need to increase the state's minimum wage or cut taxes and environmental regulations to improve the economy? Should we construct more **affordable housing** or allow local government interests to limit such development? How should the state address the challenges of a changing **population** that is not only growing, but getting older?

What should the state do to ensure enough **water** is available for both residents and the **agriculture** industry? Can the state thrive economically by changing the types of **energy** sources that power our utilities and provide our **transportation**? Is the state doing enough to protect a fragile **environment** impacted by both an ever- increasing population and industrial development?

As **health care** costs continue to rise, what can the state do to make health insurance not only available to more Californians, but affordable as well? Is the answer repealing the Affordable Care Act and turning more control over health care to the states, is it keeping the Affordable Care Act intact and amending it, or is it moving to a single payer system where the government exclusively oversees health care?

Concerning **education**, what steps can California take to improve the quality of education for our K-12 students, and maintain a system of higher education that Californians can access? Should K-12 standards be set by the state, or should national standards be incorporated? What can be done to make college more affordable, especially for students whose families earn too much to qualify for financial aid, but not enough to cover the ever-rising tuition rates CSU and UC have imposed?

Finally, given the extraordinary circumstances the world faces with the COVID-19 pandemic, how does California navigate its way through this health crisis? Well past a year into closed businesses, online instruction, and limited social interaction Californians, like everyone else, have developed COVID-19 fatigue. Facing a potential Recall Election in the Fall of 2021, Governor Gavin Newsom will have more difficult decisions to make based on if the virus continues its destructive path through the population or diminishes. Will there be a requirement for individuals to prove they have been vaccinated as a basis to board a plane, enter a theatre or ballpark, or attend in person classes in college? The Governors in Texas and Florida have issued executive orders prohibiting proof of vaccination be required in their states.

There is optimism that the virus has run its course, but the Spanish Flu 100 years ago lasted two plus years and was devastating in the number of deaths globally (estimated to be 50 million). Hopefully, we will not see such horrific casualties from this pandemic.

In considering all of these issues in this first chapter, we have discussed how California is interwoven with the federal government in attempting to craft solutions under the structure of Federalism created by our U.S. Constitution. As described, **Federalism involves two or more governments exercising power and authority over the same people and the same territory.** Under this system, though, problems can develop when sovereignty disputes erupt between states and the federal government, and in California the state faced a number of such disputes during the Trump Administration (examined in this first chapter) over immigration, funding of the bullet train, protecting endangered fish in the Delta, and health care. The state filed a flurry of lawsuits (approximately 100) against Trump administration policies dealing with the potential construction of a border wall, failing to enforce clean air standards, and the threat of withholding federal funds in response to California becoming a sanctuary state (to name a few). Donald Trump is no longer President, but the critical issues and challenges for California this first chapter has examined existed long before Donald Trump took office. Joe Biden's election as President in 2020 will end much of the litigation California became entangled in during the Trump Administration. However, the problems outlined in this first chapter persist in the Golden State.

The goal of this text is to help the student understand how California government functions in our American constitutional system. California is a large, diverse, and complex state, and even though Democrats currently control the state government, large geographic sections of the state (located in the rural north and Central Valley) comprise residents that have differing political ideologies from their urban and coastal counterparts. In fact, most of the northern and Central Valley counties voted for Donald Trump in 2016 and 2020, and over the years these counties have consistently been Republican territory. In stark contrast, the coastal and urban parts of the state (where a majority of the population resides), is solidly Democrat.

In the coming chapters we will examine the evolvement of California's government in the American system after it became the 31st state in 1850, describing how California and the federal government's political institutions compare and contrast. Learning about these differences illustrates why politics (the decision-making process) is anything but swift in an American system of government where states and the national government share power.

2
CHAPTER

CALIFORNIA POLITICAL HISTORY

In September, 1542 Portuguese explorer Juan Rodriguez Cabrillo, under the flag of Spain, led two small vessels up the California coast, sailing into what is today San Diego harbor. Cabrillo's ships proceeded northward on the seven month voyage, entering the bay near Los Angeles, but bypassing the Monterey and San Francisco bays during their trek up the coastline. Cabrillo died during the expedition, yet his exploits led to the beginning of Spanish influence in California.

Two centuries later, in 1769, California's first Spanish Mission was established in San Diego by Captain Don Portola and Father Junipero Serra. **California's Missions were created by the Spanish in the 18th century to begin Spanish colonization of California and convert the Native Americans to Christianity and allegiance to Spain.** Spain established a total of 21 Missions in California from San Diego to Sonoma. The Missions were located in soil rich locations where crops could be grown and were strategically separated some 30 miles apart (a day's horseback ride).[1] **The El Camino Real was the road established by the Spanish to connect California's 21 Missions.** The Missions also allowed Spain to permanently cement a strong military presence in California.

By the early 1800's, Spanish dominance of their American Colonies created resentment from the colonists, who grew weary of a system of government that fostered social discrimination and economic inequality. During this time, Spain became occupied in wars with France and England. The mother country was losing control of its remote colonies, including California. The end came in 1821 when revolutionaries discarded the yoke of Spain, taking control of

Mexico City and creating the government of Mexico. California accepted the Mexican government, and several former Spanish officials swore allegiance to the new ruler in Mexico City, Agustin Iturbide.[2]

Territorial disputes between Mexico and the United States over the Texas border led to war between the nations from 1846-1848. California did not see much fighting occur, but by January 1847 American forces had taken control of Los Angeles and Monterey Bay. **The Treaty of Guadalupe Hidalgo (1848) ended the war between the United States and Mexico, ceding California and New Mexico to the United States. Mexico received $15 million in payments from the United States for the two territories.**[3]

STATEHOOD AND CALIFORNIA'S 1ST CONSTITUTION

Article IV, Section 3 of the United States Constitution allows for the admission of new states by Congress, and in 1850 Congress admitted California as the 31st state of the union. California statehood was significant given that fifteen states allowed slavery and fifteen states banned slavery when California entered the union as a free state. Southern states in Congress accepted the Compromise of 1850 which granted California admittance as a free state in exchange for future Territories (New Mexico and Utah) being allowed to decide whether slavery would be legal if they became states.[4]

On June 3, 1849, acting as the military governor of the territory, General Bennett Riley issued a proclamation calling for the selection of delegates to draft California's 1st Constitution. The 48 delegates were elected through the region, and assembled in Monterey, California in September 1849. These delegates created California's 1st Constitution with the following provisions:

- Slavery would be prohibited
- California's boundary line would be drawn east of the Sierra crest and along the desert floor
- Created a two-house legislature
- Created an executive branch with a governor
- Created a judicial branch with four levels of courts
- Established separate property rights for married women
- Official state documents would be printed in English and Spanish
- Only white males 21 and over could vote

California's 1ˢᵗ Constitution was approved by a near unanimous vote of white males on November 13, 1849. Peter H. Burnett was elected California's 1ˢᵗ Governor in 1849 and San Jose became the state's first capital that same year. Less than a year later, on September 9, 1850 President Millard Fillmore signed the admission bill and California was admitted to the union.[5]

THE TRANSCONTINENTAL RAILROAD

When James Marshall discovered gold at Sutter's Mill on the American River in January 1848, an accelerated emigration to California began. President James Polk highlighted the discovery of gold in California during a presidential address in December 1848. A year later, California's population grew from 26,000 to 115,000. By 1850, San Francisco swelled to 25,000.[6]

The gold rush was on, and people were scrambling to California, but getting to the Golden State was a challenge, especially for those travelling from the Eastern United States. Trekking overland from back East was difficult. Railroad tracks ended at the Mississippi River. From there, adventurers, gold seekers, and settlers attempting to reach California drove hoarse drawn wagons through rugged terrain and hostile Native American lands. Thousands perished, and even if they made it to California, the formidable Sierra Nevada Mountains were a nearly impassable barrier during winter.

In October of 1846, a party of Illinois settlers led by George Donner entered the Sierra Nevada Mountains. An early snowstorm trapped the Donner Party near what is today the town of Truckee, and 34 of the 79 members died, including George Donner and his wife. It is believed that the survivors, lacking food, consumed the remains of the deceased, making the Donner tragedy an enduring saga. The Donner Party's woes also reinforced the dangers of journeying to California overland.

Sailing in a ship from the Eastern Seaboard took 6 months around South America's Cape Horn. With the gold rush and statehood, California needed to be connected to the rest of the nation, which lay east of the Mississippi River. The answer was the Transcontinental Railroad.

Theodore Judah, an ambitious civil engineer from Troy, New York, spent the summer of 1860 in the Sierra Nevada Mountains, plotting out a railroad route through the rugged mountains east of Sacramento. When Judah attempted to secure funding for the railroad from San Francisco investors, he failed. However, four Sacramento shopkeepers were intrigued by Judah's idea and agreed to help him finance the project. **The Big Four (Leland Stanford, Collis Huntington, Charles Crocker, and Mark Hopkins) financed the western portion of the Transcontinental Railroad during the 1860's and created a monopoly of power in California.**

Judah and his colleagues convinced Congress to subsidize the railroad and in 1862 Congress passed the Railroad Act, authorizing two companies (the Union Pacific and the Central Pacific) to construct the Transcontinental Railroad that would connect California with the rest of the nation. The Union Pacific began building west from Omaha, Nebraska while the Central Pacific (headed by Judah and the Big Four) undertook the herculean task of laying track through the Sierra Nevada Mountains. As construction began east of Sacramento, Judah found himself alienated from his partners, who were motivated by the prospect of large profits. Frustrated with the Big Four, Judah set out for New York to find new investors. Since time was of the essence, Judah attempted to reach the east coast by sailing to Panama, crossing the isthmus then boarding another vessel for New York. In Panama, he contracted a fatal case of yellow fever. Theodore Judah died on November 2, 1863, leaving the Big Four to profit from his ingenuity.[7]

However, constructing the western portion of the railroad was no easy task. Despite federal government subsides to build the railroad, three years into the project the Central Pacific was deeply in debt. Construction commenced during the Civil War, creating expenses not foreseen by the Big Four. Wood for the ties was easily obtained in California, but the rail, cars, and engines all had to be shipped from back east because manufacturing of such goods did not exist in California at the time. The war generated high demand for manufactured goods, inflating prices. Twenty-pound iron rails that sold at $55 per ton before the Civil War began spiked to $262 per ton by the end of the war in 1865.[8] Insurance rates for materials shipped from the east coast also soared as a result of the war. Confederate warships, constantly seeking powder and iron, harassed shipping lanes off the Atlantic coast, driving up the price of insuring the supplies.[9] The supply line itself was mind boggling (15,000 miles sailing around Cape Horn followed by the long truck up into the Sierra Nevada Mountains).

Facing such challenges, the Big Four each undertook important tasks during the project. Leland Stanford was elected Governor of California in 1862, and though he served only two years in office, he used his political power to obtain state subsidies for the Central Pacific Railroad that included public funds from local governments, and a $10, 000 warrant from the state treasury for every mile of track laid east of Sacramento.[10]

Collis Huntington, the shrewdest member of the Big Four, spent most of his time in New York and Washington raising money, purchasing equipment, and lobbying Congress. Due to the lobbying efforts of Huntington, and Theodore Judah before he died, the Federal Government, through the Railroad Act of 1862, provided extensive land grants and federal subsidies to both railroad companies. The Federal Government agreed to pay the Central Pacific Railroad

$16,000 per mile of track laid on flat land, $32,000 per mile of track laid in the foothills, and $48,000 per mile of track laid in the Sierra Nevada Mountains.

Charles Crocker took control of construction, the most critical task of the four. He later admitted to having no experience with railroads and literally learned on the job. But Crocker had a load of self confidence, once boasting, "Everyone was afraid of me."[11] The biggest challenge initially was a reliable work force. Many Caucasian laborers simply did not show up to work, and those that did only remained until they earned enough money to get themselves to the silver mines in Nevada. In desperation, Crocker brought in a team of 50 Chinese workers and discovered statistically they were doing a better job than the heavier Caucasians.[12] Immediately more Chinese were hired, and by 1865 the Big Four were contracting with companies to ship more Chinese from their homeland to work on the western portion of the Trans Continental Railroad. By 1866, some 10,000 Chinese performed the dangerous tasks of building the railroad through the Sierra Nevada Mountains.

Mark Hopkins served as the treasurer of the Central Pacific, administrating the day-to-day operations of the business. Coordinating the accounting was difficult given that costs were higher due to the Civil War, and government subsidies were tied to completing so many miles of track. Hopkins, realizing the importance of a reliable labor force, assisted Crocker by developing companies that would recruit and transport to California more Chinese railroad workers. The hiring of the Chinese in such large numbers combined with the huge monopoly created by the Central Pacific Railroad led to deep resentment by Caucasians (particularly the Irish in San Francisco) of the Chinese and the Big Four.

The construction of the Trans Continental Railroad took seven years to complete. To this day, accurate numbers of how many died in building it are not known. One estimate suggests some 2000 Chinese workers perished during the project. Blasting through cliff faces in the Sierra Nevada was extremely dangerous, and Charles Crocker, facing pressure to meet quotas, tried nitro glycerin, a violent explosive that increased their production, but at a very high price. After several fatal accidents, the nitro glycerin was discarded, but the black powder used in blasting away at the granite also accounted for many fatalities. Avalanches in the Sierra Nevada during winter carried entire work crews down the mountainside, and their bodies would not be recovered until the spring thaw. The bitter cold winter was responsible for many deaths as well given no adequate shelter was available for the thousands of workers toiling away in the remote mountains.[13]

Despite these hardships, and the sheer enormity of the project, the Central Pacific Railroad hooked up with the Union Pacific Railroad at

Promontory Point, Utah on May 10, 1869. Now, someone traveling from New York to San Francisco could reach their destination in ten days riding a train.

THE BIG FOUR'S MONOPOLY

The nation and California fell on hard economic times during the 1870's fostered by the national panic of 1873. **The National Panic of 1873 involved twenty-five railroad companies across the nation defaulting on their interest payments and a major investment firm (Jay Cooke and Company) filing for bankruptcy. This resulted in a panic driven sell off prompting the stock market to close for ten days.**[14] The Big Four, now operating under the Southern Pacific Railroad Company, survived the national panic of 1873, but their heavy- handed tactics in controlling shipping, land, local and state government, and the media bred contempt from farmers and blue-collar workers who blamed the railroad's monopoly for contributing to the economic hardships the state endured throughout the 1870's.

The Big Four monopoly of shipping in the Golden State was astounding once construction of the Trans Continental Railroad commenced. By 1865, the Big Four were shipping such items as timber, gold, silver, farm crops, and manufactured goods. The rate for shipping these goods was determined by the Southern Pacific which operated under the premise, "All the traffic will bear." That equated to the Southern Pacific charging inflated prices that nearly drove businesses into bankruptcy. Companies doing business with the Southern Pacific had to submit their profits to the railroad company, and then the Southern Pacific would determine what the shipping rate would be.[15]

The Southern Pacific also got into the steam ship and ferry business, lowering prices for travel when competing firms attempted to enter the market. When price gouging did not bear immediate fruit, the Southern Pacific resorted to more base tactics. Passengers exiting a competing ferry in San Francisco found themselves caked in coal dust released from a bunker by Southern Pacific employees.[16] Eventually, the competition folded, and the Southern Pacific jacked the rates back up.

The California State Legislature did nothing about the blatant price gouging, and the Southern Pacific made sure it remained that way until the early 1900's. Southern Pacific lobbyists regularly bought off state lawmakers, and each week SP lobbyist William Herrin provided a round trip train ticket from Sacramento to San Francisco for each member of the legislature.[17]

California local governments felt the sting of the Big Four's monopoly as well. County and city governments were compelled to subsidize the Southern Pacific by issuing local construction bonds for the building of bridges, trestles, overpasses, and train stations. Given the SP owned 85% of track and some 11.5 million acres of land in the state, local governments, particularly smaller communities like Fresno, Merced, Bakersfield, and Modesto had little choice but to submit to the railroad company's demands or face the grim prospect of the railroad bypassing their town.

While the media was critical of the Southern Pacific, the railroad dispensed cash to newspapers with monthly payments in hopes of receiving more positive publicity. When agents from the Southern Pacific attempted to evict farmers near the town of Hanford over a property dispute in 1880, a gun battle ensued, resulting in seven deaths. Accounts of the incident (known as the Battle of Mussel Slough) were controlled by Southern Pacific officials. In San Francisco, Charles Crocker and other SP members provided details to the local newspapers, framing the story that ruffian farmers had attacked the Southern Pacific agents and the federal marshal who accompanied them. The newspapers printed the Southern Pacific's version. Later, reports from witnesses and survivors described how one of the Southern Pacific's agents had drawn a shotgun and fired first, killing one of the farmers. It made little difference. The surviving farmers were evicted from their property.[18]

CALIFORNIA'S 2ND STATE CONSTITUTION 1879

As the 1870's dragged on, California faced economic problems. The Panic of 1873 had spooked investments, unfavorable weather conditions hurt farmers, unemployment skyrocketed, the gold rush was over, and the Big Four monopoly weighed on the state like an anvil. In San Francisco, disgruntled Irish workers under the leadership of Dennis Kearney organized the Workingmen's Party. **The Workingmen's Party was founded in 1877, consisting of some 15,000 San Francisco Irishman led by Dennis Kearney. The Workingmen's Party was anti-Chinese and anti-Railroad and had significant influence on California's 2nd State Constitution of 1879.**

Kearney was a born agitator, and given the harsh economic times, cultivated an enthusiastic following with speeches invoking populist slogans laced with bigotry and class struggle. "The Chinese Must Go!" "Rid the country of cheap Chinese labor." "Wrest the government from the hands of the rich and place it in those of the people." Kearney also declared that every Workingman should own a gun.[19] Kearney's call to arms and penchant for encouraging violence against the Chinese and the affluent eventually landed him in jail, but imprisoning the provocateur only increased his status in San Francisco. However, the Workingmen's Party was not anarchist, and eventually became a significant political force in the state. From 1878-1879, the Workingmen's Party helped elect Supreme Court judges, eleven state senators, and sixteen state assemblymen.[20] Yet their biggest influence on California politics would come at the second state constitutional convention of 1878.

On September 5, 1877, California's 2nd state constitutional convention was called by a majority of the state's voters. The convention opened the following year on September 28, 1878 in Sacramento. One third of the 152 delegates selected by California voters to the convention came from the Workingmen's Party, and their influence was imprinted upon the new constitution.

The delegates elected to the convention represented three main interests: (1) capitalists, corporations, and large landowners; (2) farmers opposed to the railroad monopoly; (3) city laborers opposed to the railroad monopoly and the Chinese.[21] The more things change, the more they remain the same. These delegates were divided over the salient issue that remains at the heart of our political discourse; how much control the government should have over the economy. The result was a document that placated the Workingmen's delegates but did little to alleviate the stranglehold the Southern Pacific had on the state. Let us review key aspects of California's 2nd State Constitution.

Taxation   Two convention delegates suggested the poor should assume the burden of future taxes unless a plan developed to equalize taxes on all groups.[22] As debate proceeded, it was agreed that the State Board of Equalization (originally created in 1870) would be empowered to assess the value of all property subject to taxes by the state. The Board of Equalization would also be able to assess the franchise, roadway, roadbed, rails, and stock of all railroads operated in more than one county in the state.[23] The Southern Pacific, the state's largest landowner, would pay more in property taxes, something the Workingmen's Party delegates strongly supported.

The Railroad Commission   The Southern Pacific's control of passenger and freight rates roiled the farmers and the Workingmen, and an elected three-member Railroad Commission was established by the delegates. The elected commissioners were to set shipping rates, not the Southern Pacific. Despite this reform, the Southern Pacific's shipping monopoly went on into the early 20th century as the Railroad Commission proved to be ineffective and subject to influence by the SP.

Chinese Restrictions   Anti-Chinese sentiment was strong amongst the Workingmen's delegates, one such delegate suggesting Dennis Kearney's battle cry, "The Chinese must go!" be inserted in the new constitution. Language approved in the 2nd constitution prohibited the employment of Chinese by private corporations. This provision would subsequently be ruled a violation of the U.S. Constitution, but at the time it satisfied the Workingmen.

As already discussed, the Big Four hired some 10,000 Chinese to build the western portion of the Transcontinental Railroad, a fact that continued to fester like a boil upon the collective conscience of the Workingmen. Spurred by such animosity for the Chinese, the Workingmen's delegates successfully placed a clause in the 2nd constitution that banned Chinese employment on any state, county, municipal, or other public works project. The California Legislature and the voters did not officially eliminate the clause until 1952.

Anti-Asian sentiment has historical roots in California from how the Chinese were treated in the 19th Century to the internment of Japanese Americans during World War II. And that anti-Asian bias has reared its ugly head today as the nation deals with the pandemic. The labeling of the Corona Virus as "The China Virus" and "Kung Flu" by President Donald Trump as COVID-19 savaged the nation in 2020 have critics of the former President attributing his remarks to a rash of hate crimes and hate speech targeting Asian Americans. Between March 2020 and February 2021, the Stop AAPI (Asian American Pacific Islander) Hate Reporting Center received 1,691 reports of anti-Asian discrimination in California.[24] Reports of people yelling at Asian-Americans and spitting on them have been documented, and multiple videos of Asian-Americans (particularly elderly ones) being physically assaulted in public have sprouted up on the internet and television. In February 2021, an 84-year-old Thai man died when an attacker cruelly shoved him to the ground in San Francisco.[25] The deadliest episode occurred in Atlanta, Georgia in March 2021 when a gunman killed eight people at three massage parlors. Six of the victims were of Asian descent. It is suspected that the Corona Virus originated from China, and President Trump did denounce the physical and verbal attacks against Asian Americans. But as far as Donald Trump's critics are concerned, words have meanings, especially when those words are uttered or tweeted by the President of the United States.

The terrible economy of the 1870's created the environment for the Workingmen's Party to blame the Chinese for the lack of jobs available to San Francisco Irish workers, prompting the convention delegates to support a prohibition of Chinese employment in California's 2nd Constitution of 1879. In 2021, Asian-Americans are being scapegoated once again. For no other reason besides race, Asian-Americans find themselves targeted, as if they are responsible for the spread of COVID-19 when the truth is they have nothing to do with it.

The State Legislature - The delegates at the 2nd State Constitutional Convention of 1878 increased the size of California's two-house legislature to its' current number of seats (80 in the State Assembly and 40 in the State Senate).

The Legislature did suffer a loss in appropriation power as the delegates prohibited state funds from being spent to aid private institutions (including religious schools and hospitals)[26]

The Executive Branch   Convention delegates granted the Governor of California authority to call the State Legislature into a special session, and if the Governor did so the Legislature could only consider the issue the Governor requested. This power has been used by governors over the years, most recently by Governor Jerry Brown in 2015, summoning the Legislature to deal with funding for the state's roads and Medi-Cal. Governor Arnold Schwarzenegger called the Legislature into a special session in 2006 due to the overcrowding of inmates in the state's prisons, an issue we will address later in the book. However, in 2020, some California lawmakers grew frustrated Governor Gavin Newsom did not call the Legislature into a special session so lawmakers could be included in managing the state through the pandemic. Republican Assembly-member Kevin Kiley indicated his disappointment with Democratic leaders in the Assembly and Senate for not pressuring Governor Newsom to call a special session, *If the legislative leadership said, 'Look, we want to be a coequal partner in managing these next several months and beyond and we would like you to summon us', I think that would create a lot of pressure for the Governor to agree to it, but the legislative leadership has had no interest in that.*"[27]

The Judicial Branch   California's 2nd Constitution expanded the State Supreme Court to its current size (one chief justice and six associate justices). The delegates allowed the State Legislature to create lower courts, and today the California judiciary consists of county Superior Courts, six Appellate Court Districts, and the State Supreme Court.

California's 2nd State Constitution was approved by the state's voters in May of 1879. The lengthy document is the current constitution of the Golden State and has been amended over five hundred times since its inception. The dizzying number of amendments in California's Constitution highlight a key difference between the state's constitution and the U.S. Constitution. Over 200 plus years, the U.S. Constitution has been amended only 27 times given the Framers made it extremely difficult to amend the document. **In order to amend the U.S. Constitution, a two-thirds vote of the U.S. House of Representatives and the United States Senate is required. The proposed amendment would then have to be ratified by three fourths of the states (38 states).** The Framers knew achieving such super majorities would make amending the U.S. Constitution extremely difficult.

California's Constitution can be amended by the voters through state-wide elections, and each election season, Golden State voters are confronted with a plethora of propositions, several of them proposed amendments to the State Constitution. These amendments can be sent to the voters by a two-thirds vote of the State Assembly and State Senate. Proposed amendments also qualify for the ballot through the initiative process which involves gathering the required number of signatures to force the measure before the voters.

Amendments to the 2nd Constitution, many of them voter approved, have restricted the legislative and executive branches concerning state budget appropriations and taxes. Given the intractable political environment of today, many government analysts believe California is no longer governable under the 2nd Constitution. However, attempts to call for a third state constitutional convention fell flat in 2010. Why do we have so many voter-approved amendments imbedded in California's 2nd Constitution? The answer comes from the Progressive movement of the early 20th century.

THE PROGRESSIVES

Collis Huntington, the last surviving member of the Big Four, died in 1900, but even though the railroad barons were all gone, the Southern Pacific's monopolistic grip on California shipping, land, and government endured at the turn of the century. However, with Theodore Roosevelt becoming President in 1901, a wave of populism swept over the nation. **Populism is a continuing American political philosophy embraced by large numbers of rural and urban poor, who seek by democratic means to use the power of government to cope with the financial giants of business, industry, and commerce.** Roosevelt opposed the corruptive influence of corporate monopolies and supported the rights of workers to organize and collectively bargain with their employers. Like minded reformers Charles Evan Hughes of New York (who went after the insurance industry) and Robert M. La Follette of Wisconsin (who investigated the lumber and railroad monopolies in the Badger state) were signs that populism was spreading.

In 1907, a group of California professionals consisting of merchants, doctors, lawyers, teachers, and skilled workers organized into what became known as the Progressives. **The Progressives were a California political movement that formed in 1907. Their purpose was to get the Southern Pacific Railroad Monopoly out of California politics.** Like Teddy Roosevelt, the California Progressives were Republicans, but not the kind of Republicans that supported big business interests. In 1910 these renegade Republicans took control of both houses of the State Legislature and captured the Governor's office. A significant reason for the Progressives' success stemmed from the introduction of the Direct Primary in the 1910 election. **A Direct Primary allows voters to choose their party's nominee for an elected office.** The California State Legislature, in 1909, approved use of the Direct Primary for the 1910 election. Prior to the Direct Primary, the Southern Pacific, in league with party leaders, chose party nominees that would serve the railroad's interest. That changed in the 1910 election, leading to the Progressives' victory. The Progressive candidate for Governor, Hiram Johnson, campaigned across California, travelling in an automobile and refusing to ride on a train. His rousing speeches included the signature Progressive refrain, "Kick the Southern Pacific machine out of California politics."[28]

Broken campaign promises have been a part of the American political experience, contributing to the apathy, disgust, and cynicism of the citizenry. But in the case of the Progressives, once they gained power in California, this reform minded movement backed up their words with deeds. Here are some of their key reforms that changed California's political landscape.

Women's Suffrage   The Progressives gave women in California the right to vote in 1911, nine years before the passage of the 19th Amendment to the U.S. Constitution that granted women the right to vote across the nation.

Non-Partisan Local Elections   Party affiliated candidates in local government elections made it easier for the Southern Pacific to exert its influence. The Progressives ended this by making all municipal and county elections non-partisan, which meant all candidates running for any local government office would have no party affiliation next to their names on the ballot. Today in California, a candidate seeking office on a county board, school board, special district board, or city council seat runs as a non-partisan candidate.

Cross Filing   The Progressives created Cross Filing in 1913, allowing a candidate to seek the nomination of more than one political party during the primary election. This was designed to further dilute the power of the state political parties and the Southern Pacific's influence on prospective candidates seeking political office. "Vote for the best person, not the party", was the Progressives' message to voters with the passage of Cross Filing.[29]

The Public Utilities Commission   In 1911 the Progressives changed the ineffective Railroad Commission by creating what is today the Public Utilities Commission (PUC), which regulates the rates charged and services provided by water, energy, communications, and transportation industries. The PUC consists of five members, nominated by the Governor. Each nominee must be confirmed by a majority vote in the State Senate. PUC members serve six-year terms that are staggered by design to prevent the Governor from loading the commission in one fell swoop. At the time the Progressives established the PUC, breaking the railroad's price gouging in shipping was the priority, but more recently, as demonstrated by the 2001 energy crisis fiasco discussed in Chapter 1, the PUC's decisions on what giant private utility companies (Pacific Gas and Electric and Southern California Edison) can charge the millions of Californians dependent on their services makes this one of the most important Governor appointed commissions in the state. In 2019, there was an attempt by the State Legislature to approve a bill that would grant California lawmakers authority over approving or rejecting rate hikes private utility companies can charge their customers, but the legislation did not pass.[30]

However, recent episodes over the past several years have called into question who the PUC is serving; California ratepayers or the utility corporations the PUC is charged with regulating. In 2017, the PUC allowed Southern California Gas Company to reopen its' natural gas facility in the San Fernando Valley less than two years after the facility was the site of the largest methane gas leak in U.S. history. When the San Onofre nuclear power plant shut down, a 2014 secret settlement agreement between Southern California Edison (who operated the facility) and PUC officials required Southern California ratepayers to bear 70% of the closing costs.[31] The 2010 natural gas line explosion that killed eight and leveled a San Bruno neighborhood was the result of Pacific Gas And Electric's failure to maintain gas line safety procedures. Despite PG&E's responsibility, revealed e-mails indicated then PUC President Michael R. Peevey was offering public relations advice to PG&E as the PUC was investigating the San Bruno accident.[32]

In 2021, the PUC has approved rate increases for PG&E to levy on their customers after the giant private utility (which serves over 5 million in Northern and Central California) emerged from bankruptcy after negotiating a $25.5 billion dollar settlement for their culpability in the destructive wildfires of 2017, 2018, and 2020.[33]

Such controversial episodes from the Public Utilities Commission have caused the California State Legislature to consider bills to reform the utility regulatory commission which oversees some $50 billion in utility rates each year. Governor Jerry Brown, though, was opposed to stripping the PUC of its powers, arguing replacing commission members not in bed with utility corporations would be a better approach. That has not satisfied PUC critics, and in 2017, Assemblyman Mike Gatto proposed a constitutional amendment be sent to the voters to dissolve the PUC (which failed to make it to the ballot) through the process of Direct Democracy, which we will next examine.[34]

DIRECT DEMOCRACY

In addition to these reforms, the Progressives also banned child labor, created workmen's compensation (allowing a worker injured on the job to be compensated a set amount of time until they could return to work), and provided free school textbooks.[35] However, arguably the most enduring legacy of the Progressive movement was the establishment of Direct Democracy in 1911. **Direct Democracy allows the voters to make laws and enact policies separate from elected officials.** The three tools of Direct Democracy the Progressives established for Californians were the **Initiative**, the **Referendum**, and the **Recall**.

The Initiative

The Initiative is a process where citizens can vote for state laws and amendments to the State Constitution. Any proposed initiative must be given a title and summary of what the initiative would do by the state Attorney General. Once the title and summary has been issued by the Attorney General, a required number of signatures must be gathered within **180 days**. Prior to Governor Jerry Brown in 2014 signing into law a measure that extended the time of gathering the signatures by 30 days, the deadline to collect the signatures had been 150 days. If the proposed initiative would be a **statute (law),** an amount of signatures equal to **5%** of the total votes cast in the last Governor's race would need to be gathered. A proposed initiative **amending California's Constitution** requires collecting an amount of signatures equal to **8%** of the total votes cast in the last Governor's race. Once the required number of signatures have been accumulated within the set time period, the proposed law or constitutional amendment will be placed before the voters in the next statewide general election. Most of the state propositions California voters consider each election are initiatives.

In 2016, California voters approved initiatives increasing taxes on tobacco products, legalizing marijuana for recreational purposes, and accelerating parole for non-violent felons, while beating back proposals to lower the cost of prescriptions drugs and ending the death penalty. In 2020, initiatives approved by Golden State voters included providing more funding for stem cell research, allowing those on parole to vote, and strengthening consumer privacy protections. California voters in 2020 rejected initiatives that would have increased property taxes on commercial and industrial properties, allowed 17-year-olds to vote, and reinstated Affirmative Action policies.

The Referendum

The Referendum is a tool California voters can use to block a recently enacted law from taking effect. With the exception of **Urgency Laws (laws passed by the State Legislature and signed by the Governor which take effect immediately),** the budget, and laws calling for a special election, legislation approved by state lawmakers and signed by the Governor will not take effect for at least 90 days (in most cases the following year). Opponents of the new state law have **90 days** to gather signatures equal to **5%** of the total votes cast in the last Governor's race. Upon successful collection of the signatures, the law will not take effect as scheduled, but will instead go to the voters who will decide its fate in the next statewide general election. While there have been 386 Initiatives that have qualified for the California ballot since 1912, only 50 Referendums were considered by the voters during the same period of time, highlighting the Referendum's infrequency of use.

In the 2016 election, Golden State voters in a Referendum approved banning the use of plastic bags in grocery stores. The law had been passed by the Legislature and signed by Governor Brown in 2014 but was challenged when the required number of signatures were gathered by opponents of the law, forcing it onto the 2016 ballot. In the 2020 election, California voters rejected a law passed by the State Legislature and signed by Governor Brown in 2018 that would have ended cash bail requirements for pre-trial inmates.

The Recall

California voters can remove an elected official from office before their term expires through the Recall. Recall of a statewide officer (like the Governor or State Supreme Court Justice) requires that signatures be gathered equal to **12%** of the votes cast for that specific office in the previous election. Recall signatures must be gathered within **160 days**. If the required signatures are obtained, the Governor (usually) calls for a special election. Lieutenant Governor Cruz Bustamante scheduled the Recall election for Governor Gray Davis in the fall of 2003.[36] The voters removed Governor Davis from office and elected Arnold Schwarzenegger as his replacement.

In 2021, Governor Gavin Newsom is most likely to face a Recall election to potentially remove him from office. Initially, it did not appear proponents of the Recall effort against Governor Newsom were going to be successful in gathering the 1.5 million signatures they needed to qualify the Special Election within the 160-day time frame specified by California law. However, Sacramento Superior Court Judge James Arguelles granted a 120-day extension of the deadline for the Recall group, citing the pandemic that prevented Recall organizers from having access to large public gatherings across the state because of the COVID-19 virus.[37]

Recall is also allowed for members of the California State Legislature, all California judges, and local government elected officials. Signatures equal to 20% of votes cast in the last race for state lawmakers and superior court judges are required to qualify a recall election for that office. Recall signature gathering requirements vary for elected local government officeholders ranging from 10% to 30% of registered voters in the electoral jurisdiction depending on the population of registered voters in that jurisdiction (30% required for a registered voter population less than 1000, 10% required for a registered voter population exceeding 100,000).[38]

In 2017, two Recall attempts commenced, one involving a recently elected Southern California State Senator, Democrat Josh Newman. Senator Newman won a closely contested race over a Republican challenger in 2016, and his victory gave Democrats a two-thirds majority in the State Senate (significant since a two-thirds vote is required to raise taxes). The Recall was triggered when Senator Newman voted for increasing the aforementioned gasoline tax. In response to the Recall effort being orchestrated by Republicans, Democrats in the State Legislature passed, and Governor Brown signed, a law ensuring the Recall election would not be a special election, (an election held on its' own) but take place during the next scheduled primary election on June 5, 2018, assuring higher voter turnout and benefitting Senator Newman. Republicans were incensed about the law as noted by GOP Assemblyman Chad Mayes, *"Dems know the gas tax is toxic and Newman will likely lose. They control everything and need to rig the system to protect their political power."*[39] Despite GOP criticism about Democrats placing the Recall election of Senator Newman on the June 2018 primary ballot, it did not matter. Senator Newman was Recalled. But in November 2020 Josh Newman won back his State Senate seat.

A second 2017 Recall effort was launched against Santa Clara County Superior Court Judge Aaron Persky. Judge Persky faced statewide criticism following his sentencing of former Stanford swimmer Brock Turner, convicted of sexually assaulting an unconscious woman behind a campus dumpster. Turner was given a six-month sentence by Judge Persky and based on the conviction, could have received up to 14 years in prison by the judge for the crime. Outraged with the light sentence Persky gave Turner, a group, led by a Stanford University law professor, began a campaign to Recall the judge, and once the required signatures were obtained, the Recall election took place in Santa Clara County in 2020 where the voters removed Judge Persky from office. Attempts to Recall state lawmakers and judges are rare, but these two Recall attempts were successful.

The Procedures for Gathering Signatures

For an Initiative, Referendum, or Recall signature to be valid, the signer of the petition must be a registered voter in California. **Verification of all signatures is the responsibility of the Secretary of State, the state's top election official.** Since verification of all signatures is not possible, the Secretary of State's office conducts a sampling of the signatures. If a percentage of the signatures sampled are invalidated, the petition will have failed to qualify for the next election. Interest groups funding the signature collection for Initiatives, Referendums, and Recalls will submit thousands of signatures beyond the required amount to maximize their chances of qualifying the measure for the next ballot.

This process to collect the required number of valid signatures is onerous and expensive for interest groups due to the increased voter turnout from the 2018 California general election. Based on the amount of voter signatures required to qualify an Initiative Statute or a Referendum being 623,212 (the number reflecting 5% of the total votes cast in the 2018 Governor's race) that is a significant increase from the required number of signatures (365, 880) needed to qualify an Initiative Statute or Referendum after the 2014 Governor's election, when voter turnout was much lower. Qualifying an initiative amending California's Constitution is more difficult as well given 997,139 signatures must be gathered as of the 2018 Governor's election compared to the 585,407 signatures needed prior to 2018. Gathering signatures to qualify Initiatives, Referendums and Recalls is a costly exercise. In 2020, signature gathering expenses averaged a record-setting $7.22 per valid signature, and the average total cost to qualify a proposition in 2020 was $4.8 million.[40]

THE PROGRESSIVE LEGACY, NOT WHAT THEY EXPECTED

The Progressive legacy on California politics over the past 110 years is an enduring one, yet their primary goal of ridding the state of special interest and political party influence through these reforms proved impossible to achieve. Hiram Johnson ran as the Vice-Presidential candidate with Theodore Roosevelt in the 1912 presidential election, but Roosevelt's Bull Moose Progressive Party (like any third party) had no chance of winning election under the two-party Electoral College system. In 1916, Johnson got himself elected to the U.S. Senate, and soon after the Progressive movement waned in California as more business-friendly Republicans took over the State Legislature and Governor's office. Between the mid 1920's and the late 1950's pro business Republicans controlled California, ironically benefitting from one of the Progressives' reforms, Cross Filing. Despite only having some 40% of registered voters, Republicans thrived in the Cross-Filing system as Democratic voters elected them on their primary ballots, assuming the candidates were Democrats. Once Democrats regained control of the Legislature and Governor's seat, Cross Filing was eliminated in 1959.[41]

The Progressives believed that party politics and special interests created an intractable barrier to practical, non-biased political solutions to public problems. California is currently entrenched in the very political gridlock the Progressives' reforms were designed to mitigate. Direct Democracy, created to undermine the two-party system and the special interests they served, has metastasized into political weapons for these institutions.

Pluralism is the concept that various elite interest groups actively compete with each other to obtain government policies beneficial to their interests. Because of Direct Democracy, California is experiencing hyperpluralism, where the Initiative is a tool incorporated by any well-funded and well-connected special interest. Today, California ballot measures represent a larger share of campaign expenditures than legislative campaigns. In 2018, California's state legislative campaigns raised some $260 million, nowhere the $785 million spent on the 12 statewide ballot measures in 2020.[42]

California's political parties have benefitted from the Initiative as well, utilizing ballot measures to advance the party agenda, encourage voter turnout for their candidates, and undermine opposing parties. The California Republican Party earned political capital from ballot initiatives banning same sex marriage, ending affirmative action programs, cutting property taxes, and requiring state officials report undocumented immigrants to federal authorities. Conversely, the California Democratic Party used ballot measures mandating levels of public school funding, approving stem cell research, and reducing greenhouse gas emissions to their political advantage.

Based on a 2011 law (SB 202) passed by the Democratic controlled Legislature and signed by Governor Brown, all future initiatives and petition referendums will be placed on the November general election ballot. For several decades, initiatives and petition referendums that qualified were allowed on either the primary or general election ballot. **Primary elections (in which voters nominate candidates to represent the party in the general election)** traditionally have lower voter turnout than general elections. Conventional thinking is that higher voter turnout increases the chance Democratic supported initiatives would be approved by Californians while lower voter turnout improves the odds that Republican backed measures placed before the electorate will pass.

In the 2016 election, initiatives (supported by Democrats) legalizing marijuana, requiring background checks for gun ammunition, and taxing tobacco products all passed. Republican backed initiatives were noticeably absent from the ballot save for one accelerating the appeals process for capital punishment cases (which passed), though the state GOP had to be pleased initiatives setting price controls on prescription drugs and placing a prohibition on the death penalty failed. With that said, the November 2016 ballot had seventeen ballot measures for the California voter to consider, and in 2020 12 propositions qualified for the ballot, enough to make even the most conscientious citizen's head spin.

The Progressives gave California Direct Democracy in hopes of curtailing the power of special interests and political parties. Twenty-eight other states have some version of Direct Democracy, but the U.S. Constitution does not permit the federal government to employ Direct Democracy. The only form of democracy available at the federal level is Representative Democracy. **Representative Democracy is a form of government in which representatives elected by the people make and enforce laws and policies.** American citizens are not given the authority to directly vote on whether the U.S. should go to war with another nation or whether health insurance should be provided to everyone nationwide. Such decisions are left to the elected representatives in the U.S. Congress and the President of the United States. Representative Democracy is also employed by the states, whose citizens elect representatives to make, enforce, and interpret the law. We consider in Chapter 3 California's ever evolving election institutions emanating from American Federalism.

3
CHAPTER

CALIFORNIA ELECTIONS

Doug LaMalfa, a **conservative** Republican representing a rural Northern California State Senate district stretching from Marysville to the Oregon border, was holding a town hall meeting in Paradise in 2011 when a constituent proffered the following question, "Any chance we can create a separate state?" State Senator LaMalfa supported the idea but responded that splitting the state into an inland Eastern California and a coastal Western California was unlikely given the U.S. Congress has the authority under the U.S. Constitution to create new states. "It would mean two more **conservative** senators," LaMalfa noted, "That's where the politics get rough in D.C. and we'd need a friendly White House, Senate, and House for the kind of state you would be creating."[1] LaMalfa left the State Senate after winning a seat in the U.S. House Of Representatives during the 2012 election.

Congressman LaMalfa's frank assessment of the federal government's reluctance to divide the Golden State has not deterred proponents of a new state in Northern California. Residents in 21 rural Northern California counties have advocated for seceding from Californian and creating the 51st state of Jefferson. However, only five (Siskiyou, Modoc, Glenn, Sutter, and Yuba counties have obtained from their governing Board of Supervisors "declarations of separation" to leave California. The state of Jefferson movement wants other Northern California counties to adopt similar "declarations of separation". These secessionists believe California's government (controlled by the Democrats) imposes **liberal** policies on them they oppose (reducing greenhouse gas emissions, tough gun control laws, expanding abortion rights, and the construction of the bullet train as examples). State of Jefferson supporters justify breaking from California, complaining they have no representation in the State Legislature because their populations are sparse. Legislative districts, based on a 1964 U.S. Supreme Court ruling, must be equal in population. This **Redistricting (the redrawing of the boundaries of the congressional districts and state legislative districts within each state)**, which we will discuss later in this chapter, has resulted (as far as the state of Jefferson proponents are concerned) in large urban California regions in the Bay Area and Los Angeles controlling the government.

Such sentiments provide a picture into the political divide that currently exists in the Golden State. California has a total of 58 counties, and of the 25 counties that voted for Republican Donald Trump in the 2016 presidential election, the bulk of them were rural inland counties consisting of more **conservative** minded people, including the 21 counties advocating for the state of Jefferson (all of which Trump carried). Similar results occurred in the 2020 presidential election with Joe Biden winning the California coastal counties and handily defeating Donald Trump (who won most of the rural counties) by 63% to 34% in the final statewide popular vote tally.

Conservatism is a political philosophy that is opposed to government regulation of the economy, heavy government spending, and tax increases. Conservatives believe it is the individual's responsibility to take care of themselves, not the government's responsibility. Conservatism also advocates the prohibition of abortion, same sex marriage, and euthanasia. In California, inland counties, a number of them in the agricultural rich Central Valley, are home to more conservatives. Congressman Doug LaMalfa's Northern California congressional congressional district, which stretches from Yuba County up to the Oregon border, is an area of the state consisting of more conservative minded voters.

California's counties near the coastline consist of a different electorate than their Central Valley counterparts Congresswoman Nancy Pelosi of San Francisco, the current Speaker of the House of Representatives, a **liberal** Democrat and the first woman to serve as the Speaker of the U.S. House of Representatives, represents constituents who tend to be more **liberal** minded voters. **Liberalism is a political philosophy that views government as a means to correct the abuses and shortcomings of society. Liberalism advocates greater government regulation of the economy, increased government spending on social programs to assist the poor, and taxation policies in which the affluent pay higher rates of taxes. In addition, Liberals supports abortion rights, same sex marriage, and euthanasia.** Congresswoman Nancy Pelosi, serving as Speaker, was instrumental in getting Congress to pass the controversial health care bill of 2010 discussed in Chapter 1, a law conservatives (like Congressman LaMalfa) adamantly opposed.

While a political chasm exists in California between rural inland counties and urban coastal counties, Republican voter registration overall in the state has been on the decline, resulting in shrinking representation in the State Legislature and the U.S. Congress. Republicans have not held one of the state's two U.S. Senate seats for over twenty years, and currently Democrats control all statewide executive positions (including the Governor's office). A key factor attributable to the Republican drop in voter registration is the demographic population shift described in Chapter 1. In addition, more people live in the urban, coastal counties of the state compared to the Republican dominated Central Valley, and only one coastal county (Del Norte County) voted Republican in the 2020 presidential election, Joe Biden capturing the rest and winning the state with 63% of the popular vote. These changing demographics in population have contributed to the erosion of registered Republican Party voters, but it was not always like this for Republicans in California.

As discussed in Chapter 2, Republicans held power in the state once the Progressive Movement faded in the 1920's. Democrats regained control of state government in the late 1950's, winning majorities in the State Legislature and getting Edmund G. Brown elected Governor in 1958. However, Republican Ronald Reagan was elected Governor in 1966, defeating Edmund G. Brown's attempt to serve a third term. Ronald Reagan became the flag bearer for conservatism, and his ability to coalesce blue collar workers (Reagan Democrats), along with his conservative Republican base, drove him to the White House in the 1980 election. Concerning job creation, President Reagan was very good to California during the eight years he served as President (1981–1989). Reagan's buildup of the U.S. military during the **Cold War** steered millions of dollars in defense contracts to the Golden State as defense contractors like Lockheed and General Dynamics created thousands of manufacturing jobs, indirectly fueling an increase in service sector employment as well. **The Cold War was the ideological, political, and economic impasse that existed between the United States and Soviet Union following World War II that resulted in the escalation of military spending by both nations, particularly in the field of nuclear weaponry.** Despite criticism by Democrats of Reagan policies that attempted to turn social programs over to the states and reduce Federal funding of those social programs, coupled with tax cuts (tenants of conservatism), President Reagan remained popular not only nationwide, but in California, which was known as "Reagan Country". After Governor Jerry Brown ended his first stint as the state's chief executive in 1982, Republicans controlled the Governor's seat from 1983-1998, and even briefly recaptured control of the State Assembly in 1994.

Cracks in "Reagan Country" began to appear in the 1988 presidential election. Though George H.W. Bush defeated Democrat Michael Dukakis in

California, the vote was close 53% to 47%.[2] In 1992, California voted for Bill Clinton, the first time a Democrat had carried the state in a presidential election since 1964. The 1992 election began a slow, but steady decline of the Republican Party in California. This chapter will describe California's election and campaign system including the **Primary Elections, the General Elections, the Electoral College, and Redistricting.** Not only will we consider how these institutions operate at the state and Federal levels, but we will also examine the political shifts taking place in California that are prompting suggestions of splitting the state by rural, inland Republicans who see their political power rapidly evaporating.

PRIMARY ELECTIONS

A Primary Election is an election in which voters nominate a candidate to represent that party in the general election. The Republicans, Democrats, and third parties conduct primary elections in California for the 120 seats in the State Legislature, the 53 seats California currently has in the House of Representatives, the state's two U.S. Senate seats, the 4 Board of Equalization Districts, the 8 statewide executive offices (including the Governor), and the U.S. presidency. In primary elections, voters choose a candidate who will square off against candidates nominated from other political parties. The winners of the primary elections move on to the general election, where the voters decide who will be elected to the office. Article I, Section 4 of the U.S. Constitution grants states the authority to determine the "manner" of elections. Concerning primary elections, states have created different types of primaries that include **Closed Primaries, Blanket Primaries, Open Primaries, and Caucuses.**

Closed Primary

A Closed Primary is a primary election in which voters must be registered with the party in order to vote in the party's primary election. The closed primary ballot only lists candidates from one party, and the party voters select from the list of candidates for each office. The closed primary ensures that only registered party members can participate in a political party's primary, and thus eliminates non-party members from having an influence on which candidate wins the party's nomination for a particular office. Closed primaries also strengthen the ability of the two main parties (Democrats and Republicans) to elect candidates more in line with the Party Platform. **A Party Platform is a statement of principles and objectives advocated by a party or candidate that is used during a campaign to win support from voters.**

Since 2000, California has used a modified form of the closed primary. The Republican Party, also known as the Grand Old Party (GOP), limited participation in the GOP primary to registered Republican voters, but the Democratic Party allowed registered Democrats and decline to state voters (those with no party affiliation) to participate in their primary elections. Some California political analysts believe the state Republican Party's prohibition of decline to state voters in their primary elections contributed to the reduction of voters registered with the GOP, and the election losses Republicans have endured over the past decade. In hopes of improving their chances of victory, the California Republican Party did allow participation of decline to state voters in their 2010 primary election, but Democrats in the Golden State still won big in the November general election.[3]

Blanket Primary

During the June 2010 primary election, a California ballot initiative was approved by the voters that eliminated the closed primary and replaced it with a **Blanket Primary. A Blanket Primary is a primary election in which all the candidates, regardless of party affiliation, are listed on the same ballot, and voters can pick from the list. Voters in Blanket Primaries need not be registered with a political party to participate.** This type of primary was approved by California voters in 2010 (Proposition 14), and under the new primary, the top two vote getters in the primary election, regardless of party affiliation, will face each other in the general election. The blanket primary weakens the influence of political parties given that candidates in such primary elections are not constrained by having to appeal to a particular party platform in order to win the nomination. Third parties, theoretically, can also benefit from the blanket primary given they have an opportunity to campaign and appeal to voters outside of their party. However, since only the top two candidates from the blanket primary will face each other in the general election, third party candidates will not be on the general election ballot unless they finish first or second in the primary election.

This is not California's first experiment with the blanket primary. In 1996, Golden State voters approved an initiative replacing the closed primary with a blanket primary. During the 2000 presidential primary election, the state Republican and Democratic parties sued in state court to block the voter approved blanket primary. Both parties argued that the Blanket Primary was unconstitutional because it allowed non-party voters to participate in the selection of a party's nominee for President of the United States. The California State Supreme Court ruled in favor of the Democrats and Republicans. However, the ruling came after the state had printed the 2000 blanket primary ballots. To comply with the State Supreme Court's ruling, the 2000 presidential primary ballot was coded, and if a voter was not registered with the political party of the presidential candidate they selected, their vote did not count. The U.S. Supreme Court upheld the unconstitutionality of the blanket primary in 2000, and California went back to the Closed Primary.

The current blanket primary approved by the voters in 2010 exempts the presidential primary, but a lawsuit challenging it constitutionality was filed in 2010 involving two provisions of Proposition 14. The first provision that was challenged orders write in votes to be discarded. The second provision that was challenged allows candidates the option of not listing their party affiliation/preference on the ballot.[4] The lawsuit was appealed to the U.S. Ninth Circuit Court of Appeals, but in December 2010, the California Supreme Court refused to block implementation of Proposition 14, and the blanket primary law remains in effect.

Open Primary

An Open Primary permits voters to choose the party primary ballot of their choice without disclosing party affiliation. In this primary, the voter is limited to casting votes for candidates of only one party. California has not utilized this type of primary, though the current blanket primary has been referred to as an open primary, it is not an open primary. In an open primary, the voter could choose the party ballot (Democrat, Republican, or third-party ballot), but they are limited in casting votes for candidates of only one party. In the blanket primary **all** of the candidates from every party are listed on the ballot.

Nominating Caucus

Some smaller populated states, the most notable one being Iowa, hold **nominating caucuses** during the primary election season. **A Caucus is a closed meeting of party leaders or rank-and-file members to select party candidates. Participants of party caucus meetings must be registered voters of that party.** Caucus meetings can last for two hours, and given the time requirements, attract only the most politically active members of a party. The Iowa Caucus is well known because it is the first state to choose a potential party nominee for President of the United States, kicking off the presidential primary season every four years. **California does not use a nominating caucus.**

California's 2020 Presidential Primary Moved to March

The State Legislature approved, and Governor Brown signed in September of 2017 a bill that moved California's Presidential Primary to March for 2020. In the 2016 Presidential Primary the Golden State held the primary in June, and by then both Hillary Clinton and Donald Trump had secured their party's nominations. By moving the 2020 Presidential Primary to March, the state attempted to have more of an influence on who would be nominated by the Democrats and Republicans for the Presidency. For the Republicans, it was a forgone conclusion that President Donald Trump would win the nomination in 2020. However, the Democrat Presidential Primary was more competitive with a slew of candidates seeking the nomination. Senator Bernie Sanders defeated Joe Biden in California's 2020 Presidential Primary, securing over 2 million votes to Biden's 1.6 million total. But in the end, Joe Biden won the 2020 Democratic Primary, California joining Nevada, Utah, Colorado, North Dakota, New Hampshire, and Sanders' home state of Vermont as the only states voting for the Progressive Sanders. Joe Biden, with the exception of Pete Buttigieg winning Iowa, carried the rest of the states, easily securing the Democratic nomination.

CALIFORNIA'S GENERAL ELECTIONS

California holds general elections on the first Tuesday in November every two years. By design, the state holds general elections for the statewide executive offices (including the Governor's seat) every four years. In 2018, Democrat Gavin Newsom defeated Republican John Cox in the race for Governor. The 2018 California general election was held on the same day national mid-term elections for the U.S. House of Representatives and the U.S. Senate were conducted nationwide. National mid-term elections occur on the first Tuesday in November of even numbered years during the "mid term" (the midway point of the current President's four-year term). In 2020, all fifty states and the District Of Columbia held the presidential general election won by Democrat Joe Biden over Republican incumbent Donald Trump. Let us consider both of California's general elections beginning with the general elections for statewide executive offices.

The general elections for California's statewide executive offices transpire every four years on the same first Tuesday in November that national mid-term elections for Congress take place in each state.

During this general election, all eight statewide executive positions that include the Governor, Lieutenant Governor, Attorney General, Secretary Of State, State Controller, State Treasurer, Insurance Commissioner, and Superintendent of Public Instruction are on the ballot. Voters statewide select the candidate they want to fill these eight statewide executive positions. In addition, voters also choose during this general election (based on the district they are in) a Board of Equalization member, lawmakers in the State Assembly and State Senate, and a member of Congress. If one of California's U.S. Senate Seats is on the ballot (U.S. Senators serve six year terms), a statewide election for the seat will take place that day as well. In 2010, Democrat **incumbent** Barbara

Boxer defeated Republican challenger Carly Fiorina in the race for U.S. Senate. **An incumbent is a person currently holding a political office that is up for re-election.** Senator Boxer, who held the U.S. Senate seat since 1992, announced she would retire from the U.S. Senate in 2016. In the 2016 U.S. Senate race, California Attorney General Kamala Harris defeated Congresswoman Loretta Sanchez, capturing Boxer's seat. In the 2020 Presidential Election, Joe Biden selected Kamala Harris to be his Vice- Presidential candidate, and with the two of them defeating the incumbent ticket of Donald Trump and Mike Pence, Kamala Harris relinquished her U.S. Senate seat and became the first woman to ever serve as Vice President of the United States. Governor Newsom filled the vacant Senate seat by appointing Alex Padilla to replace Harris as U.S. Senator, making Padilla the first Latino in California history to serve the state as a United States Senator. California's other U.S Senator is Diane Feinstein, who has been a member of the U.S. Senate since 1992, winning her latest re-election in 2018 by defeating fellow Democrat Kevin de Leon.

California's 2010 general election for Governor pitted Republican Meg Whitman against Democrat Jerry Brown. Whitman, the former CEO of E-Bay, the online retail giant, spent an unprecedented $160 million of her own money to become Governor. In comparison, Brown, a longtime California politician, won the election with campaign expenditures of $25 million.[5] The election results of the 2010 Governor's race reinforced two demographic traits influencing California politics we have discussed. First, inland counties supported Whitman and coastal counties voted for Brown. Second, the growing influence of the Latino vote became apparent in this race. Polling and election analysts concluded Whitman could not win the election without at least 30% of Latino support, which she did not receive. Four years later, Governor Brown faced a relatively unknown Republican, Neel Kashkari, who had nowhere near the financial resources Meg Whitman possessed four years earlier. Six weeks before the election, Kashkari reported having only $700,000 in funds compared to Brown's $24 million.[6] Brown went on to defeat Kashkari 54% to 41% to serve an unprecedented fourth term as Governor.

In 2018, Democrat Gavin Newsom handily defeated Republican John Cox for the Governor's seat by a 62% to 38% margin. If the Special Recall Election against Governor Newsom is called in 2021, John Cox has indicated he will run on the ballot to replace Newsom. In the 2010, 2014, and 2018 California general elections, Democrats also won every other statewide elected office, maintained strong super-majorities in both houses of the State Legislature, and in 2018 won 45 of the 53 House seats in Congress. Voter turnout in the 2018 election was high with 64% of registered voters casting ballots in the Golden State, the highest percentage of registered voters participating in a mid-term election since 1982. Some 12.7 million Californians cast ballots in the 2018 election, the highest number of mid-term voters in the state's history.[7] Mindy Romero, director of the California Civic Engagement Project at the University of Southern California suggested opposition to the policies of the Trump Administration played a key role in the high voter turnout of 2018.[8]

Every four years, California, along with the other 49 states and the District of Columbia, hold the **general election for President of the United States.** In California, during this general election, more voters will cast ballots than in the Mid-Term general election when the Governor's race occurs. Presidential general elections draw more attention, impacting voter turn out. The President of the United States is chosen in the general election through the **Electoral College** as required by the U.S. Constitution.

THE ELECTORAL COLLEGE

The Framers of the U.S. Constitution, contrary to popular belief, were not enamored with democracy, crafting a document that would only allow voters (white male landowners) to select members of the U.S. House of Representatives. U.S. Senators (until passage of the 17th Amendment in 1913) would be chosen by state legislatures, not the people. Concerning the selection of President and Vice President, the Framers wanted to avoid giving the mass public the ability to vote for these offices. The result was a system in which each state would select a group of electors who would cast ballots for President. Originally, the state's electors would only vote for a presidential candidate, and the candidate which finished second in the race would become Vice President. **The 12th Amendment of 1804 requires that electors vote separately for President and Vice President.** Over the years, as democracy expanded and more people were allowed to vote, the states granted voters the ability to select the electors. Let us consider how the Electoral College currently operates.

Each state is allotted Electoral College votes based on the number of seats that state holds in the U.S. House of Representatives plus their two U.S. Senate seats. **The District of Columbia (due to the 23rd Amendment of 1961) is currently granted three Electoral College votes.** A state is given a number of House members based on the state's population (determined every ten years by the U.S. Census), and each state, regardless of population, has two U.S. Senators. California is the largest populated state in the union (40 million), and currently holds 53 seats in the House of Representatives. Coupled with its two U.S. Senate seats, **California has 55 Electoral College votes**, more than any other state. The number of House seats nationwide is 435, and Congress has not increased that total since 1912. The U.S. Senate consists of 100 seats. That brings the number of Electoral College votes to 535, but remember, the District of Columbia also gets 3 Electoral College votes, culminating in a total of **538 Electoral College votes** up for grabs every four years in the general election for President of the United States.

When the general election for President and Vice President of the United States is held, voters in each state and the District of Columbia cast ballots for a Party Ticket, (for example: Donald Trump and Mike Pence or Joe Biden And Kamala Harris in the 2020 general election). In all but two states, (Maine and Nebraska) whoever wins the popular vote in the state wins all the state's Electoral College votes. Maine and Nebraska award their Electoral College votes based on who wins the popular vote of a congressional district, with the remaining Electoral College votes being given to the statewide popular vote winner. **In order to be elected President of the United States, a candidate must receive at least 270 Electoral College votes**, 50% plus 1 of the 538 Electoral College votes available. While the formula for awarding Electoral College votes to a state is based on the number of seats a state holds in Congress, members of Congress are not electors. For example, California has 55 Electoral College votes, and before the presidential general election, the California Republican Party will select 55 electors, the California Democratic Party will select 55 electors, and any third party that qualifies candidates for the ballot will select 55 electors. It is a winner-take-all system in California. Whoever wins the popular vote wins all the state's 55 Electoral College votes. As the results come in on election night from around the country, whichever presidential candidate reaches **270** Electoral College votes is declared the winner.

Article II, Section 1 of the U.S. Constitution says *Each State shall appoint, in such Manner as the Legislature thereof may direct, a Number of Electors, equal to the whole Number of Senators and Representatives to which the state may be entitled in the Congress.* This part of the U.S. Constitution allows the states to determine how presidential electors will be chosen, explaining why Maine and Nebraska have a different system from the other 48 states. However, several states are in the midst of changing how they award Electoral College votes, California being one of them. In August of 2011, California Governor Jerry Brown signed **Assembly Bill 459 (AB459), an Interstate Compact, that would award all of California's 55 Electoral College votes to the winner of the national popular vote in the general presidential election, regardless of whether the state's popular vote selection differed from the national popular vote results.**[9] **An Interstate Compact is an agreement between two or more states.** Article I, Section 10 of the U.S. Constitution requires such agreements or compacts have the consent of Congress, and those opposing AB 459 argue Congress would have to grant consent for such a compact to be enacted.

Under AB 459, the law would only take effect if the required number of states needed to obtain a majority of Electoral College votes (**270 needed to capture the presidency**) agreed to award their Electoral College votes to the winner of the national popular vote. Currently, 15 states (including California) along with the District of Columbia have agreed to the **Interstate Compact**, but the 196 Electoral College votes comprising these states falls short of the 270 needed. In 2021, the group National Popular Vote, an organization in support of the compact, is concentrating on nine other states with a combined tally of 88 Electoral College votes that would be enough to reach and surpass the required 270. However, the nine states, five of which include Republican controlled legislatures, make enacting the compact any time soon a dubious prospect. Republicans have shown little appetite for moving to a national popular vote.

Public support in California for AB 459 is rooted in opposition to an Electoral College system which allows a presidential candidate to win the presidency by securing a majority of Electoral College votes despite losing the national popular vote. Such a scenario occurred in the 2000 general election for President when Republican George W. Bush won the Electoral College vote but lost the national popular vote to Democrat Al Gore. The election was laced with controversy, and after a month of legal challenges over who won the Florida popular vote (whoever won Florida would have the required number of electoral votes to capture the White House), it was determined that George W. Bush bested Al Gore in Florida by a mere 537 votes, allowing Bush to defeat Gore in the Electoral College 271-267.[10] In the 2016 race, Donald Trump secured victory in the Electoral College with 306 Electoral votes despite losing the national popular vote to Hillary Clinton by 3 million votes. The popular vote margins in 2020 were even wider with Joe Biden defeating Donald Trump by 7 million votes, California providing a big chunk of the nationwide popular vote margin as Biden bested Trump in the Golden State by 5 million votes. And even though Biden won the Electoral College vote over Trump in 2020, the race was decided by much narrower margins in a small number of swing states that did not include California.

A second reason California would benefit from having Electoral College votes determined by the winner of the national popular vote involves making the nation's largest populated state a "player" in the race. In the 2008 presidential general election, California (except as a place to hold fundraisers) was ignored by both campaigns, a point made by the editorial board of the Chico Enterprise Record in the paper's editorial from June 13, 2011 supporting passage of AB 459, *In the 2008 election, Barack Obama and John McCain came to California for private fundraisers and left with $150 million in contributions. But only 2 % of that was spent on ads here, and neither returned for even one campaign stop after the nominating conventions because the result was never in doubt in this state. Ohio got 26 candidate visits, Pennsylvania 23, Florida 22, and Virginia – a state with less than a quarter the population of California – 18.* The same scenario the Chico Enterprise Record's editorial board complained about in 2008 applied to the 2012, 2016, and 2020 Presidential General Elections. In the 2020 race the Biden and Trump campaigns visited Pennsylvania 47 times, North Carolina 25 times, Michigan 21 times, Wisconsin 18 times, Arizona 13 times, and Nevada 11 times, but California garnered zero stops by either campaign.[11]

Whether enough states pass the compact to achieve the 270 Electoral College vote threshold needed by the 2024 presidential general election is questionable. Many of the states considering the change are smaller in population, and may fear losing influence to the larger populated states if Electoral College votes are apportioned based on who wins the national popular vote, not the state popular vote. It is also worth noting that part of the debate at the Constitutional Convention in 1787 involved satisfying the interests of the smaller populated states and is one of the reasons the Electoral College system, antiquated as it may be, has endured over the years.

REDISTRICTING

Reapportionment

As mentioned in the discussion of the Electoral College, every ten years (as required by the U.S. Constitution) a census is taken to determine the population of every state for the purpose of determining the number of seats in the House of Representatives and Electoral College votes a state receives. In addition, the census is the basis for how some $1.5 trillion in federal dollars will be dispersed amongst the states. Once the census is complete, **Reapportionment** takes place. **Reapportionment is the allocation of seats in the U.S. House of Representatives based on the state's population count resulting from the census.** States with growing populations will receive more House seats. States with stagnant or declining populations will lose House seats. As a result of the 2010 census, California continued to have 53 U.S. House of Representative seats, more than any other state. Ten states (mostly in the Northeast and upper Mid-West) lost at least one House seat while 8 states (located in the South and West) gained at least one House seat through Reapportionment based on the 2010 census.[12]

The 2020 Census, The Pandemic, and Politics

As COVID-19 beset the nation in 2020, the U.S. Census Bureau faced the daunting task of conducting the country's population count amidst the pandemic. Due to the spreading virus, the U.S. Census Bureau had to temporarily suspend field operations, but the work resumed later in 2020. COVID-19 prompted the U.S. Census Bureau to rely more heavily on tabulating population counts via the phone, mail, and internet contacts. But even with these pandemic-safe options, the Bureau still needed staff to venture out into the field to reach traditionally undercounted groups that included minorities, college students living on campus, seniors in nursing homes, and the homeless.

Politics became infused in completing the 2020 census as the Trump Administration attempted to have a citizenship question placed on the census form, something the United States Supreme Court rejected in 2019. In addition, President Trump issued a directive in 2020 to exclude undocumented immigrants from being counted in the U.S. Census for the purpose of determining the number of House of Representatives seats a state would get. These actions by the Trump Administration coincided with cutting short the census count in California. Predictably, California sued the Trump Administration over these census policies, but litigation by California over the census count ended when Joe Biden became President in January 2021. One of the first actions Joe Biden undertook as President was to revoke the Trump Administration's order to prevent undocumented immigrants from being counted in the census.

Redistricting, One Person, One Vote

Redistricting is the redrawing of the boundaries of the congressional districts and state legislative districts within each state. In 1964, the U.S. Supreme Court ruled that state legislative districts must be drawn so that all districts are equal in population. The Court also required U.S. House of Representative districts in every state be equal in population. These rulings were made by the U.S. Supreme Court to ensure a "one person, one vote" standard applied to all legislative districts.[13] However, a case originating out of Texas challenged the premise that legislative districts be created equally based on total population. Texas Republicans argued those legislative districts should comprise only **eligible voters, not the total population**. The U.S. Supreme Court heard the Texas case in 2016 and ruled unanimously (8-0) that legislative voting districts must be based on everyone who resides in the district, not just registered voters.[14] According to Alan Clayton, a redistricting consultant who advises Latino elected officials, if the U.S. Supreme Court had determined that legislative districts be crafted based on eligible voters, not the total population, it would decrease the ability of Latino, Asian, and African American candidates to win seats in California's Legislature and the U.S. Congress.[15] Lawyers representing the Texas Republicans maintained that only counting eligible voters as a basis for drawing legislative districts would "ensure that voters are afforded the basic right to an equal vote."[16] Given U.S. Supreme Court decisions apply nationwide, the Court's ruling that legislative districts be equal in population maintains the "one person, one vote" standard of the 1964 decision.

Gerrymandering and Redistricting Battles in California

In California, the drawing of the 53 U.S. House districts and the 120 state legislative districts every ten years became a partisan affair known as **Gerrymandering** given the State Legislature had the power to re-draw the districts. **Gerrymandering is the process of drawing legislative districts to intentionally benefit one political party.** The goal of gerrymandering is to draw legislative district maps that maximize a political party's chances of winning as many seats in Congress and the State Legislature as possible. For example, "Packing" registered Republican voters into one district will allow a Republican candidate to win that district, but surrounding districts, lacking a concentration of registered Republican voters, are districts more easily won by Democrats.

Over the past forty years, Democrats have consistently controlled a majority of seats in the California State Legislature, and thus drawn district lines every ten years benefitting their election prospects. After the 1980 census, Democrats drew legislative district lines that prompted the Republicans to qualify three referendums contesting the redistricting plan, and in 1982 California voters rejected the Democrats' district lines, prompting the California State Supreme Court to enter the fray and rule in favor of a slightly modified plan crafted by the Democrats.[17]

Redistricting bills, like all other bills passed by California's State Legislature, must be signed by the Governor. After the 1980 census, Governor Jerry Brown signed the Democrats' Redistricting plans. Such was not the case in 1991 when Republican Governor Pete Wilson vetoed the legislative district lines drawn by the Democrats. Not having the two-thirds votes required in the State Assembly and State Senate to override Governor Wilson's veto, the Democrats and Governor Wilson arrived at an impasse. Once again, the California State Supreme Court intervened and in 1992 appointed a group of retired judges to draw the state's legislative district maps.[18]

In 2001, the drawing of the legislative district lines was accomplished with little rancor. Democrats held strong majorities in both the State Assembly and State Senate, and the party also controlled the Governor's seat after Gray Davis was elected in 1998. Republicans in the State Legislature capitulated when the district maps protected incumbents in both parties, and the vote to approve the redistricting plan was 40-0 in the State Senate and 58-10 in the State Assembly.[19]

Incumbent Gerrymandering and Ideological Dogma

Regardless of the political bickering that has transpired over the decades concerning California redistricting, a common thread in drawing the maps has been **Incumbent Gerrymandering, a process in which district lines are drawn, irrespective of party, to protect incumbents.** Between 2001 and 2011, a mere 5 out of 173 California congressional and state legislative seats changed parties as a result of elections.[20] The results of incumbent gerrymandering are entrenched lawmakers with no motivation to compromise with members of the opposing party. Strict ideological dogma permeates throughout California's State Legislature and Congressional Delegation. Conservative Republican Congressman Doug LaMalfa and Liberal House Democratic Minority Leader Nancy Pelosi represent California districts in which a solid majority of the registered voters are from their party. Both of them, along with other Golden State lawmakers in districts heavily Republican or Democrat, have little incentive to consider policy offered by the other side. In fact, independent thinking on any substantive issue (taxes, the budget, the environment, health care, immigration, guns, etc.) by California lawmakers in these incumbent gerrymandered districts could lead the lawmaker to face a primary challenge from within their own party at the next election, and a fall from grace with the party leadership.

In July, 2001, Republican Assemblyman Dick Dickerson of Redding voted for the state budget after Democrats agreed to tax cuts on farm equipment and additional funding for rural police agencies.[21] Dickerson was one of four Assembly Republicans that crossed over and gave the Democrats the votes they needed to approve the state budget, which, at the time, required a two-thirds vote of both chambers of the State Legislature. The following year, when Dickerson ran for a State Senate seat, he lost in the primary to another Northern California Republican lawmaker, Sam Aanestad. During the primary campaign, Dickerson was branded a sell-out to the Democrats for his 2001 budget vote.

In 2011, Democrat Assemblyman Anthony Portantino was the only Assembly Democrat that did not vote for the state budget, prompting The Speaker of the Assembly, John Perez, to slash Portantino's staff budget and remove him from a spacious capital office. Portantino responded by calling for full public disclosure of all Assembly staff budgets, and proposing that the Assembly Rules Committee strip from Speaker Perez the power to allocate Assembly staff budget funds and office space.[22] Given his defiance to the party leadership, Assemblyman Portantino became ostracized from his party (like former Assemblyman Dickerson in 2002). However, in 2012 two reforms were put in place for California elections. The first was the previously discussed blanket primary. The second involved California's new legislative district lines, which were drawn not by the State Legislature, but by a fourteen member citizens' commission.

Redistricting Reform

California redistricting has been significantly reformed with the passage of **Proposition 11 in 2008 and Proposition 20 in 2010.** Both propositions amended California's Constitution, replacing the State Legislature with a 14 member citizens' commission in the drawing of congressional and legislative districts. **Proposition 11 (2008) changed the authority for establishing State Assembly, State Senate, and State Board of Equalization district boundaries from the State Legislature to a 14 member citizens' commission.** Under Proposition 11, government auditors would select 60 registered voters from an applicant pool. Any registered voter in the state could apply to be a commissioner. Government auditors would remove from the pool applicants with the following conflict of interests:

- *The applicant had been a political candidate for state or Federal office.*
- *The applicant had been a lobbyist.*
- *The applicant had contributed $2000 or more in any year to a political candidate.*
- *The applicant had changed their political party affiliation in the past five years.*

In addition, applicants must have voted in at least two of the last three general elections. After 60 registered voters had been chosen, government auditors would pick eight commissioners from the field, and then the eight selected commissioners would name the other six members. The makeup of the fourteen commissioners requires that five be Democrats, five be Republicans, and the remaining four be of neither party.[23]

Proposition 20 (2010) removed the State Legislature from the process of drawing California congressional district lines, transferring that authority to the 14 member citizens' commission created by Proposition 11 in 2008. With the passage of these two propositions, California's congressional and state legislative district lines would be drawn in more geographically compact districts designed to avoid gerrymandering. Given Democrats in California have been successful over the past several decades in winning legislative and congressional seats (they won 42 of the state's 53 congressional districts and hold two-thirds majorities in both houses of the State Legislature in 2021), it is not surprising that they were opposed to stripping the State Legislature from drawing the district lines. In fact, many California Democratic lawmakers donated money to **Proposition 27,** also on the 2010 ballot.

Proposition 27 would have repealed Proposition 11 and eliminated the 14-member citizen's commission, returning to the State Legislature the power of drawing the congressional and state legislative district lines. Fourteen California U.S. House members, including Nancy Pelosi, collectively donated $160,000 to the effort of qualifying Proposition 27 for the 2010 ballot then gave more money during the campaign. Democratic lawmakers from the State Legislature also donated large sums of money in support of Proposition 27 which included $100,000 donations from Assemblymen Charles Calderon and Mike Eng.[24] Despite these efforts from Democratic lawmakers, Proposition 27 was rejected by the voters in 2010.

The 2012 general election results highlight the impact of the new legislative districts drawn by the 14 member citizens' commission, and the 2010 voter approved blanket primary. Based on data compiled by the Public Policy Institute of California, 18% of California congressional and state legislative races involving candidates from opposing parties were settled by a margin of 10 points or less in the 2012 general election, more than doubling the average number of competitive congressional and state legislative races in the Golden State over the past decade.[25] In general election contests pitting candidates from the same party, resulting from the blanket primary, the margin of victory was 10 points or less in one third of the 28 races.[26] In the 2016 election, 25% of general election races involving same party candidates were decided by 10 points or less.

In a 2018 report on the California Citizens Redistricting Commission (CRC), the Public Policy Institute of California concluded the CRC's drawing of California's legislative districts after the 2010 census created more competitive races than the legislative districts created by the State Legislature in 2001.[27] The report found the Democrats have a slight advantage based on how the legislative districts were drawn by the commission, but that may be caused by the voter registration numbers that continue to favor Democrats in the Golden State. In 2021, 46% of California voters were registered as Democrats compared to only 24% registered as Republicans.

As noted, California Democratic lawmakers donated money to the elimination of the 14-member legislative district drawing commission, but the commission's district lines benefited Democrats over Republicans in the 2012, 2014, 2016, 2018, and 2020 general elections. As of 2021, Democrats continue to hold a significant majority of the State's 53 congressional seats in the U.S. House Of Representatives (42-11). Concerning the State Legislature, Democrats captured enough seats in both the State Assembly and State Senate in 2020 to give them a two thirds super majority in each chamber, allowing them to increase taxes, override a Governor's veto, and propose amendments to the State Constitution without the need of Republican votes. Perhaps state Democrats were premature in their opposition of allowing legislative district lines to be drawn by the 14-member citizen's commission.

VOTER TURNOUT IN THE GOLDEN STATE

A criteria considered critical to democracy is participation by the people. In California, civic engagement by Golden State citizens had been in decline over the years when it came to voter turnout. Back in 1960, 70% of eligible California voters participated in the presidential election in which John F. Kennedy bested Richard M. Nixon. In 2012, only 56% of eligible California voters bothered to cast ballots in the presidential race between President Barack Obama and Mitt Romney.[28] Turnout in 2014 was much worse, with record low participation in the primaries (18% of eligible voters) and the general election (30% of eligible voters).[29] The numbers ticked back up in the 2016 general election as 58% of eligible Golden State voters participated, but that means millions chose not to participate.

What a difference a few years can make. In the 2018 general election 65% of California registered voters cast ballots, the highest percentage of registered voter participation for a gubernatorial election in the Golden State since 2006.[30] And then, in 2020 81% of California registered voters participated in the Presidential Election, the highest percentage of registered voter participation in any California election since 1976.[31]

A pair of factors can be attributed to the uptick in California voter participation the past two general elections of 2018 and 2020. One is the growth of voting by mail. Prior to the pandemic hitting in 2020, vote by mail was already popular in the state with 65% of California voters sending ballots through the mail in the 2018 general election. But in 2020, as COVID-19 proliferated, Governor Gavin Newsom issued an **executive order (a rule or regulation issued by the President, a Governor, or some administrative authority that has the effect of law)** that required all 58 counties to send registered voters ballots in the mail the voter could fill out and return via mail. *'No Californian should be forced to risk their health in order to exercise their right to vote",* Governor Newsom said when he issued the executive order.[32] Republicans responded to Newsom's executive order by filing lawsuits in both federal and state courts claiming the Governor's actions were unconstitutional on the grounds that only the State Legislature can enact changes in how the election is conducted. In response to the lawsuits, the California Legislature passed, and Governor Newsom signed legislation on June 18, 2020 expanding vote-by-mail access to every Golden State voter.[33]

A second factor driving soaring voter turnout in the 2018 and 2020 general elections centered on the presidency of Donald Trump. Love him or hate him, his presidency contributed to the increased engagement by citizens in voter participation. The former President lost California by 3 million votes in 2016, claiming millions of illegal votes were cast against him in the state, accusations that were never proven. President Trump maintained he won the popular vote nationwide in 2016 and even put together a commission to investigate voter fraud in 2017, but a year later the Trump Administration's presidential commission on election integrity disbanded after finding no evidence of widespread voting irregularities in the 2016 election.[34] In addition, as pointed out in Chapter 1 and this chapter, California became immersed in a plethora of lawsuits opposing

Trump Administration policies in such areas as immigration, the environment, and the census count, all issues of significance for California. The pandemic, and how the Trump Administration dealt with it, may also have motivated Californians to vote in larger numbers. Finally, Donald Trump's unorthodox, combative approach to the office of President, and his ability to dominate media coverage seemingly every day of his presidency no doubt seared itself in the collective conscience of the nation, including California. The result was record turnout in the mid-term elections of 2018 and the presidential election of 2020 in California. The voter turnout numbers in 2020 were impressive, some 160 million Americans voting, including nearly 18 million Californians. Joe Biden defeated Donald Trump by 7 million popular votes nationwide and that number was bolstered by the 5 million popular vote margin Biden achieved over Trump in California.

Again, as in 2016, Donald Trump cried foul concerning the results of the 2020 presidential election, only this time his opposition to the outcome was more veracious given he lost. In the litigation challenging the results of the 2020 election, the key complaint of the Trump Campaign was a proliferation of vote-by-mail ballots being allowed in the key swing states that determined the winner of the Electoral College.

Interestingly, California's results in the 2018 mid-term election provided a window into the opposition the Trump Campaign and many Republicans voiced against the vote-by-mail laws enacted by the states in 2020. In 2018 several competitive House of Representative races in California were not decided for a week after the November 6 election, one race stretching over a month before a winner was declared. The reason for the delay was some 40% of the estimated 12 million ballots cast statewide in 2018 were counted by the **counties (who conduct the elections in California)** after November 6. On election night, several GOP House candidates were ahead, but when the later counted ballots were tabulated, the Democratic candidate overtook their Republican rival and won the seat. The GOP ended up losing seven House races in California in 2018, lowering their total to just 7 held House seats out of 53 in the Golden State. Republican House Speaker Paul Ryan, commenting on the 2018 House election results in California, described California's election system as "bizarre."[35] The Republicans were critical of two things involving California's election laws in 2018; expanding vote-by-mail and a change in state law that grants voters the right to have anyone drop off their absentee ballot, rather than a family member, what Republicans claim is **Ballot Harvesting, a procedure where third party individuals gather and submit absentee or mail-in ballots, something critics claim could lead to vote misappropriation or fraud.**[36]

THE TRUMP CAMPAIGN'S LEGAL CHALLENGES AND ELECTION REFORM

The night of November 3, 2020, as election returns were coming in, many Americans may have gone to bed thinking President Donald Trump was on the way to re-election for a 2nd term given he was leading in the key upper Mid-West swing states of Michigan, Pennsylvania, and Wisconsin; states he needed to capture for victory. However, by the next morning, and over the next few days things radically changed as mail in ballots in those upper Mid-West states (along with Georgia and Nevada) were counted, and Joe Biden began over-taking Trump in those critical swing states. By Thursday, as the ballot counts mounted against him, President Trump tweeted out in frustration "STOP THE COUNT!" and began claiming millions of illegal ballots were being tabulated in Michigan, Pennsylvania, Wisconsin, Nevada, and Georgia. By Saturday, November 7, the race had been called for Joe Biden, and a flurry of lawsuits by the Trump Campaign ensued, followed by the assault on the U.S. Capitol January 6, 2021 where ardent Trump supporters attempted to prevent the Congress from officially certifying the Electoral College votes that gave Joe Biden the presidency with 306 Electoral College votes to Donald Trump's 232.

Some of the legal challenges levied by the Trump Campaign in the swing states included charges of voter fraud through the aforementioned ballot harvesting procedures, arguing mailed ballots received after election day should be nullified, and questioning the legality of state voter laws. All told, some 60 lawsuits contesting the results of the 2020 Presidential election failed at every level of the state and federal courts, the U.S. Supreme Court rejecting three appeals made to them by the Trump Campaign to overturn the election, including a Texas-based lawsuit asking the Supreme Court to throw out the election results in Georgia, Michigan, Pennsylvania, and Wisconsin. In all the litigation, the Trump Campaign and its' Republican allies failed to make a plausible legal argument that would convince conservative judges, some appointed by President Trump, of fraud in the 2020 election. The U.S. Supreme Court, despite comprising a 6-3 conservative majority that included Trump appointees Neil Gorsuch, Brett Kavanaugh and Amy Coney Barrett, voided the Trump appeals in brief written rulings, some as short as three sentences or less. And despite the attempted insurrection at the Capitol January 6, 2021, Donald Trump left office on January 20 and Joe Biden was sworn in as the 46th President.

But the unprecedented contesting of the 2020 election by Donald Trump and most of the Republican Party has resulted in a slew of states (43) proposing tougher voting restrictions like reducing early voting, ending same day voter registration, imposing a voter ID requirement, and limiting or banning mail-in-voting (to name a few). In Georgia, a traditionally Republican state, Donald Trump lost by 12,000 votes and in a special run-off election in early January 2021, both of Georgia's U.S. Senate seats were won by Democratic candidates Jon Ossoff and Raphael Warnock, giving the Democrats control of the U.S. Senate.

This led to Georgia's Republican controlled State Legislature passing and Georgia Republican Governor Brian Kemp signing in March 2021 a new election law that proponents say will expand voting, but detractors claim will restrict voting. The new Georgia law, as Governor Kemp points out, does require a minimum number of drop boxes in each county and provides an additional day of early voting. However, critics of the bill cite the stricter voter ID requirements, state lawmakers having more power over local election officials, and a controversial section that prohibits handing out food and water to voters waiting in line. The passing of Georgia's new voting law immediately generated controversy when Major League Baseball, concerned about the new voting restrictions in the law, moved the 2021 All-Star Game from Atlanta to Denver.

At the federal level, Democrats, who control Congress in 2021, have passed in the House of Representatives HR1, a bill that would reform voting laws nationwide to model some of the California voting procedures discussed in this chapter. HR1 would require states have their legislative districts drawn by independent commissions (like California does) instead of by partisan state legislators. HR 1 would also grant every American the right to vote early or by mail (like California does).

In conclusion, the California election reforms discussed in this chapter concerning the blanket primary, the proposal to award California's 55 Electoral College votes to the national popular vote winner in the President's race, the 14-member citizens' redistricting commission, and the expansion of vote-by-mail are all reforms with national implications for the country. Given what happened in the 2020 election, debates will continue between Americans over the need to safeguard the elections from voter fraud versus the need to ensure all Americans have access to vote. What will govern future elections gives credence to studying how California government operates in the American system.

4
CHAPTER

THE EXECUTIVE BRANCH

In June, 2010 California lawmakers in the State Legislature were at an impasse concerning the state budget. With no prospects of getting the budget passed before the new fiscal year began July 1, Governor Arnold Schwarzenegger ordered the reduction of some 200,000 state employees' pay to the federal minimum wage of $7.25 an hour. Given the Governor of California is the state's top executive official, one would think Governor Schwarzenegger could issue such an **Executive Order** and have it followed by the official responsible for issuing the state pay checks. **An Executive Order is a rule or regulation issued by the President, a Governor, or some administrative authority that has the effect of law. They may be used to create or modify the organization or procedures of administrative agencies.** However, John Chiang, **the State Controller,** who was the executive branch official responsible for issuing pay checks to all state employees, refused to comply with the order stating, *"The Governor's proposal to cut innocent state employees' salaries to the federal minimum wage is a cheap political trick that does nothing to solve the state's budget problems. Reducing pay and then restoring it in a timely manner once a budget is enacted cannot be done without gross violations of law."*[1]

If such resistance to an **Executive Order** issued by the President developed from a federal executive branch official, the President would have asked for the resignation of the official or fired the official. At the federal level of government, only the President and Vice President are elected indirectly through the voters, all other executive branch officials in the federal government that head up departments and administrative agencies are appointed by the President, and most are subject to confirmation by the U.S. Senate. Therefore, the President has the authority to remove these appointed officials at any time, something that occurred in the first year of the Trump administration with the firing by President Trump of National Security Advisor Michael Flynn, FBI Director James Comey, and the Secretary of Health and Human Services, Tom Price. But President Trump did not stop there, and by the third year of his term, the President had greater turnover of his Cabinet posts than the previous five Presidents did in their entire first terms. These Cabinet departures facilitated the instalment of **Acting Cabinet Members (individuals appointed to Cabinet positions without Senate confirmation)**. Under federal law known as **the Vacancies Act** acting Cabinet secretaries can serve for up to 210 days without Senate confirmation. President Trump, in 2019, indicated his preference for appointing acting Cabinet members, *"I like acting. It gives me more flexibility."*[2]

California operates under a slightly different system concerning the organization of the executive branch. The Golden State's executive branch is comprised of a **Plural Executive in which eight executive officers- the Governor, Lieutenant Governor, Attorney General, Secretary of State, Superintendent of Public Instruction, Insurance Commissioner, State Treasurer, and State Controller are all directly elected by the voters every four years in statewide elections. In addition, voters also choose members to the Board of Equalization, which is part of the executive branch as well.** Since the Governor does not appoint officials within the Plural Executive, they wield power separate from the Governor and may not feel they have to follow a Governor's directive as demonstrated by State Controller John Chiang's refusal to comply with Governor Schwarzenegger's executive order to cut state workers to minimum wage in 2010. In this chapter, we examine the Plural Executive, comparing and contrasting the executive branch of California with the executive branch of the Federal Government. We begin with the Governor's office.

THE GOVERNOR

Despite the difficulties California Governors can face from an uncooperative Plural Executive, the office is powerful and influential. The Governor of California is presiding over the largest populated state in the union with an economy that would rank as the 5th largest of the world if California were a separate nation. While Governor Ronald Reagan is the only California Governor to become President of the United States, serving as Governor of the Golden State can lead to what has been referred to as "Potomac Fever", the aspirations of Governors to run for President. Former Governor Jerry Brown ran for President three times (1976 and 1980) and once again in 1992, aggressively challenging Bill Clinton for the nomination. Governor Pete Wilson considered a run at the White House in 1996, but eventually withdrew his candidacy before the

New Hampshire Primary. Current Governor Gavin Newsom has been considered a prospect to run for President in the future, but he is facing a potential Recall election later in 2021 that could potentially torpedo his White House aspirations.

It is also worth noting that California Governor Earl Warren was tapped to be Chief Justice of the United States Supreme Court by President Dwight Eisenhower in 1953 after serving 10 years as Governor of California. Today, **Proposition 140, passed in 1990, limits the terms a Governor can serve to two four-year terms. In addition, Proposition 140 also limits the terms of the Plural Executive offices to two four-year terms.** Jerry Brown was Governor from 1975-1983 (before passage of Proposition 140), and as a result of his re-election in 2014, former Governor Brown has the distinction of being the longest serving Governor in state history, bypassing Earl Warren.

The 22nd Amendment to the U.S. Constitution (ratified in 1951) limits the terms of the President to two four- year terms, and only Franklin D. Roosevelt served more than two terms as President, dying in office in the midst of his fourth term in April of 1945.

QUALIFICATIONS

The qualifications for Governor of California are the following: (1) Must be a citizen; (2) Must be qualified to vote; (3) Must have been a resident of the state for 5 years preceding election. In contrast, **the U.S. Constitution requires that the President be a natural born citizen, 35 years of age, and a resident of the nation for 14 years**. Before Governor Arnold Schwarzenegger's approval ratings sank during his second term (as the state fell into recession), there was a movement by pro Schwarzenegger supporters to change the U.S. Constitution and allow someone not born in the U.S. to run for President (Schwarzenegger was born in Austria). No such change in the U.S. Constitution occurred, and the requirements to be President are much more stringent than the requirements to be Governor of California. During the 2003 Recall Election that removed Governor Gray Davis and elected Arnold Schwarzenegger to replace him, some 135 people qualified their names on the ballot as potential candidates for Governor. The list included the victor Arnold Schwarzenegger, Gary Coleman, porn stars, and a plethora of Californians willing to pay the application fee and earn the high distinction of having qualified themselves on the ballot to run for Governor. The bizarre 2003 Recall ballot also reinforced the lower qualification threshold California's Constitution places on those seeking the Governor's office as compared to the U.S. Constitution's qualifications for President of the United States. If there is a Recall election to potentially remove Governor Newsom from office in 2021, it will be interesting to see what novice characters end up on the ballot. But regardless of the less stringent qualifications to seek the Governorship, the powers and responsibilities of California's Governor are significant. Let us consider them.

APPOINTMENT POWERS

Because California's Executive Branch is so large, the Governor, similar to the President of the United States, is granted the power to make thousands of appointments upon entering office. Such appointments include the Governor's Cabinet Departments (Business, Transportation and Housing; Resources; Welfare; State and Consumer Services; Youth and Adult Corrections; and Finance). In addition, the Governor appoints people to some 320 State Boards and Commissions that include the Public Utilities Commission, the Agriculture Labor Relations Board, the Fair Political Practices Commission, the Coastal Commission, and the State Education Board to name a few. The State Senate is required to confirm (with a majority vote) the Governor's appointments of approximately 100 full time administrative positions and 75 Boards and Commissions.[3]

California's Governor can also fill vacancies in certain offices through appointment. If a vacancy occurs in the following offices (U.S. Senate, the other seven Statewide Plural Executive offices, a County Board of Supervisors seat, and all State Judges) the Governor can fill the vacancy. When Republican Pete Wilson was elected Governor in 1990, he had been serving as one of California's two United States' Senators. Under the appointment powers granted him, Governor Wilson was able to select his replacement for U.S. Senate, choosing fellow Republican John Seymour. Senator Seymour was defeated two years later by Democrat Diane Feinstein in the 1992 election, and Senator Feinstein has held the seat ever since.

In the 2016 election, California Attorney General Kamala Harris won the U.S. Senate seat vacated by the retiring Barbara Boxer. Upon Harris becoming a U.S. Senator, Governor Brown appointed Xavier Becerra to be Attorney General, and he was confirmed to the post by the State Senate in 2017. Attorney General Becerra retained his position in the 2018 general election, but President Joe Biden tapped Becerra to head up the Federal Department of Health and Human Services and Becerra was confirmed by the U.S. Senate in March 2021. Becerra's departure prompted Governor Gavin Newsom to appoint Rob Bonta to replace Becerra as Attorney General of California in March 2021.

When California U.S. Senator Kamala Harris became Vice President of the United States in January 2021, Governor Newsom exercised his appointment powers by selecting California Secretary of State Alex Padilla to replace Harris as United States Senator. Padilla will have to face the voters to retain his U.S. Senate seat in 2022. And once Padilla left the California Secretary of State office for the U.S. Senate, Newsom appointed Shirley Weber to replace Padilla as California Secretary of State.

Both the California Attorney General and the California Secretary of State are part of the state's **Plural Executive**, offices in which the voters select the individual to serve in that position, and Attorney General Rob Bonta and Secretary of State Shirley Weber will need to be elected by California voters in the 2022 election if they want to retain their offices.

Both the President of the United States and California's Governor are provided a personal staff that serve at the pleasure of the Chief Executive. These positions include but are not limited to political advisors, legal counsel, media representatives, legislative staff, and judicial affairs staff. Staffers serving the Chief Executive are not subject to confirmation, and Presidents and Governors can appoint and remove people "at pleasure" from these posts. The President has some 150 personal staff, approximately 80 personal staff serve California's Governor. Such personal staff, especially the ones closest to the President and Governor, have more access to the Chief Executive than many top officials leading major departments and agencies, prompting criticism at times that such personal staffers have too much power and influence over policy decisions made by the Chief Executive.

JUDICIAL POWERS

The Governor of California and President of the United States can fill vacancies created by the death, retirement, or removal of judges. All federal judicial vacancies are filled by the President (subject to U.S. Senate confirmation) and every California judicial vacancy allows the Governor to select a replacement (the Commission of Judicial Appointments must confirm all California Appellate and Supreme Court appointments made by the Governor). However, judicial appointment power is not the extent of a Governor or President's authority concerning the judiciary. California Governors and the President of the United States have other judicial powers that include reducing or eliminating the punishment of an individual found guilty of a crime in a federal or state court. These powers include **Pardons, the Commuting of a Sentence, Clemency, the Reprieve, and Parole.** Granting the President and Governors such judicial powers are consistent with the checks and balances system the Framers of the U.S. Constitution created to ensure each of the three branches of government (the Legislative Branch, the Executive Branch, and the Judicial Branch) could check the other two, a concept incorporated by state constitutions as well.

Pardon

A Pardon is an Executive grant by a President or Governor that releases someone convicted of a crime from punishment and legal consequences. A full Pardon not only eliminates the punishment or legal consequence, but fully restores an individual's civil rights forfeited upon conviction of a crime (the ability to get a professional license, serve on a jury or own a gun). Some thirty states grant their Governor the power of a pardon, including California, and the U.S. Constitution allows the President complete pardoning power for all federal offenses.[4] However, pardoning powers are not extended to the President or California's Governor for convictions involving cases of **impeachment. Impeachment is a formal accusation rendered by the lower house of a legislative body that commits the accused civil official to stand trial in the upper house of the legislature. Conviction of the civil official by the upper house leads to the civil official being removed from office.** President Gerald Ford, in 1975 granted a pardon to President Richard Nixon, ensuring Nixon would never face any criminal charges involving Watergate. President Nixon was not impeached, instead he resigned from office before impeachment procedures against him commenced, allowing President Ford the legal authority to pardon Nixon. President Jimmy Carter issued a pardon to all Vietnam draft evaders in 1977.

In 2017, President Trump pardoned former Arizona Sheriff Joe Arpaio, convicted of criminal contempt of court for failing to comply with a federal court order to stop racially profiling residents of Maricopa County, where Arpaio served as sheriff.[5] Sheriff Arpaio supported Donald Trump's anti-illegal immigrant platform in the 2016 campaign, prompting the President to pardon the controversial sheriff. In 2020, President Trump used his Pardon powers to erase the convictions of four Blackwater security guards who were convicted of murdering 17 unarmed civilians in Iraq in 2007. The victims included women and children. Ryan Crocker, U.S. Ambassador to Iraq in 2007 and David Petraeus, the commander of U.S. military forces in Iraq in 2007, issued a joint statement about President Trump's pardon of the four Blackwater security guards, *"The Pardon of these individuals can only be seen as hugely damaging, an action that tells the world that Americans abroad can commit the most heinous of crimes with impunity."*[6] Evan Liberty, one of the four Blackwater security guards pardoned by President Trump, defended his actions in Baghdad back in 2007, claiming he and his fellow guards were being shot at when they returned gunfire, *"I didn't shoot at anybody that wasn't shooting at me."*[7] By the end of 2016, Governor Jerry Brown had issued over 850 pardons since taking office in 2011, a significant difference from the previous three governors who between 1991 and 2010 issued just 28 pardons combined.[8] As of March 2021 Governor Gavin Newsom has granted 72 Pardons.

Commute

The President or Governor can issue a Commute, which upholds the conviction of the criminal offense, but allows for the suspension of the criminal sentencing, or a reduction in the length of sentencing. In 2010, not long before the end of his term, Governor Arnold Schwarzenegger commuted the sentence of Esteban Nunez, convicted of manslaughter in the stabbing death of a 22-year-old college student. Governor Schwarzenegger reduced Nunez's sentence from 16 years to 7 years in prison, citing Nunez was not the one who killed the 22-year-old even though he was involved in the knife fight that resulted in the young man's death. Esteban Nunez's father is Fabian Nunez, the former Democratic Speaker of the California State Assembly. Once Governor Schwarzenegger reduced the sentence, accusations of political cronyism between the former Speaker and the Governor surfaced. The parents of the stabbing victim sued former Governor Schwarzenegger, claiming he violated state law by failing to notify them that he was reducing Esteban Nunez's sentence. Fabian Nunez argued that his son received a tougher sentence because of his father's political career.[9] As of March 2021 Governor Gavin Newsom commuted 79 sentences.

During his two terms President Barack Obama commuted over 1,700 sentences, many of them involving individuals locked up in federal prisons on drug crimes that carried mandatory minimum sentencing. Obama opted for reducing prison sentences in large numbers through commutation as opposed to pardons, issuing only 212 pardons. In contrast, President Trump commuted fewer sentences (94) during his four years in the White House.[10]

Clemency

Clemency allows a President or Governor to reduce or eliminate sentences of convicted felons for humanitarian reasons. Clemency power can be used by a President or Governor to prevent someone from being executed if convicted of an offense in which capital punishment was the sentence. Governor Gray Davis refused the Clemency request of Manuel Babbitt, convicted of the rape and murder of a 78-year-old woman in 1982. Babbitt was a Vietnam War veteran who earned a Purple Heart, and Governor Davis had also served in Vietnam, prompting speculation that the Governor might grant Clemency to Babbitt. But in his Clemency denial, Governor Davis said the following: *"Countless people have suffered the ravages of war, persecution, starvation, natural disasters, personal calamities and the like. But such experiences cannot justify or mitigate the savage beating and killing of defenseless, law abiding citizens."*[11]

Reprieve

A Reprieve gives the President or Governor the authority to postpone a sentence (particularly an execution) if new evidence surfaces which indicates the individual charged with the offense may be innocent, or their constitutional right of appealing the conviction and sentence has not been exhausted. In such cases, the President or Governor may grant Clemency (if the state allows the Governor Clemency power) or a retrial may be conducted. On September 26, 2010 Governor Arnold Schwarzenegger issued a Reprieve, postponing the execution of Albert Greenwood Brown because appellate court scheduling prevented Brown from having his appeals completed before the execution date.[12] Four days later, the California State Supreme Court denied a request to execute Brown by refusing the state's emergency request to accelerate an appeal on the legality of California's death penalty procedures. Brown had been sentenced to death by a Riverside County jury in February 1982 for the abduction and murder of a 15- year-old girl. Governor Schwarzenegger, though issuing the Reprieve for Brown, denied Brown's request for Clemency and was frustrated with the State Supreme Court's ruling, *"Albert Brown was sentenced to death for committing the most heinous and unconscionable crimes. Now 30 years later the state is still unable to carry out his execution. It is absurd that our legal system continues to prevent the state from carrying out the will of the people."*[13]

In March 2019, Governor Gavin Newsom took the unprecedented step of using the Reprieve power to prevent the execution of all 737 California inmates on death row. Newsom's moratorium on the death penalty will only remain in place through the duration of his time serving as Governor. Newsom, in defending his decision, said, *"I have never believed in the death penalty from a moral perspective."* Newsom cited some 164 people who have been taken off death row for being wrongfully convicted of murder. However, Michael Hanisee, President of the Association of Deputy District Attorneys, disagreed with Governor Newsom's decision, *"The voters of the State of California support the death penalty. That is powerfully demonstrated by their approval of Proposition 66 in 2016 to ensure the death penalty is implemented. Governor Newsom is usurping the express will of California voters."*[14]

Parole

Parole can be administered by Governors, releasing a convicted criminal from prison who has already served a portion of their sentence. Several states have Parole Boards that can recommend that a prisoner be released early. Only three states allow the Governor to reverse Parole decisions, and California is one of them. In 2004, Governor Arnold Schwarzenegger paroled

Rosario Munoz after she served 16 years for the murder of her husband's lover.[15] In 2014, Governor Jerry Brown allowed 539 out of 672 convicted killers' parole releases to stand (80%).[16] Governor Arnold Schwarzenegger upheld 27% of such Parole Board decisions and Governor Gray Davis only allowed 9 out of 374 paroled killers to be released during his governorship. In 2020, Governor Newsom spokesman Brian Ferguson indicated that the Governor had stopped 46 paroles for murderers.[17] Jack Pitney, Professor of Politics at Claremont McKenna College suggested Governor Newsom's actions in halting all executions of those on death row might make him hesitant to approve parole board recommendations to release inmates convicted of murder.[18] At the federal level, Congress abolished the parole system for federal prisoners by passing the 1984 Comprehensive Crime Control Act, creating mandatory sentencing without parole.[19]

LEGISLATIVE POWERS

While the lawmaking function is assigned to the Legislative Branch at both the federal and state government levels, Presidents and Governors do possess legislative powers. In this section we examine these powers which include **Addressing Joint Sessions of the Legislature, Proposing Budgets, Veto Options, and Calling the Legislature into Special Session.**

Addressing Joint Sessions of the Legislature

The United States Constitution requires the President *"from time to time give to the Congress Information of the State of the Union."* Annually in January, Presidents deliver to a joint session of Congress the State of the Union address. During the address, the President recommends legislation for Congress to pass and proposes funding priorities for the upcoming federal budget. Due to the pandemic, President Joe Biden did not address Congress in January 2021, but was scheduled to make a speech before a joint session of Congress in April of 2021.

In California, the Governor (also in January) fulfills a similar requirement in the State Constitution, delivering to a joint session of the State Legislature the State of the State address. However, given the conditions created by the pandemic, Governor Gavin Newsom did not deliver the 2021 State of the State address in the Capitol before the Legislature in January, opting for the confines of an empty Dodger Stadium, one of California's largest vaccination locations, to give the annual address in March. Governor Newsom devoted the 2021 State of the State address to defend his decisions in confronting the pandemic by touting his administration's efforts to get more Californians vaccinated and provide financial relief in the form of $600 payments to poor California families. Governor Newsom, mindful of the Recall Election he may face in the Fall of 2021, also promised in the Dodger Stadium address to get California public schools reopened by April 2021 for in-person instruction.[20] But those leading the Recall of Governor Newsom, frustrated with his decisions concerning lockdowns that kept businesses and schools closed in 2020, rebuffed the Governor's State of the State address, *"He's completely out of touch with reality, and that's a pretty sad, pathetic state of the union that he lives in right now in his mind,"* Recall Committee spokesman Randy Economy said.[21]

Traditionally, these addresses include encouraging the Congress at the federal level, or the legislature at the state level to pass legislation the chief executive supports. But there is a significant difference how the federal government works compared to the state of California when potential legislation is championed by a President or California Governor. The difference between the President and California's Governor in proposing legislation is that the U.S. Constitution allows the President to send potential legislation to Congress for consideration. California's Governor is not afforded the power of formally introducing bills to the State Legislature.

Proposing Budgets

Both the President and California's Governor develop budgets with their respective legislative bodies. However, the power to pass a budget rests with the legislative branches at the federal and state levels. In 1921, Congress passed the Budget and Accounting Act which required the President prepare a proposed national budget.[22] The following year (1922) Golden State voters approved a Constitutional Amendment making the Governor responsible for preparing and submitting to the State Legislature an annual budget containing most of the anticipated state revenue, and funding priorities (the amount of money the Governor is willing to spend on state government programs for the upcoming **Fiscal Year**). **A Fiscal Year is the 12-month financial period used by a government for record keeping, budgeting, funding, revenue collecting, and other aspects of fiscal management.** The federal government's fiscal year runs from Oct. 1ˢᵗ to the following Sept. 30ᵗʰ. California's fiscal year begins July 1ˢᵗ and ends the following June 30ᵗʰ.

Veto Options

Both the Governor of California and the President of the United States can veto legislation. **A Veto is a rejection of the legislation by a Governor or President.** Presidents can veto legislation passed by Congress, and California

Governors can veto legislation passed by the State Legislature. There are differ-ent veto options available to California's Governor as compared to the President of the United States. Veto options include the **General Veto,** the **Pocket Veto**, and the **Line-Item Veto.**

The General Veto

The President and California Governor each have the ability to issue a Gen-eral Veto. In vetoing the legislation, both Chief Executives will attach a veto message explaining why the bill was rejected. The veto message can also be used by the President to give Congress direction on how they could pass the bill in a form acceptable to the President. California Governors can provide similar guidance to the State Legislature in their veto messages. Congress can **override** a President's General Veto with a two-thirds vote in both the House of Representatives and the Senate. The California Legislature can **override** a Governor's General Veto with a two-thirds vote in both the State Assembly and State Senate. **Override of a Veto refers to the legislative branch approving a law rejected by the chief executive (President or Governor).** Despite the override capability available to Congress and the California State Legislature, the procedure is rarely successful. Out of 372 General Vetoes issued by Presi-dent Franklin Roosevelt, only 9 were overridden by the Congress. Most Presi-dents enjoyed similar success rates in having their vetoes maintained. President Andrew Johnson used the General Veto 21 times and 15 of them were over-ridden by Congress, the worst success rate of any President.[23] In California, the last successful override of a Governor's veto occurred in 1979 when the State Legislature overrode Governor Jerry Brown's veto of legislation involv-ing insurance and pay raises for state employees.[24]

The Pocket Veto

The U.S. Constitution provides use of the Pocket Veto by the President of the United States. Under this type of veto, the President has the option of doing nothing with a bill passed by Congress if, upon submitting the bill to the Pres-ident, Congress adjourns (goes out of session) within the next 10 days. Such a scenario allows the President to reject the bill without explanation. The Pocket Veto is absolute, and Congress has no opportunity to override a Pocket Veto. However, the U.S. Constitution also stipulates that if Congress remains in ses-sion for 10 days after submitting the bill to the President, the bill will automati-cally become law if the President takes no action on the legislation (signing the bill or issuing the General Veto). President Franklin Roosevelt issued the most Pocket Vetoes (263) of any President.

California voters in 1966 passed Proposition 6, eliminating the Pocket Veto for the Governor. Today, California Governors have 12 days to either sign or veto legislation sent to them by the State Legislature. If the Governor fails to act within the 12-day period, the bill automatically becomes law. Each year near the end of August or beginning of September, the Legislature adjourns until January. At the end of the session, lawmakers send the Governor a high volume of legislation to be signed or vetoed. During this period, Governors are given 30 days to act on bills passed by the Legislature. In 2008, Governor Arnold Schwarzenegger vetoed a record number of bills (435). Governor Schwarzenegger defended his high volume of vetoes by citing the Legislature's historically late passage of the budget that year, which occupied Schwarzenegger to the point that he did not have enough time to review all of the bills sent to him by the Legislature at the end of the 2008 session.[25] With a Democratic Governor in office, and the budget being passed on time, things have changed since Governor Schwarzenegger's tenure, and in 2013 Governor Brown signed 800 bills and vetoed only 96.[26] 2020 saw Governor Gavin Newsom sign 327 bills and veto 56.[27]

Line Item Veto

The Line-Item Veto is a power exercised by Governors which allows them to reduce or eliminate spending in **budget appropriation bills. A Budget Appropriation Bill funds government programs like education, prisons, welfare, infrastructure, and research (to name a few).** While the Line-Item Veto allows a Governor to delete spending items in the budget, it does not allow the Governor to increase spending. In California, the State Legislature can override a Governor's Line-Item Veto with a two-thirds vote in the Assembly and Senate, but this is extremely rare, the last one occurring over 30 years ago. Until 2011, approval of California's budget required a two-thirds vote of both the State Assembly and State Senate, and many of those budgets were not passed on time because of the difficulty in achieving such extraordinary majorities in both chambers. Once a budget was approved, the chances of overriding a Governor's Line-Item Veto would be virtually impossible. Despite Democratic majorities in the State Assembly and State Senate during Republican Governor George Deukmejian's administration (1983 – 1991), Governor Deukmejian used the Line-Item Veto to slash spending on some 1700 expenditure items totaling $7 billion during his two terms, earning him the nickname "Governor No."[28] None of Governor Deukmejian's Line-Item Vetoes were overridden by the State Legislature.

In the 2017/2018 budget, Governor Brown approved $125 billion in general fund spending without issuing a single Line-Item Veto, the second year in a row the Governor refrained from slashing spending approved by the Legislature. Though a rarity for Governors, the action is not unfamiliar to Brown who approved a budget with no Line Item Vetoes during his first stint as Governor back in 1982. Before Brown, Governor Ronald Reagan in 1970 was the last Governor not to use Line-Item Vetoes in the budget, making this practice the exception, not the norm.[29] In the 2019/2020 budget, Governor Gavin Newsom used the Line-Item Veto sparingly, and only one Line-Item Veto was issued by the Governor in the 2020/2021 budget.

At the federal level, the U.S. Constitution does not grant the President of the United States the Line-Item Veto. In 1996, a Republican Congress passed legislation giving the President the Line-Item Veto, and Democratic President Bill Clinton used it on federal budget appropriation bills in 1997. The U.S. Supreme Court ruled in 1998 that the Line Item Veto Congress approved for use by the President was unconstitutional given no such veto authority existed for the President in the U.S. Constitution.[30] President Clinton is the only President in U.S. history that wielded the Line- Item Veto, if only briefly. Republicans in Congress did not especially like President Clinton (they eventually impeached him) but they gave him the Line-Item Veto, hoping future Republican Presidents would use it to cut federal spending, and thus shrink the size of the federal government. Given the federal government has accumulated over $28 trillion in debt as of 2021, support for the Line-Item Veto has resurfaced, particularly by Republicans in Congress who envision it as method for Presidents to cut wasteful spending.

Calling the Legislature into a Special Session

The California State Constitution grants the Governor "on extraordinary occasions" the authority to call the Legislature into special sessions. When such special sessions are called the State Legislature should only consider the issues specified by the Governor's special session proclamation. In 1989, after the Loma Prieta earthquake struck the San Francisco Bay Area, Governor George Deukmejian called the Legislature into a special session to address state relief efforts for Northern California victims of the quake. In 2015, Governor Jerry Brown called the Legislature into a special session to deal with funding road maintenance projects and the state's expanding health care program for the needy (Medi-Cal). As referenced in Chapter 2, Governor Newsom's reluctance to call the Legislature into a special session to deal with the pandemic in 2020 drew criticism from some lawmakers who felt the Governor was making decisions unilaterally and excluding them. The U.S. Constitution allows the President to summon Congress, or either house. into a special session "on extraordinary occasions" as well. Presidents have used this authority to compel the U.S. Senate to act on presidential appointments and treaties.[31]

COMMANDER IN CHIEF

The President of the United States is the "Commander In Chief" of the U.S. military, and Presidents have used this power to send troops into battle all around the globe. The U.S. Constitution requires a Declaration of War be issued by the Congress, but Congress has not issued such a declaration since World War II. Since World War II, Presidents have sent American military forces into battle in such places as Korea, Vietnam, Panama, Somalia, Yugoslavia, and the recent wars in Iraq and Afghanistan. **Congress attempted to restrict the President's power to send troops into battle with the passage of the 1973 War Powers Act which limited the time troops could remain deployed without congressional approval to 60 days.** However, Presidents continue to maintain a position that asking Congress for approval of military action is voluntary on their part given their authority under the U.S. Constitution as "Commander In Chief."

California's Governor assumes the role of "Commander In Chief" of the California National Guard, which consists of military reservists who have already served in the nation's armed forces. The Governor can call the National Guard into action, but in most cases a request for National Guard deployment will come from local law-enforcement.[32] Natural Disasters, Rioting, or some other event threatening public order would trigger deployment of the National Guard. The Watts Riots in 1965 prompted Governor Pat Brown to send some 1000 National Guardsman to Los Angeles. Governor Pete Wilson deployed 7000 National Guard to Los Angeles in 1992 after intense rioting broke out when four white police officers were acquitted on charges of assault against Rodney King.[33] The Governor appoints an **Adjutant General as the top administrator of the National Guard.** This appointment must be approved by the President of the United States.[34] It should be noted that while California's Governor is "Commander In Chief" of the State National Guard, National Guard troops in California or any other state can come under the control of the President of the United States.

CHIEF OF STATE

The role of the President and Governors across the country as the ceremonial head of the government is one function these executives perform as Chief Of State. Concerning the President, Chief Of State functions include, but are not limited to decorating war heroes, throwing out the first pitch at the World Series, and representing the nation at times of national mourning (President Ronald Reagan provided a skillful example of this when he spoke to the nation about the importance of continuing space exploration after the *Challenger* Space

Shuttle crashed, killing the entire crew in 1986). President Barack Obama performed such duties after mass shootings at an elementary school in Connecticut and a nightclub in Florida, and President Donald Trump followed suit in 2017, arriving in Las Vegas a few days after the worst mass shooting in U.S. history as 59 people were killed and hundreds more wounded when a gunman opened fire on 22,000 fans attending a country music concert.

Perhaps one of the most recognized duties Presidents undertake as Chief Of State involves receiving Heads of State from other countries at the White House. The White House is an imposing home court advantage for Presidents when hosting foreign government leaders at summits, meetings, and state dinners.

California Governors engage in similar activities as Chief Of State (cutting ribbons on public works projects, attending the funerals of police officers killed in the line of duty, and appearing in parades, to name a few). Golden State Governors, like the President, receive foreign dignitaries when they visit the state (in 2011 Governor Jerry Brown officially hosted the new royal couple from Britain). Unlike the President, who can dazzle guests with the White House, California's Governor has no comparable residence. In fact, no California Governor had lived in the state mansion since the 1960's.

The Governor's Mansion Restored

In 1966, newly elected Republican Governor Ronald Reagan and his wife Nancy Reagan refused to move into the Governor's Mansion, which had been purchased by the state back in 1903. The older house was considered a fire trap, was located on a busy Sacramento street, and was surrounded by commercial development. The Reagans began a drive to raise private funds for a new Governor's Mansion. Funds were secured, and a new mansion was constructed along the American River. Completion of the new mansion occurred after Ronald Reagan's second term ended. Democratic Governor Jerry Brown, who followed Governor Reagan, refused to live in the new digs, and it remained unfurnished with no landscaping for 8 years while Governor Brown resided in a Sacramento apartment.

In 1982, Republican George Deukmejian became Governor and indicated he would like to live in the new mansion. However, before leaving office, Governor Brown and the State Legislature sold the mansion and put the proceeds into a state operated trust fund. These actions resulted in no Governor's Mansion for the Chief Executive of California since the 1960's. Governor Pete Wilson and Gray Davis lived in private residences during their terms. Governor Arnold Schwarzenegger commuted each day via private jet between Sacramento and his Los Angeles home, and when Governor Jerry Brown was elected in 2010, he once again chose to live in a Sacramento apartment. However, Governor Brown, who spent time in the old mansion when his father was Governor in the late 1950's, agreed to $2.5 million in renovation funding of the historic mansion in 2014, and appropriated another $1.6 million for the project in 2015.[35] Renovations of the iconic mansion were completed in 2015, and shortly after, Governor Brown and First Lady Anne Gust Brown moved in.[36]

After Gavin Newsom was elected Governor in 2018, he and First Partner Jennifer Siebel, along with their four children, temporarily moved into the renovated mansion, but, after purchasing a private residence in Fair Oaks, just outside of Sacramento, the Governor's family moved out of the mansion and into the Fair Oaks property. Governor Newsom's spokesman Nathan Click indicated the historic Governor's Mansion would be utilized for public events and state business.[37]

We have discussed the significant powers and responsibilities of California's Governors. Let us now turn our attention to the **Plural Executive** and examine the other seven statewide elected offices.

THE LIEUTENANT GOVERNOR

The Lieutenant Governor assumes all powers of Governor when the Governor is out of the state. This provision in the State Constitution was considered necessary given travel and communication in 1849 were severely limited, and Governor's leaving the state could be gone a significant amount of time. The impact of this constitutional procedure in modern times can be political because unlike the Vice President of the United States, who comes from the same party as the President, the Lieutenant Governor is a separately elected official who can be from the opposite party of the Governor. As previously mentioned, Governor Jerry Brown ran for President in 1976 and while out of the state campaigning, the Republican Lieutenant Governor, Mike Curb, exercising his authority to act as Governor, appointed a state judge in Brown's absence.[38]

If the Governor were to leave office before their term expired (with the exception of being recalled by the voters) the Lieutenant Governor would become Governor. In 1953, Lieutenant Governor Goodwin Knight took over as Governor when Governor Earl Warren left to assume the position of Chief Justice of the United States Supreme Court. The U.S. Constitution allows the Vice President to take over as President if the President were to leave office due to resignation, conviction on impeachment charges, or death. When President Richard Nixon resigned from the presidency in 1974, Vice President Gerald Ford succeeded Nixon as President.

The Vice President of the United States is President of the U.S. Senate, but rarely presides over the U.S. Senate, only appearing to cast a deciding vote (usually on legislation) in the 100-seat body if a tie exists. In 2017, Vice President Mike Pence cast the tie breaking vote to confirm Betsy DeVos as Education Secretary, the first time in U.S. history a Vice President had to cast a tie breaking vote in the U.S. Senate to confirm a presidential cabinet appointment.[39] With the United States comprising 50 Republicans and 50 Democrats after the 2020 election, Vice President Kamal Harris holds the tie-breaking vote, giving Senate Democrats the slimmest of majorities in the upper house of Congress. California's Lieutenant Governor has the same authority in the 40 member California State Senate, serving as President of the Senate and casting tie breaking votes in that chamber if the need arises.

The offices of U.S. Vice President and Lieutenant Governor of California have been lampooned as positions in which the occupant consumes most of their time inquiring about the health of the President and the Governor. With that said, Vice Presidents' Al Gore and Dick Cheney assumed prominent roles in the administrations of the Presidents they served. President Bill Clinton consulted with Vice President Al Gore on a daily basis and gave him authority to oversee reforms in the space program. After the attacks of 9/11, President Bush made Vice President Cheney a powerful figure in the development of anti-terrorism policies to protect the nation, and military actions taken in Afghanistan and Iraq. President Trump delegated the responsibility of leading the Coronavirus Task Force to Vice President Mike Pence. President Biden assigned Vice President Kamala Harris the task of overseeing the White House response to the Spring 2021 surge of migrants (many of them unaccompanied children) arriving at the U.S./Mexico border.

California's Lieutenant Governors are not given important policy roles by the Governor but do have other duties. The Lieutenant Governor chairs the Economic Development Commission, a commission designed to promote California as a business-friendly state where companies can make money. The Lieutenant Governor also serves on the University of California's Board of Regents and the California State University Board of Trustees. Before becoming Governor, Gavin Newsom served as Lieutenant Governor, voting against the tuition increases discussed in Chapter 1 levied on UC and CSU students in July of 2011.

One other responsibility bestowed upon the Lieutenant Governor by the California Constitution is to schedule the Recall Election of the Governor if it is determined the required number of signatures (1.5 million currently) have been gathered to force the special election. Lieutenant Governor Eleni Kounalakis may be required to schedule the Recall Election of Governor Newsom in the Fall of 2021.

THE ATTORNEY GENERAL

The California Attorney General is the state's chief law enforcement officer and is responsible for ensuring that state laws are enforced. This position is considered the second most powerful statewide executive office (the most powerful executive office being the Governor). California Attorney Generals offer legal counsel for the state and represent the state in **Civil Law Cases**. **Civil Law Cases occur when the government provides for the legal settlement of disputes between private parties in such matters as contracts, domestic relations, and business relations. The government may be a plaintiff or defendant in a civil lawsuit.** Over the four-year term of President Donald Trump, California, led by Attorney General Xavier Becerra, sued the Trump Administration over 100 times in a breadth of cases that included immigration, the environment, LGBTQ rights, education, health care, and the census count. By August 2020, California spent over $43 million in the litigation.[40]

Controversy developed in the Attorney General's office when Proposition 8, a 2008 voter approved measure, banned same sex marriage in California. Proposition 8 was challenged in both state and federal court, yet Attorney General, Democrat Kamala Harris (and her predecessor when Proposition 8 passed, Jerry Brown), refused to defend the ban on same sex marriage, adopting the legal position that the ban violates the California Constitution and the U.S. Constitution. Muddying the legal waters even more was the fact that Proposition 8 qualified for the 2008 ballot as an amendment to the State Constitution. The backers of Proposition 8 argued in court that they should be able to represent the legal defense of the constitutional amendment banning same sex marriage in California given the State Attorney General's office refused. The U.S. Supreme Court determined the supporters of Proposition 8 had no legal authority to defend the law and struck down Proposition 8 in 2013, then ruled in 2015 that same sex marriage was legal nationwide.

This example provides another stark contrast between California's Plural Executive and the federal government's Executive Branch structure. The U.S. Attorney General is the top law enforcement official of the federal government, but, unlike California's Attorney General (who is elected by the state's voters), the U.S. Attorney General is appointed by the President and confirmed by the U.S. Senate. U.S. Attorney Generals, while wielding enormous power, would be subject to dismissal by the President if they failed to follow a President's directives. In October 1973, when U.S. Attorney General Elliot Richardson refused President Richard Nixon's order to fire Special Prosecutor Archibald Cox, who was investigating the Nixon Administration's cover-up of the Watergate break-in, President Nixon fired Attorney General Richardson.

In November 2018, President Donald Trump fired U.S. Attorney General Jeff Sessions. Trump was disappointed Sessions **recused himself (recuse means excusing oneself from a case because of a potential conflict of interest or lack of impartiality)** from the Justice Department's investigation of Russia interference in the 2016 Presidential election. Sessions had not disclosed that he had conversations with a Russian Ambassador before becoming Attorney General, prompting Sessions to recuse himself from the Russian election tampering investigation, leading to the appointment of Special Counsel Robert Mueller who conducted a far-reaching investigation into President Trump's family finances. Contrasting these two examples of Presidents firing their Attorney Generals with California's Plural Executive system, even if a California Governor disagreed with actions taken by the State Attorney General (such as refusing to defend a constitutional amendment like Proposition 8 in court), the Governor could not fire the State Attorney General.

Another important function of California's Attorney General is to prepare the titles and summaries of all ballot propositions submitted to the voters in state elections. In 2008, California Attorney General Jerry Brown, much to the frustration of Proposition 8 supporters, altered the language of the proposition to read the proposed constitutional amendment would *"eliminate the right of same-sex couples to marry."* Proposition 8 advocates were concerned such explicit language would make passage of the measure more difficult.[41] Their fears were misplaced as Proposition 8 passed despite Attorney General Brown's editing.

In 2015, a truly bizarre ballot proposal was presented to Attorney General Kamala Harris for title and summary, the Sodomite Suppression Act, a measure that would allow the killing of gays. Attorney General Harris sought relief from a California Superior Court in providing a title and summary for the proposed law by noting it "not only threatens public safety, but it is patently unconstitutional, utterly reprehensible, and has no place in a civil society."[42] The Superior Court ruled in Attorney General Harris's favor. In response to the Sodomite Suppression Act, the State Legislature is considering raising the filing fee for ballot initiatives from $200 to $2000 to discourage fringe groups from sponsoring measures like this. In March 2021, Governor Gavin Newsom appointed Rob Bonta as Attorney General to fill the vacancy created when Xavier Becerra joined the Biden Administration to serve as U.S. Secretary of Health and Human Services. Attorney General Bonta will have to be elected by a statewide vote in the 2022 election to retain the office.

THE SECRETARY OF STATE

California's Secretary Of State is the state's top election official and custodian of all official state records. Concerning the tools of Direct Democracy, the Secretary of State determines whether a required number of signatures have been gathered to qualify an Initiative, Referendum, or Recall for the next statewide **election**. Once state propositions have qualified for the ballot, the Secretary of State will issue the thick voter pamphlet California voters receive that include the entire proposed statute or constitutional amendment, along with arguments submitted in support or opposition of the measures. After the election, the Secretary of State will publish the results of all races and propositions. Other duties include deciding every four years during the presidential primary which presidential candidates have qualified for the ballot, and monitoring campaign donations and expenditures of candidates seeking public office in California.[43]

Between 1910 and 1970, Frank C. Jordan and his son Frank M. Jordan held the post of Secretary Of State, an unprecedented tenure of a California statewide executive office. In 1970, Jerry Brown became Secretary Of State, using the office as a stepping stone to the Governor's seat, which he captured in 1974. March Fong Eu became the first Asian American to hold a statewide executive office when she was elected Secretary Of State in 1974, a significant achievement given the state's history of bigotry against Asians as demonstrated in Chapter 2's discussion of California's 2nd Constitution in 1879 and the recent slate of hate crimes targeting Asian Americans in 2021.

The U.S. Constitution specifies that the states have the authority to conduct elections, and there is no comparable office to California's Secretary Of State at the federal level. With that said, the federal government passed the **Voting Rights Act of 1965 that bans any restrictions imposed by states denying citizens their legal right to vote. The Voting Rights Act allows federal intervention of voter registration in any state or county where less than 50% of eligible voters are registered to vote.** California's Secretary Of State is required to adhere to all laws imposed by the federal government concerning the Voting Rights Act, including a provision requiring bilingual ballots be made available by all states to voters in counties where 5% or more of the population speaks a language other than English.[44] Given that California is such an ethnically diverse state, a multitude of bilingual ballots are printed in the state each election year. **There is a Secretary Of State office in the federal government, but that official is a member of the President's Cabinet and conducts international relations with foreign governments.**

In December 2020 Governor Gavin Newsom appointed Shirley Weber as Secretary of State, filling the vacancy created when Newsom appointed Alex Padilla (who had been Secretary of State) to the United States Senate. Secretary of State Weber will need to be re-elected to the office by a statewide vote in the 2022 election.

THE SUPERINTENDENT OF PUBLIC INSTRUCTION

The Superintendent of Public Instruction is the only statewide executive office in which those seeking election to the seat run as **non-partisan candidates (no party affiliation next to their name on the ballot).** The Superintendent of Public Instruction (currently Tony Thurmond) heads the State Department of Education, a 1200-member department responsible for such things as providing financial aid to California's local school districts, issuing teaching credentials, administering the state's high school exit exam (that California high school seniors must pass to graduate), and coordinating with the federal government on joint education policies (such as Common Core). While the Superintendent of Public Instruction is an important administrative position concerning education policy in California, **the 10 member Governor appointed California State Board of Education is the body that sets state standards for all California public schools in academic curriculum, textbook content, and testing.** The Superintendent of Public Instruction is charged with implementing the policies of the State Board of Education. Conflict can develop between the Superintendent of Public Instruction and the State Board of Education when education policy priorities differ.

In 1982, Bill Honig was elected Superintendent of Public Instruction and battled with members of the State Board of Education over school funding (Honig wanted increases in the funding), State Board of Education members (appointed by Republican Governor's George Deukmejian and Pete Wilson during Honig's tenure) wanted to cut education funding because of revenue shortfalls in the late 80's and early 90's. Honig responded by throwing his support behind **Proposition 98, a constitutional amendment passed by the voters in 1988 that mandated 40% of the State Budget be spent on K-14 public education.** Proposition 98 remains in effect today, and lawmakers approving the state budget must provide a minimum base funding to Kindergarten through Community College equal to 40% of the total budget expenditures. Despite the success of Proposition 98, Bill Honig's service as Superintendent of Public Instruction ended badly when he was convicted of illegally approving $337,000 worth of contracts to a non-profit education foundation run by his wife.[45]

At the federal level, Congress created the Department of Education in 1979, a Cabinet department with a Secretary of Education (currently Miguel Cardona) who is appointed by the President. This department oversees federal programs in elementary, secondary, and postsecondary education. In addition, the federal Department of Education provides funding for vocational education, adult education, bilingual education, rehabilitative education, overseas education, and education research.[46] Despite these federal education programs, education funding primarily comes from the states. Federal funding of education in the U.S. accounts for only 8% of the total expenditures.[47]

One provision in the health care reform bill signed into law by President Obama in 2010 (which had nothing to do with health care but was nevertheless inserted) allowed the federal Department of Education, not private banks (who would charge higher interest rates), to administer all college loans. Again, we can see the contrast of California's Plural Executive system and the federal government's Executive Branch system. Governor's George Deukmejian and Pete Wilson could not fire Superintendent of Public Instruction Bill Honig because he was elected by the state's voters. The Secretary of Education, an appointed member of the President's Cabinet, could be fired by the President if the Secretary failed to implement the college loan program passed by Congress in the health care bill of 2010. Arne Duncan, U.S. Secretary of Education during the Obama administration, fully supported the college loan program.

THE INSURANCE COMMISSIONER

The most recently created statewide executive office is the Insurance Commissioner, approved by California voters in 1988. Before 1988, the office had been a position filled by a Governor's appointment, but voters, frustrated with escalating auto insurance rates in the state, not only elevated the Insurance Commissioner to an independent statewide executive office with the passage of Proposition 103, but the Initiative also authorized auto insurance rate reductions. Democrat John Garamendi became the first elected Insurance Commissioner in 1990, and soon after taking office pressed California auto insurance companies to issue rebate checks to customers. Formal powers of the Insurance Commissioner include pre-approving rates for car and homeowners' insurance, issuing licenses for insurance agents and companies doing business in California, investigating insurance industry fraud, and enforcing laws and rulings applicable to the insurance industry.[48]

In 2002, Republican Insurance Commissioner Charles Quackenbush resigned from the office after state investigators determined he had mishandled insurance funds totaling $11 million intended for earthquake victims. The State Legislature was considering impeachment of Quackenbush, but his resignation from office ended the possibility of him being the first impeached officer in California since 1929.

As discussed in Chapter 1, AB 52, if passed by the State Legislature, would have given the Insurance Commissioner (currently Ricardo Lara) the authority to approve, reject, or alter proposed rate hikes by health insurance companies operating in the state. When the State Legislature failed to approve AB 52,

Proposition 45, an initiative that would have given the Insurance Commissioner the power to approve rate changes in health insurance, was rejected by the voters in 2014. While voters soundly defeated Proposition 45 (60% voted no), in that same election incumbent Democrat Dave Jones bested Republican challenger Ted Gains for the office of Insurance Commissioner despite Gaines opposing Proposition 45 and Jones supporting it.

Regulation of the insurance industry is primarily a state government function, and the **National Association of Insurance Commissioners**, comprising the Insurance Commissioners from the 50 states, the District of Columbia, and five U.S. territories is the organization that assists state insurance regulators in setting standards that support competitive markets, protect insurance consumers, and promote the financial solvency and stability of insurance institutions.[49]

The U.S. Congress has passed legislation over the years providing federal insurance for such things as natural disasters, crop insurance, terrorism insurance, and banking deposits. In addition, **the Federal Trade Commission, a five-member regulatory commission created by Congress in 1914, regulates a variety of industries, (including the insurance industry) in attempts to prevent unfair business practices that would reduce competition in business and lead to consumer fraud. Commission members are appointed by the President and confirmed by the Senate for seven-year terms.**

THE STATE TREASURER

This California statewide executive office has been referred to as "the State's Banker" given the responsibilities of the post include selling state bonds, investing state funds in financial institutions, and holding state tax revenues until the budget is passed and the revenues are appropriated to fund state programs. The selling of state bonds is a vital function of the State Treasurer given bonds finance large construction projects (like the 1960 State Water Project and the voter approved High Speed Rail Project and Water Bond discussed in Chapter 1.) In selling these bonds, it is also critical that the State Treasurer negotiate the lowest possible interest rate with investors.[50] Bonds issued by the State Treasurer with higher interest rates equates to the state owing more money when paying off the bond.

Former Speaker of the California State Assembly, Jesse Unruh, one of the most powerful figures in California state government history, was elected State Treasurer in 1974, holding the office until his death in 1987. Unruh's political clout (he had served as Speaker of the Assembly from 1961-1968, transforming the Speaker's office to a level of influence second only to the Governor) allowed him to dramatically increase the power of the State Treasurer. During Unruh's tenure as State Treasurer, he assembled the National Council of Institutional

Investors, a membership comprising 26 state employee and union pension funds with assets totaling over $100 billion. State Treasurer Unruh also was appointed by the State Legislature to a host of state commissions dealing with fiscal policy.[51] By the time of his death, Jesse Unruh had made the California State Treasurer one of the most powerful government finance positions not only nationally, but globally as well.

Currently, the State Treasurer (Democrat Fiona Ma) is responsible for the investments of $97 billion in state and local funds.[52] State Treasurer Chiang also sits on the two largest public employee pension boards in the nation, the California Public Employees' Retirement System (CalPERS) and the California State Teachers' Retirement System (CalSTRS). In 2021, both of these pension boards invested some $300 billion in U.S. and global markets.

Under the U.S. Constitution, an exclusive power of the federal government is to coin money. The Treasury Department, headed up the Secretary of the Treasury, is responsible for printing the currency (legal tender) to be used in the payment of debts. States had been allowed to issue notes used as currency, but Congress imposed a 10% tax on state currency in 1865, and by 1869 the states ended the practice of issuing currency.[53] Subsequently, while the U.S. Secretary of the Treasury heads up the Federal Treasury that prints U.S. currency, California's State Treasurer has no such authority. What the U.S. Secretary of the Treasury and California's State Treasurer have in common is the ability to sell bonds to investors.

THE STATE CONTROLLER

The State Controller of California supervises all state and local tax collection and authorizes payments of the state's bills. Anyone working for the state, contracting with the state, or eligible for state reimbursements will have pay warrants or checks issued by the State Controller's office. If the state budget is not in place by July 1, the beginning of California's fiscal year, no pay warrants or checks will be issued by the State Controller to vendors contracting with California or to many of the state's workers.

In 1992, with the state budget late by two months, State Controller Gray Davis issued state IOU notes to vendors and state workers in the hopes that banks would honor the IOUs until the budget passed and those owed money by the state would finally get paid.[54] As mentioned at the beginning of this chapter, the State Controller wields power independent of the Governor, something demonstrated by former State Controller John Chiang, who refused to comply with Governor Arnold Schwarzenegger's 2010 attempt to lower the paychecks of state workers to minimum wage until the budget passed. State Controller Chiang ignored a similar order by Governor Schwarzenegger in the 2008 budget stalemate.

Tax collection duties of the State Controller include sitting on two important California tax boards, the **Franchise Tax Board entrusted with collecting California income tax, and the Board of Equalization which collects state sales tax**. Given that the two largest revenue sources in California's budget are state income tax and state sales tax, serving on these tax collecting boards augments the power and authority of the State Controller (currently Betty Yee), who annually manages the collection and disbursements of $100 billion.[55]

THE BOARD OF EQUALIZATION

Created in 1879 after the passage of California's Second Constitution, the Board of Equalization is responsible for a number of tax policies that include ensuring **property tax assessments (determining the value of a property as a basis for taxing it)** are equal throughout California's 58 counties. The Board of Equalization also oversees the collection of sales taxes, use taxes, and fees.[56] Five members serve on the Board (including the State Controller). The other four members are elected in **partisan elections (party affiliation of candidate listed on the ballot)** in four separate districts dispersed throughout the state. Voters, depending on which of the four districts they reside in, select one Board of Equalization candidate. Taxes administered by the Board of Equalization include Property Tax, Alcoholic Beverage Tax, and Tax on Insurers.

The Board of Equalization has a long history of questionable practices and unethical behaviors that included favorable rulings in tax cases they adjudicated for corporations who contributed money to their campaigns, and suspect accounting that improperly re-directed tax revenue collected by the Board. A 2017 report by the Legislative Analyst's Office determined the Board was spending only $27 million out of its $670 million budget on what was required by the State Constitution.[57] As a result, the State Legislature passed, and Governor Brown signed legislation stripping the Board of 90% of their tax regulatory power, including preventing them from adjudicating tax appeal cases and overseeing several tax and fee programs the Board had authority over. The law (known as the Taxpayer Transparency and Fairness Act) did not eliminate the elected Board of Equalization, but severely constrained their authority to what the State Constitution grants them, namely ensuring the assessment and collection of property taxes is done fairly across the state. Under the law, tax appeal cases will be heard by administrative law judges, and tax and fee regulation will be moved to a new revenue department (the Department of Tax and Fee Administration).[58]

Current State Controller Betty Yee, who serves on the Board of Equalization, supported the plan along with other current and former Board members. However, former Republican Board member George Runner opposed the legislation, *"Contrary to its misleading title, this rushed legislation is neither fair to taxpayers, nor transparent to the public. By gutting the power of elected representatives, this bill leaves taxpayers defenseless against a revenue-hungry and powerful state bureaucracy that's unaccountable to the public."*[59] Underscoring how much the Board's authority was stripped, of the 4800 Board employees, 4400 of them were transferred to new departments.[60]

FEDERAL AND STATE TAX COLLECTION

At the federal level, an administrative arm of the U.S. Department of the Treasury is the **Internal Revenue Service (IRS), charged with collecting over $1 trillion each year in individual and corporate income taxes.** The Internal Revenue Service is led by a Commissioner appointed by the President and confirmed by the U.S. Senate. It should be noted that income taxes are levied by California and the federal government on both the employer and employee. Employers in California send what is known as payroll taxes to the state and the federal government for each employee on their payroll. In addition, the employee has, unless exempt, taxes deducted from their pay. At the end of the year, if such deductions do not cover the full tax obligation of the employee, they will send the balance of what they owe to the State of California and the federal government (usually by April 15th).

California and the federal government utilize a **Progressive Income Tax, a tax in which the tax rate set by the government increases as the amount of income subject to be taxed increases.** For example, under a progressive tax if someone earns $30,000 a year they might pay income tax at a rate of 5% of their taxable income while someone earning $100,000 a year pays income tax at a rate of 10% of their taxable income. Under this system, those who earn more pay more in income tax.

A progressive tax is in contrast to a **Regressive Tax, a tax in which the tax rate remains constant regardless of the amount subject to the tax.** Examples of regressive taxes would be the California sales tax on items purchased by a consumer in California and the federal gasoline tax placed on every gallon of gasoline purchased by a motorist. The California sales tax and the federal gasoline tax rates are fixed and do not change regardless of how much money the consumer spends on the product.

In discussing these different types of taxes, California's State Controller, Franchise Tax Board, Board of Equalization and the federal government's Internal Revenue Service are tax collection entities, collecting tax based on current tax law. Tax law, like all other laws, must be passed by the Legislative Branch, which we consider in the next chapter.

5
CHAPTER

THE LEGISLATURE

In December 1994 Willie Brown, the Democratic Speaker of the California State Assembly, was on the verge of losing the most powerful office in the State Legislature. Brown, one of the savviest politicians in California history, had been Speaker for 15 years when the 1994 elections created a political sea change nationwide. Republicans, for the first time in 40 years, emerged from the political desert and took control of the U.S. House of Representatives and the U.S. Senate. In California, the GOP won a slim 41 seat majority in the 80 seat State Assembly, assuring Assembly Republicans that they would finally have the votes to remove Willie Brown as Speaker, or so they thought. On December 5, 1994, the newly elected Republican majority in the Assembly ran into a roadblock when GOP Assemblyman Paul Horcher turned on his party and voted for Willie Brown to remain as the Speaker.[1] Horcher's stunning action left the Assembly in limbo; 40 votes had been cast for Willie Brown (including Horcher's vote) and 40 votes went to Assembly Republican Jim Brulte. Neither Brown nor Brulte possessed the required 41 votes to be elected Speaker.

Facing such a standoff, Willie Brown pulled another political rabbit out of his hat. Republican Assemblyman Richard Mountjoy had somehow gotten himself elected to both a State Assembly and State Senate seat at the same time. Assembly Democrats argued that Mountjoy could not serve in both chambers, and since he had already begun caucusing with his fellow Republicans in the State Senate he should be removed as a member of the State Assembly. However, the Chief Clerk of the Assembly, Dotson Wilson (granted authority under Assembly protocol to make parliamentary rulings) would not allow Mountjoy's removal. When Assembly Chief Clerk Wilson became ill, the rules of the

Assembly allowed the house's senior member to assume control. Willie Brown was the senior member and used his power as presiding officer to kick Richard Mountjoy out of the Assembly. With Mountjoy gone, Brown now had 40 votes and Jim Brulte only had 39. Speaker Brown maintained his reign in the Assembly for a few more months, but even the wily Brown understood the power he amassed over the years was fading, *"You're looking at a totally different speaker,"* he told the press, *"This office will never be the same."*[2]

TERM LIMITS

Willie Brown's observations about the Speaker of the Assembly were quite prophetic. Despite Speaker Brown temporarily thwarting the Assembly Republicans with some parliamentary slight of hand, significant changes were on the horizon for both chambers of the California State Legislature in 1995. By the end of 1995, Brown had left the State Assembly after 30 years of service and successfully won election as Mayor of San Francisco. Why did he leave? The answer is **Term Limits, an amendment to California's Constitution approved by the voters in 1990 that limited the terms lawmakers could serve in the State Legislature. Under Term Limits, a member of the State Assembly could serve a maximum of three two-year terms (6 years total) and a member of the State Senate could serve a maximum of two four-year terms (8 years total).** Given the law took effect immediately after passage in 1990, Speaker Brown would be forced to leave the Assembly in 1996. Term Limits was also the reason Richard Mountjoy ran for the State Assembly and State Senate during the same election in 1994. Mountjoy wanted to go to the State Senate because (like Brown) he was being termed out of the State Assembly in 1996. Term Limits had a profound effect on the California State Legislature, orchestrating a constant reshuffle of lawmakers in both chambers as termed out Assembly members (like Richard Mountjoy) ran for office in the State Senate, and State Senators (facing the end of their 8 years of service in the upper house) switched over to the State Assembly. Term Limits has also ushered in a constant class of new state lawmakers.

In addition, Term Limits, when approved by the voters in 1990, slashed the staff budgets of the State Legislature by 33%. Prior to Term Limits, some legislative staffers were actually earning higher salaries than the elected lawmakers they served. The pay reduction imposed on legislative staffers prompted a mass exodus of "senior staffers" from the Legislature to the private sector, many of these staff veterans moving into lobbying positions with special interest groups. Replacing these seasoned staffers were younger, less experienced assistants (including the author of this book). By 1994, walking through the halls of the State Capitol was like strolling the classroom halls of a college campus, and to this day, many of the staffers serving California's Legislature are fresh out of college given the positions they fill can be temporary.

It is also important to understand that Term Limits not only re-arranged lawmakers and their staffs in the State Legislature, but the law also constantly created new leadership positions in both the State Assembly and State Senate. We will discuss these leadership positions in detail later in the chapter, but for now consider this; Willie Brown served as Speaker of the Assembly for 15 years and was considered the 2nd most powerful politician in the state (the Governor being the most powerful). Since Brown's departure from the Speaker's office in 1994, there have been **thirteen** Speakers of the Assembly, some of them lasting less than a year, and none of them having the ability to maneuver, negotiate, and cajole support from the Assembly membership the way Speaker Brown could during his time. Willie Brown understood how politics worked, and his office, the Speaker's Office of Majority Services (SOMS), was filled with savvy politicos who knew how to get enough Assembly Democrats elected across the state every two years to ensure he remained Speaker during his 15-year stint.

Even when Speaker Brown faced opposition from fellow Assembly Democrats, he was able to survive as Speaker. In 1988, five Assembly Democrats (known as the Gang of 5) attempted to oust Brown by convincing all Assembly Republicans to vote for Speaker Gang of 5 candidate Charles Calderon. Three Assembly Republicans failed to vote for Calderon, and Brown won the Speakership.[3] While Assembly Republicans publically decried Brown's power, he was able to work with them and get things done. Part of Speaker Brown's success with the Republicans can be attributed to his political skills, but the Republicans also understood that Brown was going to be Speaker. That was not the case due to the Term Limits law of 1990, and lawmakers from both parties have been reluctant to negotiate with the opposing party's Assembly or Senate leaders for a number of reasons, one of them being the relatively short amount of time these legislative leaders would hold office.

California lawmakers were never enamored with the 1990 Term Limits law, and several attempts to have California voters alter Term Limits for the State Legislature failed until 2012 when **Proposition 28, an initiative allowing newly elected lawmakers in the State Senate and State Assembly to serve a maximum of 12 years,** passed. Under the new Term Limits law, State Legislators elected to the State Assembly and State Senate in 2012 and thereafter can serve a total of 12 years. The voter approved constitutional amendment allows for the Legislator to serve all 12 years in either the State Assembly or State Senate, or a combination of both chambers. With this change in Term Limits, leadership positions in the State Assembly and State Senate conceivably could last for a decade, ending the constant carousel of Legislative Leaders prompted by the 1990 Term Limits initiative.

No Term Limits for Congress

Term Limits fervor was not limited to state legislatures, and by 1994 some 20 states (including California) had approved Term Limits for their representatives serving in the U.S. Congress. In 1995, the U.S. Supreme Court ruled that Term Limits laws restricting the number of years members of Congress could serve were unconstitutional. The U.S. Supreme Court concluded that since the U.S. Constitution did not limit the terms of Congress, the states were prohibited from doing so.[4] However, when asked to rule on the constitutionality of limiting the terms of state lawmakers, the U.S. Supreme Court determined that states have the right to decide how long members of state legislatures serve in office. As a result of these U.S. Supreme Court rulings, California's 53 U.S. House of Representatives' Members and 2 U.S. Senators are not subject to Term Limits. In contrast, California's 80 State Assembly Members can now only serve 12 years maximum in the Assembly and the Golden State's 40 State Senators are limited to 12 years maximum in the Senate.

This chapter examines the Legislative Branch, comparing and contrasting California's State Legislature with the U.S. Congress. **The Structure of the Legislature, Functions of the Legislature, and Legislative Leadership Positions** will be discussed as we investigate the political complexities of lawmaking.

STRUCTURE OF THE LEGISLATURE

California's 1st Constitution of 1849 created a **Bi-Cameral Legislature (two house legislature)** the lower house being the State Assembly and the upper house being the State Senate. The U.S. Constitution also set up a Bi-Cameral Legislature for Congress (the House of Representatives the lower house and the U.S. Senate the upper house).

TERMS AND REPRESENTATION

Originally, California's State Legislature consisted of 36 Assembly seats and 16 Senate seats. California's 2nd Constitution of 1879 expanded the State Legislature to the current number of seats (80 in the Assembly and 40 in the Senate). **State Assembly Members serve two-year terms and State Senators serve four- year terms.** The 2012 voter approved Term Limits, as already discussed, limit the terms in the State Assembly to six two-year terms, and in the State Senate a lawmaker can serve three four-year terms. **No Term Limits exist for Congress.**

The U.S. Constitution set up a Bi-Cameral Legislature in which a state would be granted a number of seats in the lower House of Representatives based on the state's population. **U.S. House of Representative lawmakers get two- year terms. In the U.S. Senate (the upper house) each state, regardless of population, is granted 2 U.S. Senators who get six-year terms.** This representation plan satisfied both the larger and smaller populated states at the Constitutional Convention of 1787 and continues to be the method in determining the size of Congress. Currently, the U.S. House of Representatives consists of 435 seats, a number Congress has maintained in the House since 1912. In the U.S. Senate, each state, irrespective of its population, has 2 Senators making for a total of 100 U.S. Senate seats.

California Federal Plan Struck Down by U.S. Supreme Court

For many years California had adopted a similar method for determining representation in the State Legislature. California's **Federal Plan (modeled from the U.S Constitution's representation plan for Congress) provided that representation in the lower house (the State Assembly) be based on population, but representation in the State Senate would be determined by county, not population.** Given the State Legislature created more counties in the northern part of the state, Northern California was awarded greater numbers of State Senators than Southern California, regardless of Southern California's growing population. The U.S. Supreme Court, in three cases (*Baker v. Carr 1962, Reynolds v. Sims 1964, and Wesberry v. Sanders 1964*) prohibited any state (including California) from drawing state legislative districts, or U.S. congressional districts that were not equal in population.[5] As noted in Chapter 3, those Northern Californians advocating for the state of Jefferson maintain they have no representation in the Legislature due to these Supreme Court rulings. In 2016, the U.S. Supreme Court ruled legislative districts should be drawn based total population, not just eligible voters (discussed in chapter 3). Currently, each California State Senator represents nearly 1 million people, each California State Assembly Member represents 500,000 people, and each California U.S. House of Representative Member represents some 730,000 people.

If a vacancy occurs in a State Assembly, State Senate, or U.S. House of Representative seat in California, the Governor has a constitutional requirement to call a special election to fill the vacancy. If one of California's two U.S. Senate seats becomes vacant, the Governor has the power to fill the vacancy by appointment. Governor Gavin Newsom appointed Alex Padilla to fill the vacated U.S. Senate of Kamala Harris in 2021.

QUALIFICATIONS AND COMPENSATION

Eligibility for serving in the California State Legislature:

- Must be a U.S. citizen
- Must be 18 years of age or older
- Must have been a California resident for three years
- Must be a resident of the legislative district for one year preceding an Election

Compensation for California Legislature

Salaries for the California State Legislature are set by the California Citizens Compensation Commission, an independent commission developed after Golden State voters approved Proposition 112 in 1990. The current salary of California lawmakers (as of 2021) serving in either the Assembly or Senate is $114,877 per year plus a daily per-diem of $206 to cover meals and other expenses when working in the Capitol.

In 2010, voters passed a law that would forfeit the pay and per diem of California lawmakers for each day they were late in approving the state budget (which the Legislature is required to pass by June 15). State Controller John Chiang, who frustrated Governor Schwarzenegger by rejecting the Governor's attempt to pay state workers minimum wage, angered state lawmakers in 2011 when he determined they had not passed a balanced budget by the June 15th deadline, and as a result docked their pay. In response to Controller Chiang's actions, five Assembly Republicans sent a letter to State Attorney General Kamala Harris asking her to investigate whether Chiang had a right to determine if the budget plan the State Legislature passed was balanced.[6] Since Controller Chiang forfeited pay and per-diem for lawmakers in 2011, the Legislature has approved the budget on time every year.

The California Citizens Compensation Commission also determines other lawmaker benefits such as medical, dental, and insurance. In addition, the commission approves reimbursement for mileage, and lawmakers are paid 53 cents per mile when driving their personal vehicles on legislative business. State legislators used to be provided cars for use on state business, which included maintenance, gas, and lease payments for the vehicle, all paid for by taxpayers. In 2010, in the midst of the Great Recession, the commission not only cut lawmakers pay, but also eliminated providing them automobiles, switching to the current mileage reimbursement program.[7]

Eligibility for Serving in the U.S. Congress

In the U.S. House of Representatives, the following qualifications are required:

- Must be a U.S. citizen for at least 7 years
- Must be 25 years of age or older
- Must be a resident of the state in which they are elected

Eligibility for serving in the U.S. Senate include the following:

- Must be a U.S. citizen for at least 9 years
- Must be 30 years of age or older
- Must be a resident of the state in which they are elected

Compensation for U.S. Congress

Compensation for members of Congress in both the House and Senate is currently $174,000 a year.[8] Congress has the authority to approve compensation for its members, but the **27th Amendment to the U.S. Constitution prohibits Congress from voting itself a pay raise that takes effect before the next election.** The 27th Amendment is a political oddity. It was originally one of the amendments proposed as part of the Bill of Rights, but the amendment was never ratified by the states. In 1992, after 203 years since Congress approved it, the 27th Amendment was finally ratified.[9] Members of Congress are eligible to receive a cost-of-living increase on par with other federal employees, and the pay raises take effect each January 1st. However, Congress has declined taking the cost-of-living increases, and their pay has remained frozen at $174,000 since 2009.

Beginning in 2014, members of Congress were provided with health coverage through the 2010 Affordable Care Act (discussed in chapter 1), the very health care program so many of them wanted repealed. Since 1984, federal lawmakers have been paying into Social Security and also pay into a separate federal pension program that covers all federal employees. Given most congressional lawmakers travel great distances between Washington, D.C. and their home states, they are granted funding for travel, along with other official expenses that include staff and mail privileges.[10]

FUNCTIONS OF THE LEGISLATURE

Members of the Californian Legislature and the United States Congress engage in a number of important functions that include **lawmaking, oversight, fundraising, and service to their constituency.**

LAWMAKING

Thousands of proposed laws are introduced during the two-year legislative sessions of the California State Legislature and the U.S. Congress. Most of these bills (as they are referred to) will never become law given the long, arduous process a bill must go through to become a law of California or the United States. Both the California State Legislature and the U.S. Congress refer new bills to **Committees, the vehicle used by legislative bodies to consider proposed legislation (bills).** A bill is not debated by the entire legislative body when it is introduced, instead, it is assigned to a committee consisting of a smaller number of lawmakers who will examine the bill, hold public hearings on the proposed legislation, change the bill's contents, shelve the law (in effect ending the bill's chances of passage), or vote to send the bill to the floor for a vote from the entire membership. As mentioned, most bills will fail to become law because they die in committee. Let us consider what happens to a bill that makes it out of committee and is sent to the floor for a possible vote. We begin with the California State Legislature and then examine how the process works in the U.S. Congress.

Floor Votes on Proposed Laws in the California Legislature

When a bill reaches the floor of the Assembly, the Speaker of the Assembly manages the floor debate. In the State Senate, the Senate Rules Committee, chaired by the President Pro Tempore, manages the floor debate. Both chambers conduct floor debate in similar fashion. The bill's author will be allowed to speak in support of the legislation and any opponents are granted the opportunity for rebuttal.[11] However, floor debate in the Assembly and Senate can be ended by a majority vote of the legislative body's membership preventing **Filibusters.**[12] **A Filibuster is a legislative procedure allowing for unlimited debate on a bill or resolution before it can be brought to a vote.**

Gut-And-Amend

When floor debate commences, any lawmaker, can offer amendments (changes) to the bill, and such amendments can be voted on by a simple majority of those present.[13] Prior to 2017 a process known as **Gut-And-Amend allowed the bill to be drastically changed to the point that the bill's author would withdraw sponsorship of the legislation. In other instances, the bill's author would allow it to be stripped and completely changed to address an urgent issue.**[14] Gut-And-Amend was a common practice by the California Legislature when they had reached the end of the legislative session for the year; and last-minute revisions of bills were written, then passed by both chambers and sent to the Governor. **When Gut-And-Amend took place at the end of the legislative session, there was no time for public review or hearings on the bill** (which would normally transpire in committee) and the revised bill was subsequently approved by both houses.

At the end of California's 2011 legislative session, several bills, some controversial, were approved by the State Legislature through Gut-And-Amend. Senate Bill (SB) 292 began in February 2011 as legislation dealing with the transfer of community college units to four-year universities in California. However, by Sept. 2, 2011, with the legislative session drawing to a close, Senator Alex Padilla (D-Los Angeles), the author of SB 292, gutted the original bill and replaced it with language that would accelerate the approval of a proposed NFL football stadium for downtown Los Angeles. This action prompted the following response from Community College League CEO Scott Lay who described the revised 'transfer' bill as *"A bill to facilitate the transfer of the San Diego Chargers to Los Angeles."*[15]

Another Gut-And-Amend bill developing at the end of the 2011 legislative session was SB 202, a Senate bill initially written to increase the filing fee for California Ballot Initiatives from $200 to $2000. The bill was amended, allowing California statewide ballot Initiatives and Petition Referendums to only appear on the November general election ballots (as discussed in Chapter 2). The revised SB 202 also delayed an Initiative vote on California's rainy-day fund (monies held to cover budget shortages in future years) until November 2014. As noted in Chapter 2, voter turnout is greater in general elections as opposed to primary elections, and increased voter turnout consistently benefits Democratic supported initiatives while lower voter turnout buttresses the success of Republican backed measures.

Democrats, in control of both the State Assembly and State Senate, supported SB 202's changes (especially limiting Initiatives and Petition Referendums to the November general election ballots when more registered Democrats come out to vote). No hearings were conducted on the amended SB 202, and the bill passed minutes before the Legislature adjourned for the year. Prior to the vote on SB 202, Senator Ted Lieu (D-Torrance) was critical of the process, *"Sometimes we need to do Gut-And-Amends. This is not one of those bills."* Critical as he may have been, Senator Lieu voted for SB 202. When Senator Lieu's vote was recorded, Senate Republicans on the floor jeered.[16]

In 2012, Gut-And-Amend was employed when a bill originally about curbing air pollution from older automobiles was stripped of that language, and in its' place, provisions were inserted granting the right of some 2 million undocumented immigrants to legally work and reside in California, making them subject to paying state income taxes.[17] At the end of the 2014 legislative session, Senator Kevin de Leon added a last-minute amendment into a bill which created significant tax breaks for the film industry.[18]

The use of Gut-And-Amend has been both vilified and justified by California lawmakers. Republican State Senator Jim Nielsen held a dim view of Gut-And-Amend, *"It compromises a citizen's opportunity to participate in their government, and I am screaming and yelling about it every day around here."* Former State Senate President Pro Tem Darrell Steinberg, a Democrat from Sacramento, defended Gut-And-Amend, noting that lawmakers have a limited time to introduce legislation, *"Sometimes a gut and amend is necessary to deal with a pressing situation."*[19] California voters were given the chance to eliminate Gut-And-Amend in 2012, but rejected a proposition that would have required three days of public review before the State Legislature could vote on any legislation.

Gut-And-Amend Regulated in 2016

In 2016, California voters approved **Proposition 54, a law banning the Legislature from passing any bill unless it has been in print and published on the Internet for at least 72 hours before the vote, (except in cases of public emergency) essentially ending the practice of Gut-And-Amend.** The measure passed with 65% voter approval after pro Proposition 54 advocates linked the Initiative's passage to protecting democracy, *"We have long opposed the California Legislature's practice of making last minute changes to proposed laws before legislators, the press, and the public have had a chance to read and understand them. Such practices make a mockery of democracy,"* noted Peter Scheer, representing the First Amendment Coalition, a public interest group promoting policies to increase citizen participation in government.[20]

But like most laws, loopholes always have a habit of emerging. In 2017, several Assembly bills passed after being amended less than 72 hours prior to the floor vote. These bills were then sent to the State Senate for approval (bills must pass both chambers in identical forms before they can be sent to the Governor). Assembly Democratic leaders argued that Proposition 54 only applied to a vote in the second house (in these instances the State Senate). After threats of legal action by those who placed Proposition 54 on the ballot, Assembly Democrats relented, and the bills in question were returned to the Assembly and approved in accordance with Proposition 54.[21]

The Gut-And-Amend procedure can still be employed by the State Legislature as demonstrated in September 2017 when Senator Scott Weiner allowed his bill extending drinking hours from 2 am to 4 am be changed to modify the length of time a category of sex offenders need be registered with their local law enforcement agency. The bill, known as SB 384, did not violate the provisions of Proposition 54 given there was an eight-day period between the transformed legislation passing through both the State Assembly and State Senate.[22]

Floor Votes on Proposed Laws in the U.S. Congress

In the U.S. Congress there are distinct procedures in the House of Representatives and Senate on how a bill reaching the floor can be debated and voted on. In the House of Representatives, the **Rules Committee has the authority to provide special rules under which specific bills will be debated, amended, and considered by the House when the bill is sent to the floor.** If the Rules Committee issues a **Closed Rule** on a bill sent to the floor for a vote, debate time will be strictly limited, and no amendments can be added to the bill. Since the 1970's, the majority party in the House controls 9 seats on the Rules Committee while the minority party in the House is granted 4 seats. Given this make-up, the majority party in the House can get a bill scheduled for a vote through the Rules Committee despite opposition from the minority party.

The process for debating and voting on a bill that reaches the floor of the U.S. Senate is in stark contrast to the House of Representatives. While a Rules Committee exists in the Senate, it does not have the authority to limit debate time or amendments for a bill being considered by the entire Senate. A bill reaching the floor of the Senate can be **Filibustered** by any U.S. Senator. **The Filibuster is an attempt by a Senator to prevent a vote on the bill from taking place.** Filibusters in the U.S. Senate traditionally have been associated with a Senator literally "talking the bill to death" as demonstrated by Republican Senator Strom Thurmond, who in 1957 set the record for a Filibuster when he went on for 24 hours, preventing the Senate from voting on a civil rights bill.[23] In 1922, the U.S. Senate adopted **Cloture (Senate Rule 22) which provides a method in which to end a Filibuster.** Under the Cloture rule, a petition signed by 16 Senators will lead to a Cloture vote being scheduled to end the Filibuster. In 1979, the Senate amended the Cloture rule to require a vote on Cloture within 100 hours. To invoke Cloture and end the Filibuster, a vote of **three fifths of the Senate (60 Senators)** is required. If 60 votes fail to be achieved, no vote on the bill can take place and the bill dies. Unlike the House, the majority party in the Senate (unless they have 60 seats) will not be able to pass legislation without input from the minority party.

The U.S. Senate Filibuster Ends for Confirmation Votes

In 2013, the U.S. Senate ended utilizing the Filibuster as a means to require 60 votes in order to confirm nominees the President made for executive and judicial branch positions (with the exception of nominees to the U.S.

Supreme Court). The procedural change was prompted by the record breaking numbers of Filibusters employed by the Senate (averaging 130 per year) in the final years of George W. Bush's presidency and expanding to over 200 per year in President Barack Obama's administration. In contrast, the Filibuster was used sparingly in the past (under 30 per year in the 1960's), with very few ever employed on a President's nominee to the executive or judicial branches of government.[24]

After the election of Donald Trump, the new President nominated to the U.S. Supreme Court Judge Neil Gorsuch to replace the late Antonin Scalia (who died in February 2016). After Justice Scalia's death, President Obama nominated Judge Merrick Garland to fill the vacant seat, but Republican Senate Majority Leader Mitch McConnell refused Judge Garland a confirmation vote in the U.S. Senate, angering Democrats. Senator McConnell countered that President Obama (in his final year as President) should not be granted the appointment. When President Trump appointed Judge Gorsuch for the post in 2017, the Republicans held 52 seats in the U.S. Senate, 8 short of the 60 needed to break the Democratic Filibuster against Judge Gorsuch. Majority Leader McConnell then scheduled a vote to end Filibusters for Supreme Court nominees, which only required a simple majority vote of 51 Senators. The Senate jettisoned the Filibuster for Supreme Court nominees in 2017, and confirmed Judge Gorsuch to the Court.

Will the Filibuster be Terminated?

The Filibuster remains in place for most legislation in the U.S. Senate, which means **60 votes** must be secured for the bill to be approved, but a frustrated President Trump, with few legislative victories in Congress, called for a complete termination of the Filibuster. While Democrats opposed most of Donald Trump's policies, one thing many of them seem to agree on with the former President is ending the Senate Filibuster completely now that Joe Biden is President and Democrats control both the House and the Senate (they did not feel that way when Republicans controlled both houses of Congress and the White House after the 2016 election).

In 2021, Senate Democrats held the slimmest majority in the U.S. Senate 51-50 (Vice President Kamala Harris being the tie-breaking vote). Being able to convince 10 Senate Republicans to join Senate Democrats in passing legislation to deal with immigration, background checks of gun purchases, increasing the federal minimum wage, and a voting rights bill seem impossible.

Ending the Filibuster procedure for bills reaching the floor of the U.S. Senate would only require a 51-vote majority to achieve, something most Senate

Democrats support in 2021. But not all Senate Democrats are on board with killing the Filibuster. West Virginia Senator Joe Manchin, a Democrat representing a deep red state that overwhelmingly voted for Donald Trump in 2016 and 2020, opposes ending the Filibuster, and without his vote, the Senate Democrats would need a Republican Senate colleague to achieve the 51 votes needed for the Senate rule change, something not likely to occur.

Senator Manchin has suggested he would back altering the Senate Filibuster rules. The Senate Filibuster used to require the U.S. Senator keep talking in order to maintain a Filibuster so the Senate could not vote on the bill. But in 1971, another U.S. Senator from West Virginia, Democrat Robert Byrd, proposed new rules which allowed a Filibuster to be maintained without the Senator being required to continue speaking. The rule changes were approved in 1971, and since then the use of the Filibuster has grown exponentially from an average of 16 Cloture Votes to break Filibusters per year in the 1970's to over 53 Cloture Votes to break Filibusters per year by 2018.[25] Senator Manchin would support returning to the pre 1971 rules which would require the Senator to keep talking on the Senate floor to maintain the Filibuster. As of April 2021, the U.S. Senate had not enacted any rule changes concerning the Filibuster.

Resolving Differences in Legislation – The Conference Committee

Legislation approved in a different form in the California State Assembly and California State Senate can't be sent to the Governor. Both chambers must pass the bill in identical forms before it reaches the Governor's desk for consideration. A similar legal requirement is placed on the U.S. House of Representatives and the U.S. Senate; and legislation sent to the President of the United States must also be passed in uniform fashion by both houses of Congress. To resolve the differences in legislation, both the California Legislature and the U.S. Congress utilize **Conference Committees, joint committees consisting of members from both chambers that attempt to reconcile differences when a bill passes the two houses in different forms.** Members selected to the Conference Committees are drawn from lawmakers that served on the **Standing Committee (the committee that originally considered the legislation when it was introduced).** If the Conference Committee can resolve the differences and approve a uniform bill, that bill will be sent back to both houses for a vote. Only legislation approved in identical forms in both houses can be sent by the California Legislature to the Governor. The same requirement is placed on both houses of Congress in passing legislation for the President's consideration.

Extraordinary Majority Votes of the Legislative Branch

The California Legislature approves most bills with a simple majority vote (50% plus 1), however, there are certain areas that call for a two-thirds vote of both houses (27 votes in the State Senate and 54 votes in the State Assembly). **Areas requiring a two-thirds vote in the State Legislature include:**

- Any proposed amendment to California's Constitution
- Votes to override a Governor's veto
- Urgency Measures (a law that would take effect immediately)
- Votes to raise taxes or fees
- A State Senate vote to convict and remove from office an impeached official

The U.S. Congress is also bound by extraordinary vote requirements which include:

- A two-thirds vote in both houses for an amendment to the U.S. Constitution
- A two-thirds vote to override a President's veto
- A two-thirds vote by the U.S. Senate to ratify treaties with foreign nations
- A two-thirds US. Senate vote to convict and remove from office an impeached official
- A three-fifths vote by the U.S. Senate to break a filibuster

Extraordinary Majorities and Gridlock

At both the Federal and California level of government, citizens have often been frustrated with a system that generates what is known as **Gridlock, the inability of the government to address and develop solutions for a host of pressing issues.** Gridlock can be partly explained by the intransigence of lawmakers unwilling to compromise because of political ideology. Yet these extraordinary majorities needed in the State Legislature and Congress to approve measures also foster gridlock. Until 2011, the California Legislature required a two-thirds vote to approve the state budget, and before 2011, state budgets in California were consistently late (missing the July 1 deadline by over 2 months in 2010). In Congress, Senate Filibusters, as noted, have increased so much in frequency that literally every major piece of legislation requires 60 votes in the Senate to be approved. However, depending on which party controls a majority of legislative seats and the governorship or presidency, extraordinary majority votes can be beneficiary to the minority. This had been true for Republican lawmakers in the California Legislature, who despite their minority status, still maintained the ability to influence budget decisions given a two-thirds majority vote is required in the State Assembly and State Senate to raise taxes and fees. But given the woeful election results over the past decade for the California GOP in the State Legislature, Democrats hold super two-thirds majorities in the Assembly and Senate. The 2016 election gave Democrats super two-thirds majorities in both chambers of the State Legislature, granting them the ability to approve tax increases on gasoline in 2017 (as discussed in Chapter 1). Those super majorities were maintained for Democrats in both houses after the 2020 election.

OVERSIGHT

Not only does the Legislative Branch have the responsibility of making the law, but this branch of government is also charged with **Oversight, ensuring the laws it has passed are being executed, the money it has appropriated is being spent as intended, and that government officials are following the law.**

Oversight by the California Legislature

With budget funding problems existing for a majority of state governments and the federal government, legislative oversight of government spending is something Republicans and Democrats should agree upon. Such bipartisanship developed in the California State Senate in August 2011 when on a vote of 36-1, the Senate approved SB8, authored by Senator Leland Yee (D-San Francisco), which required the University of California, California State University, and California Community Colleges make public the financial records, contracts, and correspondence of **foundations** and **auxiliaries** operating on California's college campuses. **Foundations and Auxiliaries are nonprofit organizations that raise funds for its own charitable purposes or donate raised funds to other nonprofit organizations.** California State University campuses operate 87 auxiliaries and foundations that in 2009 accounted for $1.3 billion according to the CSU Chancellor's office.[26] When California's colleges faced budget cuts during the Great Recession of 2008, concerns were raised that auxiliary and foundation money was not easily distinguishable from state funding. SB8 passed overwhelmingly in the State Assembly and Governor Jerry Brown signed the legislation a few weeks later in early September. The bill is noteworthy for requiring these auxiliaries and foundations to open their books for public scrutiny (Sacramento State President Alexander Gonzalez spent over $27,000 from the campus auxiliary money to remodel his kitchen in 2007).[27]

As mentioned in Chapter 4, a state audit of the Board of Equalization compelled the Legislature to severely erode the authority of the tax regulatory agency in 2017 after reports of improper use of taxpayer money and other management problems surfaced, another example of legislative oversight. In 2021, another state audit revealed that the Employment Development Department (EDD), the state agency responsible for administering unemployment payments to millions of Californians who lost their jobs due to the pandemic, found that as much as $10.4 billion in fraudulent payments may have been approved by the EDD, including $810 million in unemployment benefits to 45,000 inmates in prison.[28]

However, because of Term Limits, a constant change of legislators has made conducting oversight all the more difficult. Term Limits have also curtailed staff resources available to California lawmakers for oversight.[29] SB8 is and the fraudulent unemployment claims unearthed by a state audit are examples of oversight, but California's budget (which we will discuss in Chapter 7) is $200 billion each year. Conducting oversight on so much money is a daunting task, especially for freshman lawmakers, of which there were many after the passage of Term Limits in 1990. For the 2015/2016 California legislative session, 72 out of the 120 lawmakers had two years or less of experience as state lawmakers.[30] The 2012 Term Limits change allows legislators to serve longer terms, but whether that improves the Legislature's ability to conduct effective oversight remains an open question.

To assist California lawmakers in the oversight function, several non-partisan independent bodies have been created by the State Legislature. **The Bureau of State Audits** is the State's auditor and provides independent and nonpartisan assessments of financial and operational activities within California's government. This bureau discovered the $1.5 billion the California State University was hiding from the public in 2019 (discussed in Chapter 1) and the $10.4 billion in unemployment fraud mistakenly paid out by the Employment Development Department in 2020/2021. **The Little Hoover Commission** is an independent State oversight agency that investigates government operations and (through reports issued) recommends policies that promote efficiency and improved service of California government. A third office that provides vital oversight and review for California's State Legislature is **The Legislative Analyst's Office (LAO),** a non-partisan, independent office that provides concise summaries of all proposed legislation currently being considered. The LAO also provides detailed analysis of the state's revenues and expenditures to assist lawmakers and the Governor in adopting the state budget. In addition, the LAO will issue an unbiased, comprehensive analysis of all statewide ballot measures.[31] None of the people serving in these oversight offices are elected politicians, allowing them to provide objective analyses.

In 2008, former Senate President Pro Tempore Darrell Steinberg created the Senate's Office of Oversight and Outcomes to investigate the functions of a plethora of state departments and agencies. Steinberg's oversight office unearthed a host of problems that included a state mortgage lender improperly foreclosing on homeowners who made current payments, the hiring of convicted sex offenders to treat drug addicts at state rehab clinics, and the spending of public funds by local government redevelopment agencies (which we discuss in chapter 7) without any oversight.[32] However, when Senator Steinberg left office in 2014, the new Senate President Pro Tempore, Kevin De Leon, axed the funding for the Office of Oversight and Outcomes. Those that worked at the oversight office were staff members of Senator Steinberg, and once he was termed out, their positions were eliminated, another casualty of Term Limits.

Oversight by Congress

At the Federal level, Congress in 1946 passed the Legislative Reorganization Act which placed oversight responsibility within **Standing Committees (permanent committees established by each house of Congress)**. These Standing Committees in the House and Senate are responsible for ensuring the laws passed are being executed as intended by Congress.[33] Such oversight responsibilities include reviewing how money appropriated by Congress is being spent, and whether the executive branch is acting in accordance with the law.

Intel on Iraq

After Democrats regained control of Congress in 2006, oversight investigations in the House and Senate commenced over the inaccurate intelligence provided by the Central Intelligence Agency (CIA) concerning the threat Iraqi leader Saddam Hussein posed to the world. The CIA claimed Hussein had significant stockpiles of biological weapons and was developing nuclear weapons. President George W. Bush's administration used the inaccurate intelligence to justify the military invasion of Iraq in 2003, something Congress approved and the American public supported. Once American military forces removed Hussein from power, American weapons inspectors could find no weapons of mass destruction in Iraq, prompting Congress to investigate why the CIA had been mistaken in their assessment of Saddam Hussein's Weapons of Mass Destruction capability.

Benghazi and a Private E-Mail Server

The September 11, 2012 attack on a diplomatic compound in Benghazi, Libya, which resulted in the deaths of four Americans, including Ambassador Christopher Stevens, triggered several congressional investigations of the Obama Administration to determine why there was not adequate protection for

Ambassador Stevens and the others in a country with limited security after the toppling of Muammar el-Qaddafi's government.[34] During the oversight investigation, Hillary Clinton, Secretary of State when the Benghazi attack took place, faced intense scrutiny over her State Department's inability to safeguard the Americans.

In 2014, a House Select Committee opened up yet another inquiry into the Benghazi tragedy that continued for two years, coinciding with Secretary Clinton's presidential run. During that investigation, it was discovered Secretary Clinton had been using a private e-mail server over the four years she served as Secretary of State. That revelation opened up an F.B.I. inquiry of Secretary Clinton possibly mishandling classified material, an inquiry that dogged her throughout the 2016 campaign. A popular refrain "LOCK HER UP!" by Donald Trump supporters at his campaign rallies clearly indicated the Benghazi episode was a political liability for Secretary Clinton.

Impeachment Squared

But the worm turns, and after Donald Trump won election as President in 2016, his administration became engulfed in a series of congressional oversight investigations by three separate committees (one in the House and two in the Senate) and a Special Counsel inquiry. The investigations centered on Russian influence in the 2016 presidential election and possible links between the Trump Campaign and the Russians. The President only ratcheted up suspicions by firing F.B.I. Director James Comey in May 2017. The firing of Director Comey, who was investigating Russian interference in the election, created more questions about the Trump Campaign. When Attorney General Jeff Sessions recused himself from the Russia election tampering inquiry in 2017, Deputy Attorney General Rod Rosenstein appointed Special Counsel Robert Mueller to oversee an investigation of Russian government influence in the 2016 presidential election. Special Counsel Mueller issued a 700-page report in 2019 and while the Mueller Report cited numerous Trump associates lied to federal investigators, and several of them were convicted of perjury and obstruction of justice, there were no recommendations in the report to charge President Trump. However, the Mueller Report claimed what they found "does not exonerate" the President, and that Congress should continue the investigation.[35]

Conventional thinking suggests that Congress is more aggressive in conducting oversight investigations when the presidential administration in office is from the opposite party controlling Congress. And things certainly ramped up concerning congressional oversight of the Trump Administration after the Democrats regained control of the House of Representatives in the 2018 midterm elections. When details of a phone call President Trump made to the

President of Ukraine (Volodymyr Zelensky) revealed Trump may have been soliciting foreign assistance to discredit Joe Biden, congressional Democrats cried foul. The Democrats charged that President Trump was threatening to withhold military aide to Ukraine unless the Ukrainian President disclosed dirt against Joe Biden's son, Hunter Biden. President Trump was allegedly seeking information from the Ukrainians that would confirm Hunter Biden was hired and paid a huge amount of money by a Ukrainian natural gas company during the Obama Administration (with Joe Biden as Vice President) in exchange for political favors by the Obama Administration.

President Trump's actions with the President of Ukraine, as far as House Democrats were concerned, were an impeachable offense, and in December 2019, the House of Representatives impeached President Trump. In the impeachment trial, which took place in the U.S. Senate, President Trump was acquitted on February 5, 2020, **the Senate failing to achieve the two-thirds vote needed to convict President Trump and remove him from office**. Senator Mitt Romney was the only Republican Senator that voted to convict President Trump in the 2020 impeachment trial.

And then came the January 6, 2021 insurrection at the Capitol with thousands of fervent Trump supporters overcoming the Capitol police and storming into the Senate and House chambers. Prior to the Capitol being invaded, President Trump addressed the insurrectionists and thousands more just down the street from the Capitol where (at the time) Congress and Vice President Mike Pence were certifying the Electoral College votes that would make Joe Biden President on January 20. President Trump told the crowd the election had been stolen from him, imploring them to *"Fight like Hell or you won't have a country."* What followed was complete chaos as a mob of Trump supporters muscled their way into the Capitol, clashing with Capitol police as they entered. Five people died, including a Capitol police officer, Brian Sicknick, as a result of the riot. House Democrats moved swiftly to impeach President Trump a second time for his role, as they saw it, in inciting the insurrection, and a week later, on January 13, the House voted 232-197 for impeachment. No House Republicans voted to impeach President Trump the first time, but ten GOP House members voted to impeach the President for inciting the rioters, including Wyoming Representative Liz Cheney, the daughter of former Vice President Dick Cheney.

By the time the 2nd impeachment trial for Donald Trump took place in the U.S. Senate, Trump was out as President and Senate Republicans argued there should not be an impeachment trial for someone who no longer is President. But the Senate trial commenced, Democrats insisting the former President should be convicted and barred from ever seeking Federal Office again for his actions associated with the January 6 insurrection. However, once again, on February 13, 2021, Donald Trump was acquitted in the Senate despite 57 Senators out of 100 voting to convict him; that number falling short of the **67 votes (two-thirds of the Senate)** needed for conviction in an impeachment trial. While Mitt Romney was the only GOP Senator voting to convict Trump in the first impeachment trial, six other Republican Senators joined Romney and voted to convict the former President in the second impeachment trial.

In four years of endless investigations of the Trump Administration, the former President was defiant after being acquitted in his second impeachment trial, *"This has been yet another phase of the greatest witch hunt in the history of our Country."*[36] Regardless of what people think of Donald Trump, one thing is true about him; he made history by conducting his presidency in unorthodox fashion. President Trump was like a bull in a china shop when it came to how he governed, breaking presidential norms with reckless abandon. No President had ever been impeached twice (only two; Andrew Johnson in 1868 and Bill Clinton in 1998 had been impeached prior to Trump). The last time the Capitol was breached was in the War of 1812 when the British arrived in August of 1814 and nearly burned the Capitol to the ground. It is astounding to think January 6 could have happened at all given what the nation went through on 9/11 twenty years ago. Given all the investigations and the two impeachments of Donald Trump, the January 6 Insurrection, and the former President's brazen approach to governing, Oversight by Congress has a new meaning.

FUNDRAISING AND SERVICE TO THE CONSTITUENCY

It is important to remember that once elected by the voters, lawmakers don't spend all of their time in the Capitol. While lawmaking is arguably the most important function of any legislature, elected representatives serving in Sacramento or Washington, D.C. return to their states and districts on a regular basis to hear from constituents and attend fundraising events. Huge amounts of money are required not only to initially win election, but to remain in office, and a cruel reality any lawmaker discovers (no matter how committed they are to changing the system) is fundraising needs to occur. Securing a seat in the California State Assembly costs on average $800,000, in the California State Senate the average cost for victory is $1 million.[37] In 2019, the average cost of winning a seat in the U.S. House of Representatives was $2 million, and in the U.S. Senate the tally came to $15.7 million.[38]

Members of the California State Legislature and U.S. Congress have district offices located in the districts they represent. Staff members that serve in these district offices help to coordinate constituent service the lawmaker provides the district. Such service will include scheduling events back in the district for the lawmaker to attend (town hall meetings, public festivals, parades, dinners, etc.). District staff (particularly the Chief of Staff for the district) will attend an event if the lawmaker is not available. The district office also handles problems constituents are having with a government agency. Savvy citizens who request intervention on their behalf by a member of Congress or a California lawmaker understand a government agency (which depends on funding from the legislative branch) is more likely to pay attention when a lawmaker's office contacts them about a constituent problem.

LEGISLATIVE LEADERSHIP IN THE STATE ASSEMBLY AND SENATE

The Speaker of the Assembly

The Speaker of the Assembly has been considered the second most influential political leader in California behind only the Governor. While Term Limits have eroded the ability of someone to remain Speaker and consolidate power like Jesse Unruh and Willie Brown, the position continues to be a powerful one. The Speaker is the top leader in the State Assembly and will come from the party holding a majority of the 80 Assembly seats. Sometimes, Speakers need to curry favor with minority party Assembly members (as demonstrated by Willie Brown) to be elected Speaker, but in most cases the party with the majority of Assembly seats will choose a Speaker and a formal vote will take place of the entire Assembly membership. In 2015, Democrat Anthony Rendon was elected as the Speaker of the California Assembly, Replacing Toni Atkins, who moved on to a seat in the State Senate.

The Speaker wields enormous power in the State Assembly which includes:

- Appointing all Assembly members to committees
- Appointing all committee chairs and vice chairs
- Scheduling the Assembly business
- Assigning office space to all Assembly members
- Determining the staff budget of all Assembly members
- Assisting fellow party Assembly members in their re-election campaign

Members from both the majority and minority party depend on the Speaker to give them committee assignments and chairmanships that improve their ability to advocate or oppose legislation important to constituents in the district they represent. For example, if a member of the Assembly is from an agricultural rich Central Valley district, they are going to desire being placed on the Agriculture Committee. Remember, in our discussion of lawmaking, proposed legislation is first assigned to a committee and that committee will determine if the bill makes it to the floor for a vote. A lawmaker from an agricultural district will have the best chance to influence agriculture related legislation if they are assigned to the Agriculture Committee. Given the Speaker appoints all committee assignments (Republicans and Democrats alike) lawmakers from both parties are dependent on the Speaker.

The Speaker is someone **Interest Groups (a group whose members share common objectives and attempt to influence government policy to their benefit)** will gravitate to, and former Speaker Jesse Unruh understood the political opportunities afforded him in raising large sums of money through campaign contributions provided by interest groups.[39] Speakers have followed the Unruh model, raising huge amounts of money and doling it out to fellow party Assembly members for their re-election campaigns.

Assembly lawmakers that refuse to cooperate with the Speaker find themselves literally isolated, and such isolation goes beyond being denied plum committee appointments. The Speaker assigns office space in the Capitol to all members of the Assembly and determines their staff budget. Willie Brown was once asked why he gave a newly elected Assembly member who had been critical of him a tiny, windowless office. Speaker Brown answered directly, "Because I didn't have anything smaller."[40] However, in 2011 Assembly Democrat Anthony Portantino challenged the authority of Speaker John Perez to allocate Assembly staff budgets and office space (as discussed in Chapter 3) after Portantino's staff budget was slashed and office size reduced. Such defiance of the Speaker is another by product of Term Limits, and an indication that Assembly lawmakers are not as easily disciplined by the Speaker as compared to the Jesse Unruh and Willie Brown eras.

In 2017, a Recall effort was launched against Speaker Rendon by progressive Democrats upset that the Speaker refused to allow a vote in the Assembly on the Single Payer health care law that passed in the Senate. Speaker Rendon derailed the bill because no financing mechanism to pay for the estimated $400 billion cost of offering health care to all was included in the Senate legislation. It is most unlikely that Speaker Rendon will be Recalled, but the fact progressive Democrats are making the attempt is another reminder the Speaker, though a powerful position, is subject to Recall like every other California state lawmaker.

Speaker Pro Tempore

The Speaker Pro Tempore (currently Democrat Kevin Mullin) would exercise the powers of the Speaker when the Speaker is not present, and during floor sessions the Speaker Pro Tempore can preside over the Assembly, allowing the Speaker to work the floor for votes if such a need arises. A majority vote of the full Assembly is required to elect someone as Speaker Pro Tempore, but the office will be filled based on the Speaker's preference and the lawmaker chosen for the post comes from the majority party in the Assembly.

Assembly Majority and Minority Leaders

The Assembly Majority **Party Caucus (a Party Caucus refers to the total number of lawmakers representing a distinct political party in the legislature)** selects the Assembly Majority Leader (currently Democrat Eloise Gomez Reyes) and the Assembly Minority Party Caucus selects the Assembly Minority Leader (currently Republican Marie Waldron). It is worth noting that Minority Leader Waldron ascended to the leadership position in 2018 when Brian Dahle left the post in order to run for a seat in the State Senate.[41]

The Assembly Majority Leader will coordinate strategies with the Speaker in an attempt to keep the Majority Party Caucus unified on such important votes like the budget. The Assembly Minority Leader will also consult with the Speaker on Assembly business, but given the Democrats hold 60 of the 80 Assembly seats in 2021, Minority Leader Waldron has no leverage given the Democrats have a super majority and do not need Republican support to pass anything in the Assembly.

Assembly Rules Committee

The Assembly Rules Committee consists of 9 members, four chosen by the Majority Party Caucus and four selected by the Minority Party Caucus. The Chair of the Rules Committee is appointed by the Speaker. The Rules Committee has the authority to refer bills to other committees and is also responsible for hiring and firing all Assembly staffers. Assembly Member Anthony Portantino, the Democrat who ran afoul of Speaker John Perez in 2011, wanted the Assembly Rules Committee to set staff budgets and assign lawmakers their Capitol offices, not the Speaker.

President of the Senate

The President of the Senate is the Lieutenant Governor of California (currently Eleni Kounalakis), and as discussed in Chapter 4, has limited influence in the State Senate despite the important title. The Lieutenant Governor would only appear in the State Senate to cast a tie breaking vote or preside over an impeachment trial.

President Pro Tempore

This is the position of power in the State Senate, but unlike the Speaker of the Assembly, **the Senate President Pro Tempore does not individually wield power, but shares this authority with four other members on the Senate Rules Committee**. The President Pro Tempore Chairs the Rules Committee, which also consists of two Senators nominated by the majority party and two Senators nominated by the minority party. Democratic Senator Dave Roberti was elected President Pro Tempore in 1980 (the position is chosen by a vote of the entire State Senate membership) and held the post until 1994. President Pro Tempore Roberti (like Speaker Willie Brown) influenced policy, authoring legislation in 1989 to ban specifically identified semi-automatic assault weapons in the wake of a Stockton elementary school shooting tragedy in which a deranged gunman opened fire and killed five children.[42]

The current Senate President Pro Tempore is Democrat Toni Atkins, who along with Assembly Speaker Anthony Rendon, has shepherded legislation limiting the ability of landlords to evict tenants and provide billions in economic stimulus to assist low-income Californians and small businesses during the pandemic.

Senate Rules Committee

The Senate Rules Committee, chaired by the President Pro Tempore, and consisting of four other members (2 Democrats and 2 Republicans) maintains the following powers:

- Appoints all Senators to committees
- Appoints all Senate committee chairs and vice chairs
- Refers new bills to committees
- Determines Senate staff budgets and office space
- Hires and fires all Senate staff

As already pointed out, the President Pro Tempore does not wield individual power like the Speaker of the Assembly, sharing it instead with the Senate Rules Committee. However, the State Senate is granted distinct authority to confirm gubernatorial appointments to an array of state boards and commissions, making the Senate President Pro Tempore a key player in the confirmation process of a Governor's appointees within the Executive Branch. When it comes to budget negotiations, the Senate President Pro Tempore is on equal footing with the Speaker of the Assembly.

Senate Minority Leader

The Senate Minority Leader (currently Republican Scott Wilk) is chosen by a vote of the Senate Minority Party Caucus, and (like their Assembly Minority Leader counterpart) possesses a degree of influence on budget matters given increasing taxes and fees requires a two-thirds vote of both legislative chambers. In 2011, Republican Assembly Minority Leader Connie Conway and Republican Senate Minority Leader Bob Dutton kept their respective party caucuses unified in refusing to allow any two-thirds votes to be achieved for the purpose of raising taxes or fees in the State Assembly or State Senate. However, Democrats, after the 2020 elections, gained two-thirds majorities in both the Assembly and Senate, making it more difficult for Republicans to thwart tax and fee increases, bond measures, and constitutional amendments, all of which require a two-thirds vote of both chambers.

LEGISLATIVE LEADERSHIP IN THE U.S. CONGRESS

The Speaker of the House

The top leadership position in the U.S. House of Representatives is the Speaker of the House who is elected by a vote of the entire House membership. In 1975, the Speaker's powers were significantly enhanced as House rules were changed allowing the Speaker to choose the chair and majority party members on the House Rules Committee (the committee that determines the rules of procedure for all bills sent to the House floor for a vote). Legislation the Speaker wants enacted will prompt the Rules Committee to limit debate time on the measure and prevent any amendments from being added to the bill. As already discussed, if a bill passes in different forms in the House and Senate, a Conference Committee is formed to work out a compromise measure that can possibly be approved by both chambers. All House members serving on a Conference Committee are appointed by the Speaker.[43] The Speaker is also second in line concerning presidential succession following the Vice President.

Other powers granted to the Speaker of the House include deciding who will be recognized to speak on the House floor during debate, referring all new bills to a Standing Committee for review, and scheduling votes on legislation reaching the House floor. After the 2006 election, Democrats were in control of the House and made Nancy Pelosi of San Francisco Speaker, the first woman in the history of the United States to serve as Speaker. Pelosi's tenure as Speaker lasted 4 years, and in 2010, Republicans won back the House, selecting Ohio Republican John Boehner to be Speaker.

Speaker Boehner faced criticism from conservative House members for not doing enough to undue President Obama's policies, facilitating his exit as Speaker in 2015. Before leaving, the Speaker initiated a debt and spending plan to prevent the federal government from defaulting on its' debt and shutting down, but Boehner had enough of being Speaker, once referring to the job of keeping the House Republican Caucus unified as "Herding Cats." Wisconsin Republican Paul Ryan became Speaker in 2015, and though optimism for promoting a Republican agenda of tax cuts, de-regulation of industry, and the repeal of Obamacare grew after Republican victory in 2016, Speaker Ryan faced similar dissatisfaction from conservative House Republicans and President Trump that more was not accomplished by Congress in the first two years of the Trump administration. Speaker Ryan decided in April 2018 that he would not seek re-election to Congress. In the mid-term elections of 2018, the Democrats won back control of the House and Nancy Pelosi once again became Speaker of the House.

The House Majority Leader

The House Majority Leader is elected by the majority party caucus in the House, working closely with the Speaker to develop the party's legislative program. Republican Eric Cantor of Virginia was selected to be the Majority Leader of the House in 2011, but inexplicably lost re-election in 2014 to a Tea Party Republican in the primary election. California House member Kevin McCarthy became the House Majority Leader in 2015, and, along with Speaker Paul Ryan, worked to keep House Republicans united in supporting Republican Party priorities such as repealing the Affordable Care Act (Obamacare") passed in 2010, defunding Planned Parenthood (an organization associated with providing women health care services that include abortion), opposing President Obama's nuclear deal with Iran, and promoting President Trump's policies to cut taxes, end international trade deals, de-regulate industry, and make it more difficult for undocumented immigrants to enter the country. With the Democrats victory in 2018, Steny Hoyer, a Maryland Democrat once more became the House Majority Leader, having served in that position when Nancy Pelosi first became Speaker in 2007.

The House Minority Leader

The House Minority Leader is the losing candidate in the House election for Speaker, representing the minority party. The Minority Leader encourages minority congressional members to remain unified in opposition to the majority party, but given the procedures in the House, the minority party is limited in preventing legislation they oppose from being voted on and passed. If the Speaker is having trouble getting his party caucus to support legislation the Speaker wants, the Minority Leader can be consulted by the Speaker for possible minority party votes. Representative Nancy Pelosi, who previously served as Speaker of the House, became House Minority Leader for the Democrats, and Speaker John Boehner, much to the dismay of conservative Republicans, was compelled in 2015 to seek support from Pelosi in securing House Democrat votes to avoid a shutdown of the Department of Homeland Security. Speaker Boehner needed the House Democrats' help after a number of House Republicans refused to fund the Department of Homeland Security unless the House provided no funding for President Obama's executive order granting amnesty to some 5 million undocumented immigrants. Boehner's working with Pelosi only aggravated his House Republican detractors even more, but the Speaker resigned (as previously noted) later in 2015. After the 2018 victory by the Democrats in the House, Nancy Pelosi assumed the Speaker's office once again and Republican Kevin McCarthy of California became the House Minority Leader for the Republicans.

The President of the Senate

The Vice President of the U.S. is the President of the Senate but would only show up to cast a tie breaking vote, which rarely occurs. As pointed out in chapter 4, Vice President Mike Pence cast the tie-breaking vote to confirm Betsy DeVos as Education Secretary and was in the Senate to provide the tie-breaking vote to repeal the Affordable Care Act (which proved unnecessary since only 49 Senators voted for repeal, one short of a 50-50 tie). Current Vice President Kamala Harris, in February 2021, cast the tie-breaking vote in the Senate to advance $1.9 trillion COVID-19 relief bill. There is a good chance Vice President Harris will be able to cast more tie breaking votes in the Senate in 2021 and 2022 given the Senate currently comprises 50 Democrats and 50 Republicans. When the President of the United States appears before a joint session of Congress to speak (such as the yearly State of the Union address) seated directly behind the President will be the Speaker of the House and the President of the Senate.

The President Pro Tempore of the Senate

Since the President of the Senate seldom presides in the chamber, Senators elect a President Pro Tempore to be the temporary presiding officer of the Senate, presiding over the Senate in the Vice President's absence. Senate tradition has allowed the majority party's most senior member to be chosen President Pro

Tempore, and West Virginia Democrat Robert Byrd, who served in the Senate since 1959 (the longest tenure in Senate history), was the President Pro Tempore until his death in 2010. His replacement as President Pro Tempore was Senator Daniel Inoyue (D – Hawaii), who just happened to be second behind the late Senator Byrd in length of service in the U.S. Senate, having been first elected in 1962. After Republicans wrested control of the U.S. Senate from the Democrats in 2014, Senator Orin Hatch (R-Utah) became the President Pro Tempore. With Democrats retaking the Senate in 2020, Patrick Leahy (D-Vermont) is the current President Pro Tempore. The position is more honorary than powerful, but the President Pro Tempore is third in line for succession to be President of the United States (following the Vice President and the Speaker of the House).

The Senate Majority Leader

This is the top leadership position in the U.S. Senate, and Chuck Schumer (D – New York) is currently the Senate Majority Leader, having been chosen by his Democrat Senate colleagues per the rules of the Senate. The Senate Majority Leader is granted the right to be recognized first in any debate on the Senate floor and schedules all floor business (including votes on legislation, resolutions, and filibusters).[44] However, due to the filibuster being retained by the Senate, the Majority Leader regularly consults with the Senate Minority Leader concerning the scheduling of floor business. It takes 60 votes to break a filibuster and end debate so a vote can be taken on most measures reaching the floor of the Senate. Subsequently, the Senate Majority Leader will work with the Senate Minority Leader because votes will likely be needed from minority party Senators to end filibusters, which have (as noted earlier in this chapter) increased significantly in numbers over the past decade.

As previously discussed, former Senate Majority Leader Mitch McConnell (R – Kentucky) took a calculated political risk in preventing a confirmation vote on President Obama's Supreme Court nominee Merrick Garland in 206, banking on President Trump's victory over Hillary Clinton. McConnell's gambit worked, and conservative Justice Neil Gorsuch is now on the Supreme Court because of it.

McConnell was also able to get a confirmation vote for Supreme Court Justice Amy Coney Barrett, who filled the vacancy caused by the passing of Justice Ruth Bader Ginsburg in the Fall of 2020. Senate Democrats complained of hypocrisy by their Republican colleagues. Justice Barrett was confirmed a week before the 2020 Presidential Election. Back in 2016, McConnell and the Republicans were fine with keeping a Supreme Court seat vacant for a full year so the Presidential Election would decide who would get to fill the vacancy. That was not the case in 2020.

The Senate Minority Leader

Senator Mitch McConnell (R – Kentucky) is the current Senate Minority Leader, and like his counterpart (Majority Leader Chuck Schumer D – New York) has the right to be recognized first in any Senate floor debate. The Senate Minority Leader is selected by a vote of the minority party's Senators.

Prior to Republicans regaining control of the U.S. Senate in 2014, Senator Harry Reid was the Senate Majority Leader for the Democrats and Senator Mitch McConnell held the Senate Minority Leader position for the Republicans. Once the Republicans took back control of the House in 2010, Senate Minority Leader McConnell's influence grew, and he was able to extract Senate Democrat votes after the 2010 election to extend President George W. Bush's tax cuts for all income earners (including those making over $250,000). Senate Democrats had little choice but to go along with extending the tax cuts not only because of the election results in the House, but also due to the fact that President Obama needed Republican Senate votes to ratify a nuclear weapons reduction treaty with Russia. Under the U.S. Constitution, **the Senate is required to ratify with a two-thirds vote all treaties the President enters into with a foreign government**, prompting the need for Senate Republican votes to ratify the treaty. Such **extraordinary majority votes** in the Senate make the Senate Minority Leader a more powerful position than the House Minority Leader.

As a result of the 2020 election, the U.S. Senate is currently a 50-50 split between Republicans and Democrats, but since the Democrats won the White House in 2020, Vice President Kamala Harris casts the tie-breaking vote, if need be, in the Senate. Technically, the Democrats are the majority party in the U.S. Senate, but by the slimmest of margins. Chuck Schumer and Mitch McConnell agreed to an arrangement where Democrats are the majority, but Senator McConnell has insisted the Filibuster, which requires 60 votes to end debate and vote on a bill, be maintained in the Senate. So far, this arrangement has held, but as discussed earlier in this chapter, many Democrats want to see the Filibuster be eliminated.

THE GOOD, THE BAD, AND THE UGLY

This chapter has focused on the structure, functions, and leadership differences between the California Legislature and the United States Congress. Lawmaking is anything but easy, especially when considering how difficult it is to get legislation passed, something the Trump Administration confronted over four years and the Biden Administration faces in 2021. With that said, historic laws have been approved at the federal level through Congress to strengthen civil rights for millions, expand voting rights to more Americans, and provide retirement and health care for senior citizens. Over the years, the California Legislature has approved measures to protect the environment, create an unmatched system of higher education, foster the construction of major transportation projects, and provide Direct Democracy to the people.

Yet the passage of laws inevitably create conflict. Republicans in the U.S. Congress remain committed to repealing 'Obamacare', toughing up our immigration laws, cutting taxes, and easing regulations on business and industry. Congressional Democrats want stricter gun control laws (their fervor re-ignited by the unprecedented 2017 mass shooting in Las Vegas that left 59 dead, and another rash of mass-shootings plaguing the nation in 2021), legislation curbing greenhouse gas emissions, and laws addressing the widening income disparity between the affluent and everyone else.

In California, controversy abounds with Governor Newsom's executive actions to confront the pandemic that resulted in lockdowns, closed businesses, and millions of California children being educated through zoom. Governor Newsom's directives to shut down a significant portion of the state over 2020 and 2021 as a result of COVID-19 has grown the movement to Recall the Governor. Governor Newsom did not help himself when he was caught dining in a swank Napa County restaurant in November 2020, contradicting his own lockdown procedures he expects Californians follow to combat the pandemic. Critics of the Governor also lay the blame at his feet for the woeful record of the Employment Development Department (discussed earlier in this chapter) as billions of dollars in fraudulent payments were released by EDD. And EDD's problems have been compounded by their slow response in providing unemployment payments to millions of unemployed Californians trying to pay rent and buy groceries. With a Recall Election looming in the Fall of 2021, these criticisms of Governor Newsom will be highlighted by those who want him removed. Special interest money is already being raised for the potential Recall Election of Governor Newsom, and there are no limits on how much money can be raised in support of removing Governor Newsom or in support of retaining the Governor. California law equates the Recall Election to a ballot measure, and there are no spending limits for ballot measures.[45] However, the Recall Ballot will have two parts, the first asking the voter if Governor Newsom should be Recalled, but the second part allows the voter to choose from a list of candidates for Governor if Newsom is Recalled. Any candidate on the second part of the ballot is subject to campaign fundraising limits ($32, 400 donation-limit for individual contributors).[46]

Given the ever-spiraling growth in spending by special interest groups who fund legislative and executive branch campaigns, state propositions, and lobbying firms, is it any wonder that the average citizen feels jaded, powerless, and disgusted with our political system? Such antipathy only intensifies when lawmakers are caught in uncompromising situations. In 2005, a Republican congressman from San Diego, Randy 'Duke' Cunningham, was convicted of accepting $2.4 million in bribes by leveraging his membership on the powerful House Appropriation and Intelligence Committees, ensuring generous government contracts were granted to those that could provide him the finer things in life (a Rolls Royce, yachts, Persian rugs, and a multi-million-dollar home in San Diego).[47] Cunningham served seven years in jail, but what was perhaps the most galling aspect of his wrongdoing involved him collecting an annual federal pension of over $42,000 for his 15 years of service in Congress, something Congress addressed by passing legislation in 2007 which bans members of Congress from pension benefits if they are convicted of bribery, witness tampering, or perjury.[48] The law is not retroactive, and Cunningham still receives his pension.

Former California State Senator, Democrat Leland Yee, pleaded guilty to racketeering charges in 2015 that were stunning in their detail. Yee not only confessed to trading political favors for money, but also admitted he was willing to coordinate a multimillion-dollar weapons deal for shoulder-fired missiles and automatic weapons involving a group linked to Muslim rebels in the Philippines.[49] The fact that Yee was a strong advocate for government oversight (he authored the college oversight law mentioned earlier in this chapter and supported tougher gun control laws) leaves him vulnerable to criticism of being disingenuous. At the time Senator Yee was indicted on the racketeering charges, he continued to receive his full salary given the State Constitution does not allow a lawmaker's pay to be withheld unless the legislator is expelled from the office. An amendment to California's Constitution that would grant the State Legislature the ability to suspend a lawmaker's pay prior to expulsion was approved by the voters in the 2016 election.

These two examples, though dramatic in scope, are not isolated incidences involving lawmaker indiscretions. The former Speaker of the U.S. House Of Representatives (Republican Dennis Hastert) faced a federal indictment in 2015 for lying to the FBI (Federal Bureau of Investigation) about $3.5 million Hastert agreed to pay a former student of his to keep quiet about an improper relationship between the two. Hastert's problems were magnified by the fact that during his Speakership, another Republican member of Congress (Mark Foley) was texting sexually explicit text messages to male teenagers who were part of the House Page Program (high school students serving as federal employees in the House of Representatives).[50] Hastert was a favorite of social conservatives, opposing laws that strengthened the rights of homosexuals, and Foley had supported creating stricter punishments against child sexual predators.

In 2016, another sexting episode with a minor surfaced as former Democratic congressman Anthony Weiner was convicted of asking a 15-year-old girl to engage in sexually explicit conduct for him online. Weiner was sentenced to 21 months in federal prison. As repulsive as the behavior was, compounding Weiner's criminal acts involved the discovery on his seized computer of e-mails belonging to Weiner's wife, Huma Abedin, a top aide to Hillary Clinton. The revelation of the discovered e-mails resulted in F.B.I. Director James Comey reopening the closed investigation of Mrs. Clinton's e-mails a week before the Presidential election, possibly contributing to Donald Trump's victory.[51]

After California Democratic State Senator Ben Hueso was arrested on suspicion of drunk driving in 2014, it came to light the following year that the California State Senate had initiated a late-night transportation service for the senators. Once the media made public the 24-hour program, it only took Senate President Pro Tempore Kevin De Leon a few days to announce the end of the late-night ride service through one of his aides, who said the decision to ax the program demonstrated De Leon's goal of *'vigorously working to restore the public's confidence in government and be trusted stewards of the taxpayer dollar."*[52]

In December 2019 U.S. Representative Duncan Hunter, a California Republican, plead guilty to illegally using $250,000 in campaign money to finance trips and other personal expenses; some of the money allegedly spent to pursue romantic affairs with five women. Hunter resigned from Congress in January 2020 and was sentenced to 11 months in prison by a federal judge.[53]

These sordid episodes partly reflect the public's disdain for politicians while also calling into question how disconnected some lawmakers become from the constituents they are supposed to be serving. Public opinion polls have indicated that root canal is more popular than Congress, and similar ill sentiments by the public were directed toward the California State Legislature after the Great Recession of 2008. Though Americans tend to bristle at the legislative branch as a whole, they are more inclined to support the lawmaker who represents them at the state and federal level, reinforcing the notion that **'all politics are local'**. With that said, citizens who are struggling to pay bills, find adequate employment, live in affordable housing, and provide for their kids, especially in the COVID-19 era, have little time for politicians they perceive as self-indulgent creatures whose actions speak much louder than their words.

6
CHAPTER

THE JUDICIAL BRANCH

During the 1970's Baretta, a weekly cop television show began each episode with a theme song: "Don't do the crime if you can't do the time." In 1994, California voters took that theme song to heart by approving **Three-Strikes-And-You're-Out, a law requiring anyone convicted of three violent or serious felonies to serve a sentence of 25 years to life in state prison**. While Golden State voters were more than willing to throw the book at convicted felons, the state's electorate was reluctant to finance the building of more prisons to house the swelling inmate population the three strikes law and other minimum sentencing statutes created. This resulted in California's prison population (by 2011) being at 180% of prison design capacity. In 2011, California incarcerated 143,435 inmates, however the state's prisons are suitable for housing only 80,000 convicts.[1]

Responding to this discrepancy, a 2011 United States Supreme Court decision ordered California within the next two years to cut its' prison population by a whopping 33,000. The U.S. Supreme Court, in issuing this ruling, upheld a lower federal court decision requiring the inmate reduction in California. Reaction to the U.S. Supreme Court's order was mixed, *"If that doesn't have a negative impact on the safety of the people of California, I don't know what does,"* California Republican Congressman Dan Lungren said. Like Congressman Lungren, other Republican lawmakers objected to the Supreme Court's opinion, fearing it will trigger an early release of dangerous felons, *"People that go to the state prison system aren't there because they stole a pack of gum,"* noted Republican State Senator Bob Dutton.[2]

Despite these criticisms, judges at the federal level (like the U.S. Supreme Court) are insulated from the public's displeasure when they decide cases like this one given federal judges are not subject to retention by the voters, something the framers of the Constitution had in mind. In *Federalist Paper No. 10,* James Madison believed that the success of the U.S. Constitution would be determined by whether it could provide a system of both majority rule and protection against majority tyranny. Writing in *Federalist Paper No. 78,* Alexander Hamilton suggested that without an independent judicial branch, constitutional protections against unlimited power for elected officials *"would amount to nothing."*[3]

In this chapter, we explore the different aspects of the California judicial branch and the federal government's judicial branch. Areas of emphasis will include **The California Court System, The Selection Of California Judges, How California Judges Can Be Removed, Common Law and Judicial Review, The United States Court System, The Selection Of Federal Judges, and How Federal Judges Can Be Removed.** We will conclude the chapter with a review of the **California Criminal Justice System (Police, District Attorneys, Juries, Public Defenders and Prisons).**

THE CALIFORNIA COURT SYSTEM

The California court system has gone through some changes over the years. Like the United States court system, California's courts are divided between trial courts that exercise **Original Jurisdiction (the authority of a court to hear a case first)** and appellate courts maintaining **Appellate Jurisdiction (the authority of a court to review the decisions of a lower trial court).** California used to have two separate levels of trial courts, but in 1998 California voters approved Proposition 220 which allowed counties to consolidate their municipal trial courts into superior courts.[4] By 2001, all 58 counties in California had made the switch, eliminating municipal courts and elevating all previous municipal court judges to the superior court. Today, all California trial courts, the courts of original jurisdiction where the trial is conducted, are superior courts.

California Superior Court

The California Superior Courts are the courts of **original jurisdiction** where the trial would be held. These courts hear cases involving **Civil Law, where the government, through the courts, provides a forum for the settlement of disputes between private parties in such matters as contracts, domestic relations, business relations, and accidents.** In civil law cases, one party is seeking some kind of compensation from another party.

California Superior Courts also hold trials in cases involving **Criminal Law, laws defining acts committed against the public as being offenses to**

society. In Criminal Law cases, the government is always the prosecutor against individuals charged with violating the law. The bulk of criminal law is adopted by the states, but over the years, more federal criminal statutes have been enacted.[5] In criminal law cases, the government is attempting to convict an individual of the crime being charged, and upon conviction, punish the individual.

An important distinction to be made when examining the judicial branches of government in California and at the federal level is that California courts have jurisdiction over civil and criminal law cases involving California law, while cases dealing with federal government civil and criminal law are under the jurisdiction of the United States court system. For example, Scott Peterson was charged and convicted in California Superior Court of murdering his wife and unborn child because the offense occurred in California. In contrast, Timothy McVeigh was charged and convicted in a federal court for murdering 160 people in the Oklahoma City bombing. Because McVeigh bombed a federal building and killed federal employees, the jurisdiction for trying McVeigh rested with the federal government, not the state of Oklahoma where the crime took place.

California Superior Courts operate out of each county and some 10 million cases are annually filed in these courts, of which 8 million are criminal (most of them traffic violations) and 2 million involve civil law issues. Currently, some **2,100 judges (some of them temporary) fill California's Superior Courts**.[6] Judges serving in California's Superior Courts get six-year terms and must be retained by the voters in the county they serve when their six-year term ends. Superior Court vacancies are filled by the Governor, but there is no government body that confirms a Governor's Superior Court appointments in California.

California Courts of Appeal

If one loses their case in Superior Court, they can appeal the verdict to the State Courts of Appeal. California Courts of Appeal operate under **appellate jurisdiction**, reviewing decisions from the lower Superior Court. When a case is appealed, the appellate court will not conduct a trial. Instead, three appellate court justices will review what happened in the lower court, allowing lawyers from both sides to come before them and make arguments. However, unlike the trial court, no witnesses testify, and no jury is selected to render a verdict. The decision rests with the three appellate court justices who can do the following:

- Uphold the decision of the lower court
- Reverse the decision of the lower court
- Send the case back down to the lower court for a re-trial

There are six Courts of Appeal districts in California. The 1st District is San Francisco, the 2nd District is Los Angeles, the 3rd District is Sacramento, the 4th District is San Diego, the 5th District is Fresno, and the 6th District is San Jose. Case loads are extremely high, averaging over 20,000 cases filed for appeal annually, a huge number given that only **105 California appellate court justices exist** to review all of these appeals.[7]

All California appellate court justices are nominated by the Governor and their nominations must be confirmed by the **Commission on Judicial Appointments, consisting of the Attorney General, the Chief Justice of the Supreme Court, and the senior presiding judge of the Courts of Appeal.** A vote of 2 out of 3 commission members confirms the Governor's appointment. Confirmation of a Governor's judicial nominee is usually routine. Since the Commission on Judicial Appointments was created in 1934, only two nominees have been rejected by the Commission.[8] Once an appellate court justice is confirmed, the jurist must be elected by the voters in the appellate court district they will serve during the next statewide election. Courts of Appeal justices are given 12-year terms.

The California Supreme Court

The California State Supreme Court consists of 7 justices (six Associate Justices and one Chief Justice). Unlike the Courts of Appeal, the California Supreme Court can be selective in the cases it agrees to review on appeal. Each year roughly 9000 appeals to the California Supreme Court are filed, and most of them will be denied for review by the justices.[9] The California Supreme Court averages some 83 reviews of appealed cases from the 9000 filed. If a majority of the justices deny review of a case, the decision is made public by a brief order (usually one paragraph). However, Supreme Court Justice Goodwin Liu, in 2015, did issue two lengthy dissents against majority decisions denying reviews of a 10-year-old being capable of waiving his 5th Amendment right to silence, and life sentences being given two marijuana growers for a killing a jury determined they did not personally commit.[10] In the 2015–2016 session, the California Supreme Court issued 78 decisions.[11] If the California Supreme Court refuses to review a case, the decision from the lower court stands. It should be noted, though, that the seven State Supreme Court justices are required to review all capital punishment cases.

The high court is primarily a court of appellate jurisdiction, but the State Supreme Court exercises other powers. The seven justices have authority to review orders issued by the Public Utilities Commission, and issue **Writs of Mandamus (an order requiring an officer to perform an official duty that the law requires).** Examples of Writs of Mandamus would include having the

Governor call a special election or requiring recall signatures be verified by the Secretary of State. In addition, the California Supreme Court can issue a **Writ of Habeas Corpus, an order issued by the seven justices requesting a detained or jailed person be brought before a judge so that it can be determined if the detention is legal.**

All decisions rendered by the California Supreme Court will be final unless the case involves federal law or the United States Constitution. For example, after the California Supreme Court upheld **Proposition 8, a 2008 voter approved measure which amended the California Constitution to define marriage as between one man and one woman**, the case moved to the federal courts. In August 2010, a federal district court judge ruled that Proposition 8's ban of same sex marriage violated the Equal Protection Clause of the U.S. Constitution.[12] The United States Supreme Court struck down Proposition 8 in 2013 (as discussed in chapter 4).

Like Courts of Appeal justices, California Supreme Court justices get 12-year terms, and each justice is appointed by the Governor and confirmed by the Commission on Judicial Appointments. Before leaving office, Governor Arnold Schwarzenegger was able to appoint as Chief Justice of the State Supreme Court Tani Cantil-Sakauye. Chief Justice Cantil-Sakauye was confirmed becoming the second female Chief Justice in state history. The first female Chief Justice of the State Supreme Court was Rose Bird (who we will discuss presently). All California Supreme Court justices must face the voters to be retained, and each justice appears on the ballot statewide. In 2015, two new State Supreme Court Justices ascended to the bench, Mariano-Florentino Cuellar and Leondra R. Kruger, both appointed by Governor Jerry Brown. The newest member of the State Supreme Court is Justice Martin Jenkins, appointed by Governor Gavin Newsom in October 2020. Justice Jenkins, a former California Court of Appeals justice, filled the vacancy created with the retirement of Justice Ming Chin who served on the State Supreme Court for 24 years.[13]

REMOVING CALIFORNIA JUDGES
Rejected by the Voters

In California, there are many ways to remove a judge from the bench. First, the voters can reject the jurist when their term expires. This does not often happen, but in 1986 three California Supreme Court justices were removed by the voters (including Chief Justice Rose Bird). Chief Justice Bird had been appointed by Governor Jerry Brown to replace Chief Justice Donald Wright. Bird had no experience as a judge (however neither did U.S. Chief Justice Earl Warren when President Eisenhower selected him). When Chief Justice Bird faced her first confirmation election in 1978, she barely won (52% to 48%). As Chief Justice, Rose Bird favored school busing to desegregate public schools, opposed Proposition 13 (a popular initiative that cut property taxes for homeowners and businesses), and rejected the Legislature's ban on state funded abortions. However, the issue that generated intense opposition to her as Chief Justice involved capital punishment.

From 1978 to 1986, none of the 213 inmates on death row in California prisons were executed. In all 52 capital punishment cases the California State Supreme Court reviewed during Rose Bird's tenure, the Court reversed the lower court's death sentences, stopping the executions.[14] In 1986, Chief Justice Bird and two Associate Justices (Joseph Grodin and Cruz Reynoso) faced retention by California voters in a statewide election. Rose Bird was easily defeated, as only 33% of voters supported her.[15] Justices' Grodin and Reynoso were also removed in the election, and to this day these three are the only California State Supreme Court justices in state history to be removed by the voters.

Recalled by the Voters

California judges are also subject to Recall, a tool of Direct Democracy that allows voters to remove an elected official (including all state judges) before their terms expire. Before Chief Justice Bird was removed by the voters in 1986, she survived a Recall election in 1985. The threat of a Recall may have impacted the California Supreme Court upholding Proposition 8's ban on same sex marriage in 2009.[16] California religious organizations, and other groups opposed to same sex marriage clearly let it be known they would start gathering signatures to qualify a Recall of Supreme Court justices if they ruled Proposition 8 unconstitutional. The threat appeared to work. In 2008, before Proposition 8 passed, the California Supreme Court ruled that same sex couples had a legal right to marry.[17] However, in 2009 the California Supreme Court upheld Proposition 8 on the grounds that it was approved by the voters as an amendment to the State Constitution.[18] That ruling became moot when a federal district court ruled Proposition 8 unconstitutional, something affirmed by the United States Supreme Court in 2013.[19]

As discussed in chapter 2, Santa Clara County Superior Court Judge Aaron Persky, in 2020, was removed in a Recall election by the county's voters after issuing a light sentence to a former Stanford University student convicted of sexually assaulting an unconscious young woman.

Impeachment

State judges, like federal judges, can be impeached. The State Assembly would vote to bring the impeachment charges (with a simple majority vote), and the trial to possibly remove a California judge would be held in the State Senate (with a two-thirds vote needed to convict and remove the judge from the bench). Judge James Hardy was impeached and convicted in 1862 on charges of using language disloyal to the United States at a trial he presided over. In 1929 Superior Court Judge Carlos Hardy was impeached for accepting a $2500 payment for legal services, but the State Senate acquitted Judge Hardy in his impeachment trial. This procedure is extremely rare, but the California Constitution provides for removing state judges through impeachment.

Removal by the Commission on Judicial Performance

The Commission On Judicial Performance, originally created in 1960, and reformed by the voters in 1994, investigates charges of misconduct or incompetence of California judges. Over the years, California judges have made degrading sounds and vulgar gestures in court, fallen asleep in court, cleared the court docket on Fridays so they could play golf, and improperly accepted gifts from litigants in exchange for favorable rulings.

In 1993, an incident involving a Santa Barbara Superior Court judge (James Slater) drew statewide attention, leading to the passage of **Proposition 190 in 1994, changing the make-up and powers of the Commission On Judicial Performance**. The judge had shown up to court, discovering a vehicle parked in his designated parking stall. Incensed, the judge began letting the air out of the car's tires even after being informed the automobile had a handicapped sticker. At the time of this incident, the Commission was comprised of a majority of judges and attorneys and could only recommend removal of a judge to the State Supreme Court. Proposition 190 changed the Commission's make-up so that a majority of the Commissioners were not from the legal profession, eliminating a conflict-of-interest problem. In addition, Proposition 190 now grants the Commission On Judicial Performance the power to remove any state judge for willful misconduct or incompetence.

COMMON LAW AND JUDICIAL REVIEW

The foundation of American law comes from the U.S. Constitution and the English system of **Common Law, the concept of using previous court judgments as a basis for determining the case currently before a court.** Common Law relies on *precedent* **(previous judicial decisions)** in determining legal rights. Anyone who has visited an attorney's office may have noticed the immense library of law books adorning the office. Those books house case law, the written decisions issued by judges in previous cases (though today these cases are more readily accessed through the internet). Attorneys find prior case law decisions that strengthen their client's legal position, using those previous rulings when arguing the case in court. This is the basis of Common Law.

The other bedrock of American law is the U.S. Constitution. When the framers of the Constitution created the three branches of the federal government, the judicial branch was given power *"to all Cases, in Law and Equity, arising under this Constitution, the Laws of the United States, and Treaties made"* (Article III, Section 2 U.S. Constitution). The term *Equity* allows a judge to provide legal remedies where there is no applicable law. However, the U.S. Constitution is silent on whether the judicial branch has the power of **Judicial Review, the authority of the courts to declare acts of the legislative and executive branches unconstitutional.** Judicial Review operates on the premise that the U.S. Constitution is the supreme law and any acts violating the U.S. Constitution (both federal and state) are void. Judicial Review assumes the judicial branch is the guardian of the U.S. Constitution.[20] The power of Judicial Review was given to the federal courts in the case of *Marbury v Madison (1803).* In this case, the United States Supreme Court ruled that an act passed by Congress was unconstitutional, creating the *precedent* that courts possess the power of Judicial Review, a power both federal and state courts have utilized over the years.

THE U.S. COURT SYSTEM

U.S. District Courts

Article I, Section 8 of the U.S. Constitution grants Congress the authority to establish all lower courts below the U.S. Supreme Court. Currently, there are **94** U.S. District Courts dispersed throughout the country, at least one in every state (with some states having four District Courts). There are presently some 700 federal judges serving in the 94 U.S. District Courts across the nation.[21] In comparison, California alone has 2100 Superior Court judges holding trials, a good example of how the states have a much higher volume of cases than the federal government. Congress has also created specialized lower federal courts for taxes, bankruptcy, and international trade. U.S. District Courts are the courts of **original jurisdiction** (the court with the authority to hear a case first), and hold trials in federal cases dealing with criminal and civil law. All U.S. District Court judges are appointed by the President and confirmed by a majority vote of the U.S. Senate. At the federal level, the U.S. Constitution provides a role for the legislative branch to confirm all judicial appointments made by the President. In California, the State Legislature has **no authority** to confirm any state judge appointed by the Governor.

U.S. Courts of Appeals

The U.S. Courts of Appeals practice **appellate jurisdiction** (the right to review decisions from a lower court) concerning federal cases tried in U.S. District Courts. Like California's Courts of Appeal, U.S. Courts of Appeals will not conduct a trial, but will review the proceedings of the lower court, allowing attorneys from both sides to appear before the appellate justices and make their arguments. In most instances three appellate justices review the case and hear legal arguments from both attorneys. As in California, appellate justices for the U.S. Courts of Appeals can:

- Uphold the decision of the lower court
- Reverse the decision of the lower court
- Send the case back down to the lower court for retrial

Congress has created thirteen U.S. Courts of Appeals regions across the country. Eleven of these regions are spread over specific geographic territories, the largest being the Ninth Circuit Courts of Appeals which include nine western states (California being one of them). The other two U.S. Courts of Appeals are located in Washington, D.C. (one of them hearing appeals from trial court rulings in the District of Columbia and the other having jurisdiction over appeals concerning patents and international trade, regardless of what part of the country the trial court decision came from). Currently, there are 179 justices serving on the U.S. Courts of Appeals, and vacancies are filled by the President and confirmed by a majority vote of the U.S. Senate.[22]

The U.S. Supreme Court

The highest court in the nation is the U.S. Supreme Court consisting of 9 justices who have the ability to bring about significant social change in the nation based on their rulings. *Brown v. Board of Education* in 1954 ended government-imposed segregation in public schools and *Roe v. Wade* in 1973 established abortion rights for women. Both of these U.S. Supreme Court decisions reinforce the significance of **Judicial Review** (the ability of a court to determine the constitutionality of laws and executive actions). Decisions of the U.S. Supreme Court are final unless a constitutional amendment nullifying the decision is passed by Congress and ratified by the states or a future Supreme Court overturns the ruling.

The U.S. Supreme Court primarily acts as a court of appellate jurisdiction, reviewing decisions from the U.S. Courts of Appeals. However, the U.S. Supreme Court can practice original jurisdiction in cases involving Foreign Ambassadors and disputes between different states. With that said, Congress has granted U.S. District Courts original jurisdiction in these areas as well.

In order for the U.S. Supreme Court to consider reviewing a case, the **Rule of Four (four or more justices agree the case is worthy of consideration)** applies. If the Rule of Four is enacted, the Court will issue a **Writ of Certiorari,**

an order to the lower court requesting the case record for the justices to review. The Court permits attorneys to make oral arguments before them, and during these hearings any of the 9 justices can ask the attorney questions. When it comes time to decide the case, the 9 justices will meet privately in conference (usually on Wednesdays and Fridays when they are in session) and discuss the case.[23]

Written Opinions by the U.S. Supreme Court

When the U.S. Supreme Court decides cases, a **written opinion** will be issued by the justices. Any justice can choose to write an opinion, and in some Supreme Court decisions all 9 justices pen written opinions. Such opinions are issued by lower court judges as well, and if the Supreme Court decides not to review the case, those lower court opinions establish the precedent. Written opinions reinforce the concept of **common law** because the opinions create precedent for future cases similar in nature. If the U.S. Supreme Court's decision is 9-0, 8-1, 7-2, 6-3, or 5-4, a **Majority Opinion is released outlining the views of the majority.** If the Chief Justice is in the majority, they will write the majority opinion. It should be noted, though, that the Chief Justice does not have any extra voting authority as compared to the other eight justices when it comes to deciding cases. Any justice can issue a **Concurring Opinion, where the justice votes with the majority, but may have a different legal view on the issue.** Justices that are in the minority will pen a **Dissenting Opinion, describing why the majority was wrong in the conclusion they reached in the case.** The dissenting opinion is important because it can create the legal precedent for a future court to reverse the decision.

The U.S. Supreme Court Justices

Originally there were 6 Supreme Court justices and Congress has the authority to determine the number of justices serving on the Court. In 1869, Congress set the number of Supreme Court justices at 9, and it has not changed since. After winning re-election in 1936, President Franklin Roosevelt attempted to add 6 more justices to the Supreme Court, but Congress refused. In 2021, President Joe Biden may be attempting to revise President Roosevelt's failed 'Court Packing' plan, tasking a special commission with studying the possibility of increasing the number of Supreme Court Justices by four. This commission will also be investigating the possibility of creating term limits for Supreme Court Justices. Under the U.S. Constitution, there are no term limits for federal judges.

As with the other federal judges, a vacancy on the U.S. Supreme Court is filled by the President, subject to the U.S. Senate confirming the Supreme Court justice. Since 2005, eight new members have joined the U.S. Supreme Court. Chief Justice John Roberts and Associate Justice Sam Alito were appointed by President George W. Bush, Associate Justice's Sonya Sotomayor and Elena Kagen were appointed by President Barack Obama, and President Donald Trump was given the opportunity to appoint three Supreme Court Justices (Neil Gorsuch, Brett Kavanaugh, and Amy Coney Barret). Justices serving on the U.S. Supreme Court (like all other federal judges) get virtually lifetime appointments once they are confirmed by the U.S. Senate. Associate Justice John Paul Stevens (at 89) stepped down in 2010 and Associate Justice Anthony Kennedy retired in 2018 at the age of 81. Former Chief Justice William Rehnquist died in office at age 80, Associate Justice Antonin Scalia (79) passed away in 2016, and in 2020 Associate Justice Ruth Bader Ginsburg succumbed to cancer at the age of 87.

REMOVING FEDERAL JUDGES

Unlike California judges that face removal from a number of methods, federal judges can only be dismissed by Congress through the process of impeachment. Over the years, 15 federal judges have been impeached by the House of Representatives and 8 have been convicted and removed by the Senate. In over 200 years, that is a small number. With that said, over the past 26 years, the House has impeached, and the Senate convicted and removed 3 federal judges, the most recent one being U.S. District Court Judge Thomas Porteous in 2010. Judge Porteous was charged with concealing cash and gifts he received from lawyers appearing before his court.

In June 2009, the House impeached U.S. District Court Judge Samuel Kent a month after Judge Kent was sentenced to 33 months in prison for lying about sexually assaulting two women. Judge Kent sought to retire from office so he could retain his annual salary as a federal judge for life. The House responded by impeaching the Judge so he could not collect the lifetime salary. Kent agreed to resign after being impeached by the House, which avoided an impeachment trial against him in the U.S. Senate.[24] Ugly behavior in government is not solely the province of elected lawmakers.

But the most unusual impeachment and removal of a federal judge involves Alcee Hastings. Judge Hastings was charged in the House with accepting a $150,000 bribe in exchange for issuing a lenient sentence to a convicted felon in his court. At his trial, the Senate convicted Hastings of the bribery charges in 1989. In Article 1, Section 3 of the U.S. Constitution it states, *Judgment in Cases of Impeachment shall not extend further than to removal from Office, and disqualification to hold and enjoy any Office of honor, Trust or Profit under the United States.* That meant the U.S. Senate, after convicting Judge Hastings, could have voted to ban him from seeking any federal office in the future, but the Senators in this trial chose not to do that. Just three years later, in 1992, Alcee Hastings ran for a seat in the House of Representatives (the chamber that impeached him) and won election. Congressman Hastings, a Democrat, continued to serve in the House of Representatives, having won re-election yet again in 2020, holding a seat on the powerful House Rules Committee. However, in April 2021 Congressman Hastings died of cancer at the age of 84. The old adage *"if you can't beat them, join them"* would certainly apply to Alcee Hastings.

THE CALIFORNIA CRIMINAL JUSTICE SYSTEM

The Police

In California, there are an estimated 80,000 police, which equates to 217 officers per 100,000 residents.[25] These law enforcement officers are disbursed among federal, state, and local governments, with a majority of them serving at the local government level. Police officers are entrusted with enforcing the law and maintaining order during natural disasters and civil disobedience (such as riots or unruly public demonstrations). How law enforcement discharge their duties has been the subject of public scrutiny, especially with the number of police shootings involving unarmed people (many of which have been caught on camera) prominently featured by the national media. Adding to the problem is that many of these police shootings of unarmed residents feature a white officer firing on a black person. In 2009, a Bay Area Rapid Transit (BART) white police officer fatally shot an unarmed black train rider (Oscar Grant) in Oakland, and in 2014 (a few weeks after the Ferguson, Missouri shooting of Michael Brown prompted the 'Black Lives Matter' movement) Los Angeles police shot a mentally ill black man in the back, claiming he was attempting to wrest a gun from one of the officers. In 2018 Sacramento police shot and killed Stephon Clark. Clark was unarmed and in his grandmother's backyard. Police mistakenly thought Clark was pointing a gun (it was his cell phone) and they opened fire.

But in May 2020, an inflection-point for the nation that became global in scope over how police treat people of color occurred in Minnesota when a Minneapolis police officer (Derek Chauvin) was caught on video pressing his knee on the neck of George Floyd for over 9 minutes, resulting in the death of Mr. Floyd. Despite Floyd pleading for Chauvin to stop, claiming he could not breathe and that he was dying, Chauvin continued applying pressure to the sprawled and handcuffed Floyd's neck, even after Floyd was unresponsive. The video, taken by 17-year-old Darnella Frazier, which also showed three other Minneapolis police officers doing nothing to stop Chauvin, went viral, and people around the country, and around the world, were shocked and outraged viewing Officer Chauvin carrying out, what many concluded to be a slow, sadistic murder of Mr. Floyd. What made Darnella Frazier's video even more significant was it clearly contradicted the initial statement by the Minneapolis Police which attributed Mr. Floyd's death to a *"Medical Incident During Police Interaction."*[26] Frazier's video was also the key piece of evidence that lead to a Minneapolis jury in April 2021 convicting Derek Chauvin of murder and manslaughter in the death of George Floyd. Sentencing in this case had not been determined, but the most serious charge of murder carries up to 40 years in prison.

The trial of Derek Chauvin was televised live every day across the nation, and the city of Minneapolis was already on edge awaiting the verdict when another police killing of an African American (Daunte Wright) occurred just ten miles from the courthouse in which the Chauvin trial was being conducted. Wright was pulled over for a traffic violation, but when a warrant showed up on his record, police decided to arrest him. When Wright resisted and attempted to enter his car, Brooklyn Center Police Officer Kim Potter, a 26-year veteran, pulled what she claimed was her taser to subdue Wright, but instead she had her service weapon out and fatally shot Mr. Wright. Potter has been arrested and charged in the death of Daunte Wright. What is so perplexing about Potter's mistake in pulling out her weapon instead of the taser is the same thing happened in the aforementioned 2009 killing of Oscar Grant at the BART station in Oakland. BART Police Officer Johannes Mehserle claimed he made the mistake of drawing his gun instead of the taser and fatally shooting Grant. Mehserele was convicted of involuntary manslaughter and resigned from the BART Police Department. In the wake of the Oscar Grant shooting, police departments supposedly changed training guidelines and protocols to prevent such a mistake from happening again. Former Philadelphia Police Chief Charles Ramsey, in response to the Daunte Wright killing, told CNN that after the Oscar Grant shooting police departments across the country switched to cross draws (which means the gun should be on one side of the belt and the taser on the other side so the officer does not confuse the two). Ramsey was puzzled how such a mistake could happen again. These incidents suggest one of the potential reforms police departments need to undertake is to improve training and protocols, something we will address presently.

Police work can be extremely dangerous, and in the past decade over 1600 law enforcement officers died in the line of duty nationwide.[27] Since California statehood, over 1500 police have been killed, including the 2015 shooting of Hayward Police Officer Scott Lunger during a traffic stop at 3 am. Four years later, in 2019, two police officers were shot and killed in the Sacramento region, both in their first year of service. 22-year-old Davis Police Officer Natalie

Corona, on patrol alone, was dealing with a minor traffic accident involving three cars when a man approached Officer Corona as she was checking one of the motorists' drivers-licenses and shot her in the neck, then continued firing into the fallen officer. Officer Corona's killer eventually retreated to his home and shot himself dead, leaving behind a note indicating his hatred of the police. Six months later, 26-year-old Sacramento Police Officer Tara O'Sullivan was shot and killed while responding to a domestic violence call in Sacramento. Officer O'Sullivan was assisting an alleged domestic violence victim when she was fatally shot. Because Officer O'Sullivan's shooter engaged other Sacramento police in a gunfight, Officer O'Sullivan lay unattended for 44 minutes. She later died after being transported to UC Davis Medical Center.

Police have also been marked for attack in response to the spate of incidents caught on film showing law enforcement officers killing someone. After an unarmed black man died struggling with police officers in New York, two New York policemen were ambushed in their squad car by an assailant who shot and killed both of them in 2014. Instagram posts of the assailant (prior to the attack) indicated he intended to target New York police officers.[28] Tensions were only inflamed in July 2016 when five Dallas police officers were gunned down by a former U.S. Army private during a peaceful demonstration in response to a pair of fatal police shootings a few days earlier in Louisiana and Minnesota. Later that year, when San Francisco 49ers quarterback Colin Kaepernick began kneeling during the national anthem to protest police shootings of African Americans, fierce arguments about disrespecting the military, the police and the American flag erupted against Kaepernick. By 2017, Kaepernick was out of the league, but his willingness to call attention to the issue caught on with other NFL players, who began taking a knee during the anthem. President Donald Trump publicly inserted himself into the debate, calling on NFL owners to fire any player kneeling or doing anything else to disrespect the flag during the anthem. The players maintained their protests were centered on the inequities of a criminal justice system that fails to protect people of color (particularly African Americans), while those opposed to their demonstrations (including President Trump) argued the players' actions were un-American.

But the George Floyd killing took things to another level, triggering massive protests around the nation, thousands marching, despite the concerns of COVID-19. Rioting and looting occurred in Minneapolis and scores of other cities, a byproduct of police shooting incidents when anger and frustration spill out into the streets and provocateurs and looters sow chaos; something California is most familiar with given the Los Angeles rioting after four white police officers were acquitted in the videotaped beating of Rodney King in 1992. California cities had their share of protesting and some violence in the Summer of 2020 over police killings of unarmed people of color, but nothing like what took place in Portland and Seattle that Summer. The sustained 2020 Summer protests against the police in Portland were extraordinary, with some 10,000 people marching on a regular basis some nights. President Trump sent in federal law enforcement to deal with the continuing demonstrations that often turned violent in Portland.[29] In Seattle, there was an attempt to permanently establish a 'People's No Police Zone' where several blocks were literally taken over for a few weeks by a group of utopians. Saner minds prevailed after two fatal shootings in the zone, and the city finally dispersed the squatters. Businesses operating in the 'People's No Police Zone' were not too pleased, suing the city for abandoning them.[30]

Body Cameras and Data Gathering

One of the great challenges not only in California, but nationwide, is to hold police accountable for their actions while at the same time ensuring that they are granted the authority to properly do their jobs in enforcing the law. A policy some communities are implementing is the use of body cameras by police. In Rialto, California all of the police began wearing body cameras the size of pagers in 2012. After a year of use by the Rialto cops, the application of force by the officers declined 60% and complaints against the police dropped by 88%.[31] By 2018, California required all statewide police departments deploy Body Worn Cameras (BWC's) and that a police department release "critical incident" BWC recordings within 45 days of the recorded incident.[32] However, some other states have been reluctant to adopt BWC requirements for their police, citing the need to protect civilians' privacy rights and to ensure an ongoing criminal investigation is not impeded by releasing BWC footage. This issue came to a head in April 2021 in North Carolina where a Black man (Andrew Brown) was shot dead by Pasquotank County Sheriff's Deputies. Nearly a week after the shooting, no BWC footage had been released to Brown's family and attorneys. North Carolina law only allows police BWC footage be released to the public with a court order. A brief 20 second clip from one Deputy's BWC was shown to the Brown family and attorneys. The Deputies were serving Brown with an arrest warrant when he apparently backed his vehicle up, attempting to drive away when he was shot.[33]

For police officers, greater public scrutiny can deflate morale if the only information residents learn of them involves violent encounters with a suspect. For instance, a 2016 Sacramento city policy requires their police department release footage (dash or body camera) within 30 days of officer-involved shootings, deaths in custody, and select citizen complaints.[34] The Sacramento Police Department claimed releasing just this type of footage masks the everyday positive interactions officers have with the public they serve. Sacramento

Mayor Darrell Steinberg advocated for adjusting the video release policy to include footage of day to day interactions between the police and residents where officers diffuse situations, instead of escalating them. *"The police have rightly complained that with our current video release policy, the only thing the public sees is the controversial shooting. Well, there is a lot more to see,"* said Mayor Steinberg.[35]

In September 2015, California State Attorney General Kamala Harris announced the creation of a state-run webpage that allows the public to access information on California law enforcement. The website features data on (1) law enforcement officers killed or assaulted when on duty, and (2) deaths of people in custody, including arrest-related deaths. Former Attorney General Harris (elected to the U.S. Senate in 2016) described the purpose of creating the webpage, *"All of these incidents have encouraged a national dialogue about what is the relationship between law enforcement and communities we have served. Part of this conversation should take place looking at the data."*[36]

The web page, gathering data from the state's 800 police departments, reported in 2016 that 157 people died in violent encounters with law enforcement officers. The police departments' data also detailed 782 violent incidents resulting in serious injury or death, or where the discharge of a firearm occurred.[37] These violent episodes involved 832 civilians of which 42% were Hispanic, 30% were white, and 20% were black.[38] Between 2016 and 2018 there has been an average of 150 people California police killed, most being shot. It is also worth noting that the data indicate a majority of individuals police shoot dead are armed themselves. Putting some perspective on the data, these use of force incidents cited in the report represent a miniscule fraction of the millions of police encounters with civilians in a state of 40 million. In addition, the report noted that six police officers were also killed in violent encounters with civilians in 2016, but despite the deaths of Officer Lunger, Officer Corona, and Officer O'Sullivan cited earlier in the chapter, there has been a steep decline in police officer deaths over the past half century (a drop of 70% since 1970). The steep decline in police deaths has been attributed to officers equipped with improved body armor and more wearing bullet proof vests, advanced trauma care when officers are injured, improved training in de-escalation and the adoption of tasers that assist police in neutralizing physical encounters that could turn deadly.[39]

Law Enforcement Salaries and Benefits

Another significant issue for law enforcement officers has been growing public angst towards them and other government employees concerning generous taxpayer funded salaries and pension benefits. In 2012, City of San Jose voters approved Measure B, a law that would have reformed the city's public pension obligation to city employees, including the police, but a California judge struck down Measure B, and the city re-opened negotiations with the police officer's union after the court ruling. Chuck Reed, the Mayor of San Jose in 2012, fully supported Measure B, and mounted an effort to curtail public pensions of government workers through a proposed statewide Initiative. The Initiative did not qualify for the 2016 election, but Reed and his supporters, vowing to return in 2018, failed once more to place the measure on the ballot.

With police facing greater public scrutiny in how they perform their jobs (cries of *'Defund The Police'* a popular refrain from Progressive Democrats and political groups such as Black Lives Matter in 2021), potential cuts to salaries and benefits, and early retirement (police in California can retire with a healthy pension at age 50) law enforcement agencies are confronting a shortage of applicants. In California, many cities have faced severe budget cuts over the years (which we will address in Chapter 7) that led to reduced salaries for metropolitan police. Both San Jose and Los Angeles have experienced a drop in qualified applicants for their police departments as potential recruits seek more lucrative employment in other areas.

The Politics of Reforming the Police

In August 2019 Governor Gavin Newsom signed AB 392, a law redefining the conditions in which California police are justified in the use of lethal force. The legislation specified two reasons that would justify a deadly use of force by a police officer.

- *To defend against an imminent threat of death or serious bodily injury to the officer or another person.*
- *To apprehend a fleeing felon if the officer reasonably believes that the person will cause death or serious bodily injury to another unless immediately apprehended.*[40]

When AB 392 was being drafted there was both support and opposition to changing the standards of when the deadly use of force could be applied by police. Cheryl Dorsey, having served 20 years as a Los Angeles Police Officer, wrote in support of AB 392, *"If the Legislature passes AB 392, departments across the state will change their policies and training to require officers to avoid shooting people if there are reasonable alternatives. That's not too much to ask."* But Julie Robertson, a Sacramento County Sheriff's Deputy had a different view on altering California law when it came to granting police the right to use lethal force, *"Rather than helping police make better decisions by improving training and clarifying use-of-force policies, AB 392 takes a punitive approach that turns cops into criminals while eroding our fundamental right to defend ourselves."*

In their contrasting views on changing deadly use of force standards for California peace officers, both Cheryl Dorsey and Julie Robertson speak about improving training for law enforcement officers, a reform that police and sheriff's departments consider vital not only to better prepare a recruit for policing, but to increase the diversity of recruits. Under proposed legislation in 2020 by California organizations representing both police chiefs and rank-and-file officers, prospective officers should have to take college classes that would prepare them, *"to meet the expectations of a modern police force."*[41] Under the proposed law, college courses that would be required as part of the police training curriculum would include classes on mental health, psychology, social services and communication. In justifying expanding the curriculum for police training, the groups advocating for these training reforms cited studies showing police officers who lacked a college education accounted for three-fourths of disciplinary actions being taken against them by their departments.[42]

At the Federal Government level, in March 2021, the George Floyd Justice in Policing Act passed in the House of Representatives, creating a number of reforms for police departments across the country. The House legislation would authorize the U.S. Department of Justice to investigate police departments demonstrating a pattern of discrimination and create a national registry to compile data on complaints and records of police misconduct. The proposed law would also make it easier to sue the police by eroding **Qualified Immunity, a legal principle that grants government officials performing discretionary functions immunity from civil suits unless the plaintiff shows that the official violated "clearly established statutory or constitutional rights of which a reasonable person would have known.'** The U.S. Supreme Court, going back to the 1980's has upheld the standard of Qualified Immunity which has shielded police officers from civil lawsuits. In the House legislation, federal law would change so that police officers could be charged for "reckless" conduct, rather than "willful misconduct".[43] Willful misconduct, under current law, is a higher standard to meet in court, making it more difficult to sue a police officer. Whether this bill can be passed in the Senate is unknown given the Filibuster, discussed in Chapter 5, would require 60 votes to get the George Floyd Justice in Policing Act over the finish line and sent to President Biden for signing.

The District Attorney

The voters in each of California's 58 counties elect a **District Attorney, whose primary function is to represent the government in prosecutions against violators of criminal laws.** The District Attorney (DA) determines if there is sufficient evidence against a suspect to warrant prosecution of the individual. DA's are granted discretion in some instances to determine what type of crime a suspect may be charged with; a **felony, which is a more serious offense that can lead to over one year in prison or the death penalty**, or a **misdemeanor, a less serious offense with shorter or no jail time.** Crimes in which DA's can use discretion are known as **Wobblers, criminal violations in which the DA can decide to either bring a felony or misdemeanor charge against the defendant.** In 2014, California voters approved **Proposition 47, a law that reduces non-serious and nonviolent property and drug offenses from felonies to misdemeanors**, thus limiting some of the discretionary authority District Attorneys have in determining what type of charge will be brought against the defendant.

Given the District Attorney is an elected official, decisions to prosecute can be extremely political, especially in high profile cases involving violent crimes like rape or murder. Public outrage of the crime puts pressure on the DA to get a conviction in such cases. DA's also face conflicting pressures when considering criminal charges against a police officer for excessive force. As previously discussed, a rash of police killings of unarmed individuals has compelled District Attorneys to determine whether criminal charges should be filed against police officers involved in the killings. The District Attorney works with county and city law enforcement on a regular basis, making the prosecution of a police officer (depending on the case) a difficult decision for the DA. In cases involving potential criminal charges being filed against a police officer for fatal excessive force, some states allow a **Grand Jury** to conduct the investigation, something that occurred in Ferguson, Missouri which led (based on the Grand Jury's examination of the evidence) to no criminal charges against the police officer who shot and killed Michael Brown in 2014. However, in August, 2015, California Governor Jerry Brown signed legislation that eliminates the ability of a California **Grand Jury** to investigate cases involving alleged excessive use of force by law enforcement which result in the death of a suspect, compelling the county District Attorney to conduct such investigations.[44]

Juries

In California, all 58 counties have **Grand Juries, a body of 11 to 23 members that can determine whether someone is charged (indicted) with committing a crime. California Grand Juries also investigate local governments for possible illegal activities.** Those selected to serve on a Grand Jury in California do so for one year and are culled randomly from a list of citizens eligible to serve on a **Trial Jury. Trial Juries are an impartial body of citizens that sit in judgement of charges brought in either criminal law or civil law cases.** In most cases, Trial Juries consist of 12 members and must return a unanimous verdict of innocent or guilty when rendering a decision. Grand Juries, unlike Trial Juries, do not determine innocence or guilt of a defendant.

In September 2020 Governor Gavin Newsom signed legislation that would expand the jury pool by requiring jury commissioners (county officials who create jury pool lists) to include anyone who files state taxes. Prior to this law being signed by Governor Newsom, jury pools were drawn from the Department of Motor Vehicles driver's license and ID card data base and from county lists of registered voters. State Senator Scott Wiener (D – San Francisco), a sponsor of the legislation, said relying on DMV and voting list data for jury selection skewed the jury pool to white and more affluent Californians. A study done by Political Data, Inc. found that 59 percent of California registered voters are not Latino, Black or Asian. Expanding the jury pool lists to include filers of state taxes would establish greater equity in the criminal justice system, Senator Wiener argued, by creating jury pool lists better reflective of California's demographics in which whites make up just 42% of the overall state population. In 2019, the California Franchise Tax Board processed over 18 million tax returns.[45] That is a lot of potential jurors.

The Public Defender

A 1963 U.S. Supreme Court decision (***Gideon v. Wainwright***) determined that the U.S. Constitution's Sixth Amendment right to legal counsel required that states provide an attorney to defendants charged with a crime who could not afford legal representation. All California counties either have a **Public Defender** office or retain the services of private attorneys to represent those unable to pay for legal counsel. San Francisco County is the only California county that elects a Public Defender, and San Francisco's Public Defender oversees an office of some 100 attorneys with an annual budget of $24 million.[46]

However, in many counties throughout the Golden State, Public Defenders face extremely high caseloads, prompting calls by advocates for equal justice that more state funding be made available to bolster the ranks of attorneys serving those who cannot afford a lawyer. In 2015, one such advocacy group, the American Civil Liberties Union (ACLU), sued Fresno County, claiming the county failed to provide adequate resources to their Public Defender's office, leaving thousands of low-income defendants without proper legal representation over the past six years. The state of California was also included with Fresno County in the ACLU lawsuit.[47]

The Prisons

As mentioned at the beginning of this chapter, the U.S. Supreme Court in 2011 ordered California to reduce its state inmate population by 33,000 due to state prisons operating at an unacceptable 180% of capacity according to the Court. Governor Brown and the Legislature responded with the passage of **AB 109, a 2011 law that transferred responsibility for a population of select criminal offenders from state prisons to county jails. In addition, the law requires that those sentenced to non-serious, non-violent, or non-sex-offenses serve their time in county jails rather than state prisons.** Combined with the aforementioned **Proposition 47**, the 2014 Initiative that reduced some felonies to misdemeanors, and a 2016 voter approved measure (**Proposition 57**) making it easier for those convicted of non-violent felonies to be granted parole, increasing numbers of lower level offenders are either being housed in county jails or released and placed on county probation.

The State Budget and Prison Reform

The California Department of Corrections had consistently taken up roughly 9% of the state budget before AB 109, Proposition 47, and Proposition 57 were enacted. Conventional thinking would be that AB 109, Proposition 47, and Proposition 57 facilitated significant cuts to the Department of Corrections' budget, but that has not been the case. Despite locking up fewer inmates in state prisons, increasing the use of county jails for low level offenders, placing more convicted individuals on county probation, and reducing some felonies to misdemeanors, Governor Newsom's budget for 2020-2021 allocates over $13 billion for corrections, representing an 8.7% portion of the state budget.[48] The explanation in maintaining such funding for corrections in the budget centers on state prisons still incarcerating over 115,000 inmates despite the prison reduction reforms begun in 2011. Also, a 2017 California State Supreme Court decision grants wide authority for state judges to reject shortening sentences for those serving time under the 'Three Strikes' law.[49]

The question remains whether these reforms will reduce the **Recidivism Rate, the rate at which inmates released from state prison returned to state custody.** Based on a 2016 report, the California Department of Corrections determined the Recidivism Rate of adult felons released from state prison was 54%, down from 61% three years earlier.[50]

Another key factor in determining the success of these reforms will be examining crime rates in the Golden State. Based on data from the FBI and the California Department of Justice, California's violent crime rate decreased by 2.9% to 430 violent crimes per 100,000 between 2018 and 2019. However, in 2020, with the pandemic spreading, the homicide rate increased by a disturbing 30%.[51] While it may be premature to make any definitive judgements on these prison reduction reforms, those opposed to early release of California felons (like prosecutors, sheriffs, and conservative lawmakers) will argue the 2020 rise in homicides bolster their position that these reforms threaten public safety. Yet other factors may also contribute to rising crime rates in California, such as strained county and city budgets, which we will examine in chapter 7.

CHAPTER

THE BUDGET AND LOCAL GOVERNMENT

In 1993, a Democratic lawmaker came to the floor of the State Assembly advocating more funding be made available to subsidize low-income housing (shortages of such housing a longstanding problem as pointed out in chapter 1). California was still feeling the effects of the early 1990's recession and the Golden State's unemployment rate doubled the national average. As the Cold War ended, the federal government slashed defense contracts, cut aerospace funding, and closed military bases in California, further damaging the state's economy.[1] In this environment, the State Legislature grappled with providing funding for programs (like low-income housing) with less revenue being available. In response to the Democratic lawmaker's request for more low-income housing funds, Assembly Republican Ross Johnson sarcastically quipped, "How do you propose to pay for it? Do you have a piggybank?"

California was sorely in need of a 'piggybank' when the Great Recession hit in 2008. As bad as things were economically in the early 1990's, the 2008 Great Recession created state budget deficits in the $20, $25, and $30 billion-dollar range. By 2009, state unemployment languished at 12%, and the housing market remained in flux as many California homeowners owed more on their mortgages than their property was worth. By 2017, economic conditions in the state had improved demonstrably, and successive budgets by the Legislature and Governor Jerry Brown between 2013 and 2019 restored funding on education, welfare, and health care after massive cuts to those programs. Yet the state has not adequately addressed fundamental long-term debt resulting from health care and pension obligations to retired and soon to be retired state and local government workers. For example, in reviewing Governor Brown's 2013/2014 budget, Legislative Analyst Mac Taylor noted that the Governor's budget failed to augment the state retirement fund for teachers or save for retiree health care costs, both of which could obligate state taxpayers for years to come.[2]

In response to the Legislative Analyst's concerns, Governor Brown took steps to enhance funding for the two giant state worker retirement programs, the California Public Employees' Retirement System (CalPERS) and the California State Teachers' Retirement System (CalSTRS). In the 2017/2018 budget, Governor Brown borrowed $6 billion from a state fund that invests money state agencies are not using, diverting those monies to CalPERS. Back in 2015, the Governor and Legislature developed a plan to increase contributions to the CalSTRS system by the state, the teachers, and the school districts.[3] But the investment portfolios of these two massive retirement systems are not delivering enough returns to cover the health care and pension obligations of future retired state workers. Governor Brown noted the reality in 2017, *"These retirement liabilities have grown by $51 billion in the last year alone due to poor investment returns and the adoption of more realistic assumptions about future earnings."* Based on 2019 estimates by CalPERS and CalSTRS, California has $245 billion in unfunded liabilities to the two giant state pension programs.[4]

California is not alone in facing economic hardships. Many other states have confronted similar revenue shortfalls, and in 2020 the **federal government only collected enough revenue each month to pay 75% of its expenditures, borrowing the rest**. A popular theme echoed by conservatives is that government needs to live within its means like average Americans do month in and month out. Liberals contend that in tough economic times the rich need to pay their fair share of taxes to ensure government can continue to provide services and programs the people rely on. If only it were that simple. The truth is crafting a $200 billion budget in a state of 39.5 million people is complex and difficult, not just because the economy is unpredictable, but also because of the structural limitations placed on California lawmakers by the state's voters and the federal government.

Developing California's budget each year also has significant implications for local governments who provide many of the services citizens depend on (such as police, fire, welfare, health care, and education). In the recession of the early 1990's, the state's general fund revenues were not sufficient to meet minimum funding obligations to public education imposed by **Proposition 98 (a 1988 voter approved initiative that mandated 40% of the state budget must be allocated to public education)**. To solve the funding shortfall, the state took control of property tax revenues (monies California local governments depended on) and used the revenues to meet the public education funding requirements mandated by Proposition 98.[5] In 1993, as this process was implemented by the State Legislature, California lawmakers were greeted with a chorus of protests in meetings with local government officials concerning the state's raiding of local property taxes. The State Legislature responded to the local government complaints by adding a ½ cent to the state sales tax and sending that money back to the counties for public safety purposes.[6]

Counties are especially vulnerable when it comes to receiving funding for services they provide because over 60% of their funding comes from **Intergovernmental Transfers, funds provided to local governments by the state and federal governments.**[7] Local school districts also rely on intergovernmental transfers for a significant majority of their funding, but Proposition 98 technically ensures them minimum funding by the state. In 2004, California local governments (including counties) were granted some relief from the state raiding their property and sales tax revenue with the passage of **Proposition 1A (a voter approved initiative that prevents the state from taking local tax revenues and compels the state to fund all mandates imposed on local governments by the State Legislature).** Though Proposition 1A protects local government revenues, a provision in the law allows Proposition 1A to be temporarily suspended if a fiscal emergency is declared by the Governor.[8] Cities and Special Districts also rely on intergovernmental transfers.

Compounding the problem in financing California local governments is the state's practice of "borrowing" funds earmarked for local government programs in lean budget years. While Proposition 98 mandates that 40% of the state budget be appropriated for public education, a provision in Proposition 98 allows the state to fund local school districts below the 40% threshold, then reimburse the schools the following fiscal year. In 2011, the state considered withholding $10.4 billion in payments to public schools.[9]

In addition, for the 2011/2012 budget Governor Jerry Brown signed legislation that gutted $1.7 billion from the 400 **Redevelopment Agencies created by California cities. These agencies were designed to improve "blighted" areas of a city by allowing a developer to build such things as shopping malls, office buildings, entertainment facilities, sports stadiums, and convention centers.** The way Redevelopment Agencies are funded is through the selling of bonds. The funds generated are used to redevelop blighted areas of a city. Once the projects are completed, the increased property tax revenue does not go to schools and other local governments, but instead is retained by the Redevelopment Agencies to pay off the bonds initially sold to finance the project.[10]

Anticipating Governor Brown's move, several California cities shifted money from their Redevelopment Agencies into other city government entities to prevent the state from taking the monies. Sacramento transferred $1.4 million from Redevelopment, Los Angeles used a series of contracts and loans to shelter $1 billion in Redevelopment money from the state, and Santa Clara moved $205 million from its Redevelopment Agency to other city departments in hopes of preserving the funds for a new football stadium for the San Francisco 49ers. Governor Brown's administration threatened legal action to prevent these cities from sheltering such Redevelopment funds.[11] The cities and Redevelopment agencies pursued litigation as well, suing in court to stop the state from seizing the $1.7 billion.[12] In December 2011, the California State Supreme Court ruled the state could legally abolish the Redevelopment Agencies and claim the $1.7 billion.

As these examples illustrate, the state budget tremendously impacts not only the millions of Californians depending on services provided by the state, but California local governments as well. This chapter will address **the budget process, state revenues, state expenditures, ballot box budgeting, federal government grants, and the basic structure of California local government.**

THE BUDGET PROCESS

As mentioned in Chapter 4, California's fiscal year begins July 1st and runs until the following June 30th and every budget the state operates under covers this time period. With that said, the planning of any California state budget begins 18 months prior to the July 1st enactment date. The early stages of preparing the budget involve state government department administrators, agency staff, and the Governor's **Department of Finance**. During this 12-month period, the **Department of Finance (the executive branch department responsible for compiling the budget proposal the Governor will deliver to the State Legislature by January 10th of each year)** reviews the budget funding requests by all the state departments and agencies. Like any government bureaucracy, funding requests from these departments and agencies during projected lean budget years will be (at a minimum) the level of funding they are currently receiving. When state revenues are projected to rise, department and agency administrators will lobby for increased funding.

The Governor's January Budget Proposal and the May Revise

Once the Department of Finance has completed this detailed process, the Governor, as required by a 1922 constitutional amendment, must submit a proposed budget to the State Legislature by January 10. The Governor's proposal in January is based on the best estimates of projected state revenues, but such estimates may be inaccurate. Governor Arnold Schwarzenegger experienced both scenarios during his governorship. In 2006, state revenues were $7.5 billion greater than estimated in January. The 2008 budget proposal was a different story as state revenues ended up $6 billion less than Governor Schwarzenegger projected in January.[13] In January 2011, the news was all bad for newly elected Governor Jerry Brown, and in his budget proposal he warned that the $13 billion in cuts he was proposing would be doubled to $26 billion if state sales and income tax rates (set to expire on July 1, 2011) were not extended. Governor Brown was optimistic he could convince Republican lawmakers to extend the tax rates (he needed two Republican votes in the State Assembly and State Senate to extend the tax rates). The Republicans refused.

In April 2021, according to Department of Finance, California collected approximately $137 billion, some 14% more than projected. California collected $15 billion more in revenue than it expected, and Governor Gavin Newsom is using some of that surplus revenue to send $600 payments to assist low-income Californians struggling during the pandemic and offer $2 billion in grants for businesses hurt by COVID-19.[14]

Proposing budgets is not an exact science, but California Governors will have a better idea about state revenues by May. The April 15th state income tax receipts have been calculated and now the Governor will release the **May Revise, an amended version of the Governor's January budget proposal.** As already discussed, the revenue available can be greater or less than what the Governor projected in January. In 2011, the May Revise projected rosier revenue projections than Governor Brown anticipated in January. However, the increased revenue projections only emboldened the Republican lawmakers in both houses of the State Legislature to reject Governor Brown's request to extend state sales and income tax rates set to expire July 1.

Revenue totals can be altered after the May Revise. For example, the 2017/2018 budget was adjusted upwards after additional revenues materialized from spring tax receipts in June 2017, allowing Governor Brown to approve an additional $1 billion in spending by the Legislature than what he had originally proposed.[15] In 2020, Governor Newsom, facing an economic slump due to the pandemic, issued a revised budget in May slashing $19 billion from what he had proposed spending in January. With rosier revenues developing in the Spring of 2021, and California set to receive $150 billion from the massive $1.9 trillion COVID-19 relief package passed by Congressional Democrats and signed by President Joe Biden, Governor Newsom's 2021 May Revise should be able to fund state spending beyond what the Governor proposed in January for the 2021/2022 budget.

The Legislature Passing the Budget by June 15

After the May Revise, the State Legislature is required to approve the budget by **June 15,** and the California Constitution requires that the State Legislature pass a **balanced budget (a budget in which government expenditures do not exceed government revenues)**. Over the years the June 15 deadline was constantly ignored by the State Legislature, causing budgets that should have been in place by July 1 to not be approved until August or September. The 2010/2011 budget was not passed until September 2010, well over two months late. There was no significant penalty imposed on the Legislature for failing to meet the June 15 deadline until voters approved in 2010 **Proposition 25**. Prior to Proposition 25, a two-thirds vote was required by both houses of the State Legislature to approve the budget, and this extraordinary majority vote was partly responsible for the Legislature's inability to pass budgets on time. **Proposition 25 allows the Legislature to approve the budget with a simple majority vote (50% plus 1)**. As discussed in Chapter 5, Proposition 25 also penalizes the State Legislature for failing to meet the June 15 deadline by forfeiting their pay for every day the budget is late. In 2011, each member of the State Legislature lost some $4000 in pay because the budget was not approved until late June.

The Governor's Budget Authority – The Line Item Veto

Once the State Legislature passes the budget, it is sent to the Governor. At this point, the Governor can exercise his budget authority through the use of the **Line-Item Veto, which allows the Governor to reduce or eliminate expenditure items throughout the budget bill.** The Legislature can override any Line-Item Veto with a two-thirds vote of the State Assembly and State Senate, but override votes are virtually impossible to obtain given Democrats and Republicans in the State Legislature would usually have to join forces to achieve such an override vote. In the 2017/2018 budget, Governor Brown, for the second year in a row, did not utilize his Line-Item Veto powers, authorizing all of the Legislature's spending. With Democrats in 2017 enjoying two-thirds super majorities in both houses of the Legislature, Governor Brown decided not to tempt fate and risk the Legislature potentially over-ridding a Line-Item Veto.

However, despite Governor Brown's reluctance to utilize the Line-Item Veto in 2016 and 2017, and his successor Governor Gavin Newsom following suit in 2019 and 2020, the Governor's initial January budget proposal and the May Revise are scrutinized by local governments, corrections officials, state government department administrators, contractors doing business with the state, education administrators, and the Legislature (to name a few) because they all understand the Governor's power under the Line-Item Veto. In the Governor's budget proposals, a clear message is being sent (based on revenue projections) on the amount of funding the Governor is willing to allocate for each area in the budget. In passing the budget, if the Legislature attempts to fund programs in excess of what the Governor proposed in January and May, the Line-Item Veto allows the Governor to slash the excess funding.

Prior to Governor Brown and Governor Newsom, the past three Governors employed the Line-Item Veto extensively, Governor Pete Wilson trimming $1.9 billion in 1998, Governor Gray Davis rejecting $1.8 billion in 2000, and Governor Arnold Schwarzenegger slashing $1.8 billion in 2009.[16] Some of Governor Schwarzenegger's spending cuts in 2009 included funding for the elderly, children's health care programs, and AIDS prevention and treatment, resulting in a lawsuit being filed by the St. John's Well Child and Family Center and other public service organizations over the Governor's use of the Line-Item Veto.[17] Governor Schwarzenegger's Line-Item Veto authority was upheld in court.

It should be noted, though, that the Line-Item Veto only allows the Governor to **reduce spending in the budget,** not increase spending. Another important fact about the Governor's Line-Item Veto power is that this type of veto can only be used by the Governor on the budget.

Budget Trailer Bills

When the Governor signs the budget, included are a number of **Trailer Bills, legislation implementing changes to state law in order to enact the budget.** In 2014, a trailer bill limiting the amount of financial reserves a public school district can save was approved, and a 2015 trailer bill allowed the State Water Resources Control Board to mandate consolidation of local water agencies if one water agency was failing to provide an adequate supply of safe drinking water.[18] Similar to the gut-and-amend procedure utilized by the Legislature prior to 2017 (discussed in Chapter 5), last minute amendments can be inserted into budget trailer bills with no public review, though because of the voter approved Initiative in 2016 (Proposition 54), they must be in print for 72 hours before approved by the Legislature.

In 2017, trailer bills were passed lengthening the timeline of Recall elections (something that could help Governor Newsom if his Recall election takes place later in 2021), widening the category of people banned from owning guns, and granting unions the ability to converse with recently hired government employees.[19] Unlike most other pieces of legislation, budget trailer bills can't be rejected by voters through a Referendum. Once the Governor signs the budget and the accompanying budget trailer bills, the enacted state budget covers spending for the fiscal year from July 1 to the following June 30. Let us now consider why approving the California budget has been such a difficult process over the years.

STATE REVENUES

Nearly 80% of revenues the state collects each year come from **Personal Income Tax and Sales Tax.** Though California's economy recovered from the 2008 Great Recession (unemployment dropped to 4.7% in 2017), the stock market remained volatile, despite record post-recession gains, dropping some 500 points one day in August of 2015. COVID-19 lockdowns in 2020 drove Golden State unemployment numbers up, but despite gloomy projections for massive revenue shortages (estimated to create a $54 billion hole in the state budget and prompting Governor Newsom to propose $19 billion in spending cuts in his 2020 May Revise budget proposal, the Governor signed a $202.1 billion budget on June 30, 2020. The Governor and State Legislature avoided some of the pain Governor Newsom laid out in the May Revise by delaying the cuts contingent on the Federal Government providing relief through a COVID-19 funding bill known as the Heroes Act.

But a pleasant surprise materialized six months later in January 2021 with the state discovering tax revenues were generating a $15 billion surplus. The reason for revenues moving into the black despite the pandemic-driven recession centered on high-income earners continuing to make money through employment and a sizzling stock market that seemed unfazed by COVID-19. State revenues can fall when unemployment grows and the stock market tumbles, but the unemployed workers hit hardest by the pandemic were in industries not conducive to working at home. Those who have been able to maintain employment by working at home and those generating income from stocks and property were not negatively impacted by the pandemic. Since these income earners continued making money, the income tax windfall developed.

It should be noted that income tax is not limited to employees, but also includes those who make money in stocks and property. These income-earners pay what is known as a **Capital Gains Tax, a tax levied by the state and federal government on the selling of stocks and property**. Over the years, the state has come to rely more and more on income tax revenue, and in 2021 California income tax accounted for 67% of the state's estimated $158 billion general fund budget for fiscal year 2021/2022.[20]

Income Tax

As discussed in Chapter 4, California utilizes a **Progressive Income Tax (the percentage of tax increases as income increases)** on income earners in the Golden State. Income tax increases, approved by Californians with the passage of **Proposition 30 in 2012**, now place the top income tax rate for those making over $1 million at 13.3%. Governor Jerry Brown attempted to convince

Republican lawmakers to prevent income tax rates from dropping (as specified by the law in 2011) to help close the 2011/2012 $26 billion budget hole, but State Assembly and Senate Republicans were not interested in voting to maintain the higher rates or in allowing California voters the opportunity to vote on retaining the taxes. These Republican lawmakers pointed to figures from the non-partisan **Legislative Analyst Office (LAO)** indicating that taxpayers with incomes over $200,000 a year contribute 50% of all state income taxes despite the fact that these income earners represent only 3% of the state's income taxpayers. In contrast, the LAO report also noted that taxpayers earning below $50,000 a year pay only 10% of all state income taxes even though they comprise 70% of the state's taxpayers.

As already highlighted, state income tax is the largest revenue generating source for California, representing two- thirds of total state revenues annually. With the state dependent on such a small minority of taxpayers bearing a large burden of the income tax, solutions for generating more revenue can't be exclusively centered on the populist theme of "soaking the rich", according to Republican lawmakers. However, despite Republican opposition to state income tax increases, **Proposition 30** passed, and, as a result, all those earning over $250,000 in the state saw their income taxes rise. Those in the state who believe the wealthy need to pay their fair share supported extending these income tax increases on the affluent for another twelve years, which the voters did in the 2016 election.

Sales Tax

The second largest revenue source for California is the sales tax, representing roughly 20% of the revenue pie, and like the state income tax, the sales tax dropped on July 1, 2011 from **8.25% to 7.25%.** Governor Jerry Brown wanted to maintain the 8.25% rate, but Republican lawmakers refused to budge on their no tax increase ideology. After the 2011/2012 budget was passed without the income and sales taxes extensions, Republican State Senator Doug LaMalfa reiterated the significance of defeating Governor Brown and Democratic lawmakers in their attempt to generate $11 billion through the tax extensions, *"Republicans, through their steadfast commitment to the taxpayers, have prevented another massive tax increase."*[21]

Senator LaMalfa and his fellow Republican lawmakers were certainly looking out for income taxpayers making over $200,000 a year given the huge share of the income tax they pay, but when it comes to protecting the average Californian from the higher sales tax, the reality is the sales tax cut did not have much of an impact. The one cent sales tax cut lowered the price of an item costing

$400 by $4, an $800 item lowered the cost $8, and on an item costing $1000, the sales tax cut saved the customer $10. Asked about the drop in sales tax, Scott Denny, owner of Hughes Ski Hut in Chico, California said, *"We haven't had a single customer talk about it at all. I don't know if they're unaware or if they don't care."*[22]

Proposition 30, approved by the voters in 2012, increased state sales tax by ¼ cent for four years, but the sales tax increase expired in 2017, lowering the state's sales tax rate to **7.25%,** however sales tax can be higher than the state-wide 7.25% rate in parts of California where sales tax rate increases have been approved by voters at the local government level. For example, voters in San Jose, Newark, and East Palo Alto all approved sales tax hikes in 2016. Adding these local government sales taxes, the average sales tax in California is 8.11%, with some California cities reaching as high as 10%.[23]

One reform that has been considered to augment state revenue is applying the sales tax to services, not just products. Estimates by the **State Board of Equalization,** the **agency overseeing sales tax,** conclude that applying sales tax to services (like a round of golf, haircuts, etc.) at the current state sales tax rate would add $122 billion in monies for state and local governments.[24] Steve Westly, former State Controller from 2003-2007 (the State Controller super-vises all state and local government tax collection) supports the idea of taxing services, *"We need to follow the lead of a growing number of US states that tax service industries. In an information age, taxing goods alone is outdated and inadequate."* Westley would not stop there. He would support California adopting New York City's taxing of sugar saturated drinks and follow what 34 other states do by taxing oil extraction.[25]

The State Use Tax

Technically, if a consumer in California buys a product online, they are sup-posed to report the purchase and pay a **Use Tax, a sales tax on an item pur-chased online and delivered to the consumer.** However, California has no tax collecting infrastructure in place to compel the consumer to pay the use tax, and most Californians don't know about it. Facing huge deficits, and an inability to maintain the 2009 tax rates, Governor Jerry Brown and Democratic lawmakers approved as part of the 2011/2012 budget a provision requiring online mer-chants (like retail giant Amazon.com) to collect sales tax on goods purchased online by Californians.[26] The state is anticipating the online sales tax revenue will generate $200 million annually.[27] Amazon.com initially responded with hostility, threatening a lawsuit against the state and the possibility of financ-ing a Referendum campaign challenging the law. A compromise was reached between Amazon.com and the state with the retailer agreeing to collect the tax.

In 2019, giant online retailers like Amazon and eBay were required to collect California use tax on behalf of smaller cyber retailers that conducted business through Amazon and eBay platforms. The law, passed by the State Legislature and signed by Governor Newsom, was designed to compel online behemoths like Amazon and eBay, who have been paying the state use tax since 2012, to collect it from out of state third party sellers using Amazon and eBay web- sites. Prior to the law passing in 2019, these small out of state retailers bene- fited by avoiding the use tax and maintaining a price advantage over California companies.[28] California State Treasurer Fiona Ma (the State Treasurer ensures state revenues are appropriated to fund state programs) supported the law say- ing, *"This new law will close this major loophole by mandating that all online retailers collect and remit all the state and local sales taxes due and level the playing field between our brick-and-mortar businesses in our state."*

Other Taxes and Fees

California also taxes corporations, insurers, gambling, liquor, tobacco, gas and automobile registration. The state has increased "sin taxes" on such things as liquor, tobacco, and gambling over the years, and in 2016 California voters approved a $2 tax increase on tobacco products. Governor Brown and the State Legislature used nearly half of the new tobacco tax revenue ($465 million) to fund the growing number of Californians eligible for **Medi-Cal, the state's health care program for the poor**. The State Legislature, in 2017, with a two-thirds vote, also increased the gas tax to grow revenue streams for state transportation infrastructure.

BALLOT BOX BUDGETING – REVENUES

Proposition 13 – 1978

In the discussion of state revenues, Governor Jerry Brown and Democratic law- makers failed to convince a single State Assembly or State Senate Republican to approve extending income and sales tax rates during the 2011/2012 budget delib- erations. The reason Democrats needed Republican support to extend the taxes is **Proposition 13, the 1978 ballot initiative that not only lowered property taxes for California property owners, but also included a provision requiring a two-thirds vote by both houses of the State Legislature to increase taxes.** After the 2016 election, Democrats achieved a two-thirds majority in the State Assembly and State Senate, achieving the vote threshold required under Propo- sition 13 to raise gasoline taxes in 2017, and Democrats retained that two-thirds supermajority in both chambers of the Legislature in 2020.

Proposition 26 – 2010

California voters approved an initiative in 2010 that will make it more difficult for the State Legislature to increase certain **Fees (regulatory charges levied by the State on oil manufacturers, businesses that treat hazardous materials, and alcohol retailers)**. With the passage of Proposition 26, a two-thirds vote of both the State Assembly and State Senate will be required to increase these types of fees. In July 2011 Governor Jerry Brown signed legislation creating a **new fee** for California rural homeowners who will be compelled to pay the state $150 per year to cover state firefighting services provided to them. The new fee did not fall under the provisions of Proposition 26, but taxpayer groups threatened to sue the state claiming the fee is actually a tax and required a two-thirds vote of the Legislature instead of the simple majority vote (50% plus 1) it received.[29] Given the devastating wildfires of 2018 and 2020 discussed in Chapter 1, California rural homeowners would appear to have received much more service from the firefighters than they paid for.

Proposition 30 – 2012

In Governor Brown's 2012/2013 budget, it factored in passage of Proposition 30 by the voters, an initiative that would increase the state sales tax by ¼ cent for four years and increase personal income tax on annual earnings over $250,000 for seven years. Governor Brown's 2012/2013 budget also featured a Plan B if Proposition 30 failed, which entailed automatic spending reductions (known as trigger cuts) that would have slashed state spending in public education by $6 billion. Governor Brown went on a statewide campaign, visiting college campuses and K-12 schools imploring voters to pass Proposition 30. Millions of dollars were also poured into the Proposition 30 campaign by both supporters and opponents of the measure. In the end, voters approved Proposition 30, and (as mentioned) in 2016 extended the personal income tax increases for another twelve years.

STATE EXPENDITURES

Public Education

The single largest expenditure in California's state budget is public education, annually accounting for 50% of the spending. Public education funding covers approximately 5.5 million children in 1000 locally controlled K-12 school districts, 2.6 million Community College students, 450,000 students through the California State University System (CSU), and 216,000 University of California (UC) students. These education institutions are immense and state lawmakers, be they Democrat or Republican, realize the importance of maintaining funding levels to ensure these institutions remain solvent. As discussed in Chapter 1, K-12 funding in the 2011/2012 budget was preserved, but mid-year cuts would have been automatically triggered if the $4 billion in anticipated extra revenue Governor Jerry Brown and legislative Democrats relied on failed to materialize. Those mid-year cuts could have shortened the K-12 school year by a week. In the 2011/2012 budget, California's Community Colleges took a $400 million hit, and CSU and UC both sustained $650 million in cuts. Deeper mid-year cuts into higher education, along with tuition increases, would have taken effect if Proposition 30 had not passed in 2012. Improved economic conditions prior to COVID-19 hitting in 2020 led to the augmentation of public education funding for both K-12 and higher education with K-12 and community colleges receiving an additional $3.1 billion in funding for the 2017/2018 budget.

The 2020/2021 budget deferred some payments to K-12 schools given the projected $54 billion in deficits the state was facing because of the pandemic. State colleges and universities were not so fortunate, facing cuts of up to 10%. But as noted, the $15 billion in surplus revenues that materialized in 2021 resulted in the State Legislature approving a series of stimulus bills that provided $6.6 billion to assist K-12 schools in re-opening for in person instruction. Another of the stimulus bills restored some $857 million in cuts endured by the CSU and the UC higher education institutions.[30]

Health and Human Services

Roughly 30 percent of the budget is taken up with Health and Human Services, which accounts for the health care and welfare programs provided by the state. Currently, ten million Californians qualify for **Medi-Cal, the State health care program for the poor.**[31] The 2011/2012 budget increased co-pays for Medi-Cal patients as part of the spending reductions, however the growing number of residents eligible for Medi-Cal created a funding problem for the state, something Governor Brown and the Legislature dealt with by approving a significant chunk of the 2016 voter approved tobacco tax for the expanding health care program. Concerning Cal-Works, the state welfare program, the amount of time an adult may receive state assistance was reduced from 5 years to 4 years, and monthly cash grants to welfare recipients were slashed by 8% in the 2011/2012 state budget.[32] Frustrated advocates for the poor claim the state did not effectively replenish these cuts despite improved economic conditions.

In his 2021/2022 budget, Governor Newsom is proposing $122 billion for the Medi-Cal program, but it should be noted that a significant portion of this funding is not part of the State's General Fund but comes from Special Funds that are separate from the General Fund. Cal-Works is set to receive

$5.3 billion, and there is $2.6 billion set aside for homeless programs, including Project Homekey (discussed in Chapter 1). Governor Newsom's 2021/2022 budget also provides money to deal with responding to the Pandemic, including $370 million for the Vaccine Distribution Task Force and $2 billion in statewide testing efforts.[33]

Corrections

The third largest item in the California budget is corrections (the prison system), comprising 8% of the state's expenditures annually. As discussed in Chapter 6, California's prison population had swelled to 180% of prison capacity, prompting the U.S. Supreme Court to order California to reduce its' prison population by 33,000 inmates by 2013. Responding to this crisis, Governor Jerry Brown proposed, and the Legislature passed a prison realignment bill that would send some 40,000 nonviolent state inmates to local jails. However, local governments (particularly the counties who house the majority of criminals in county jails) were skeptical about the state's ability to fund the transfer of the inmates, which would require nearly $1 billion in state support the first year and $700 million annually in future years.[34] Governor Brown and Democratic lawmakers needed to increase state vehicle and sales taxes to pay for the prison realignment. In order for this plan to work, it was imperative California voters approved increasing the taxes in 2012, which they did.

COVID-19, coupled with the changing sentencing and parole laws covered in Chapter 6, have resulted in a significant reduction in the state prison population. The inmate population in California's 35 prisons fell 21% since the onset of the pandemic. According to the Legislative Analysts Office, California could save in excess of $1 billion with the closing of eight state prisons, and in 2020 plans were already drawn up to close two correctional facilities.[35]

Other State Expenditures

The remainder of the budget, a scant 10%, is left for funding the Legislative, Executive, and Judicial branches of California's government. In addition, environmental protection, business, transportation, housing, state and consumer services, labor development, and general government are also included in the remaining 10%. As is evidenced by the breakdown of California's budget, slashing programs other than education, health care, welfare, and corrections won't necessarily solve the revenue problems plaguing the Golden State in lean budget years. Also, cutting into California's bigger ticket budget items is not so easily achieved.

BALLOT BOX BUDGETING – EXPENDITURES

Proposition 98 – 1988

Proposition 98, the 1988 ballot initiative that mandates **40%** of the state budget be spent on public education was a response to property tax cutting Proposition 13, passed in 1978. Cutting property taxes was fantastic for California property owners, but much of that property tax revenue went to the local schools, and when that revenue dried up, California public schools were left with huge financial challenges. Proposition 98 guaranteed minimum funding requirements for Kindergarten through Community College, and this has been a tremendous boost for public education in the Golden State, but going into every budget, state lawmakers understand 40% of the budget is already decided.

Proposition 42 – 2002

This voter approved initiative requires all gasoline sales tax revenues be spent on mass transit, roads, and highways. Moving 39.5 million people around California is no easy task, and in Chapter 1 we discussed the challenges of building effective transportations systems for future generations. It can be argued that locking in monies generated from gasoline sales tax for transportation is sound policy, but it is another example of limiting what the State Legislature can do when attempting to hammer out a budget.

Proposition 2 – 2014

Proposition 2 requires that the state set aside a portion of revenues each year to pay down state debt and augment a reserve fund that can be tapped into during lean budget years. While the state budget in theory must be balanced, the budget does not include public pension funds paid to retired state employees (discussed earlier in this chapter) that total some $50 billion annually. In years when revenues to the state are strong, Proposition 2 requires a minimum of $800 million up to $2 billion be set aside to pay down state debt, and that a minimum of $800 million to $2 billion be set aside in a "rainy day fund" for future years when revenues to the state are down.[36] Approved by the voters in 2014, this proposition, while a prudent measure given the state's debt problem and unpredictable revenue streams year in and year out, does limit options for lawmakers when crafting the budget each year. Governor Brown was committed to bolstering the reserve fund, which after the 2017/2018 budget totals $8.5 billion.[37]

The reserve fund continued to grow, reaching $18 billion by 2018, but when the pandemic arrived in 2020, Governor Newsom and the State Legislature, confronting a potential $54 billion budget hole, tapped into the reserve fund to the tune of $9.6 billion.[38] In his 2021/2022 budget proposal, Governor Newsom plans to replenish the reserve fund, adding $3 billion for 2021/2022 and nearly $6.5 billion over the next three years.

FEDERAL FUNDS AND THE STRINGS ATTACHED

In looking at the California budget, a popular refrain from fed up taxpayers is: *"Cut the welfare!" "Cut the environmental protection programs!" "Cut the free health care!"* Many of the programs California funds are set up as **Matching Funds, a financial agreement between two levels of government by which one level agrees to provide specific amounts of money for a program, activity, or project if the other will provide specific amounts of money for the same purpose.** Many of the programs California funds in the budget (be they education, health care, welfare, law enforcement, transportation, environmental protection, and more) are **matched** by federal government dollars. If the California State Legislature cuts funding in federal matching fund programs, the state loses federal dollars because the federal funding is tied to the state's financial commitment to the program. It is estimated today that for every dollar California sends to Washington, the federal government returns 96 cents. California lawmakers, when making budget cutting decisions, have to take into account how the cuts will impact the amount of federal dollars the state receives. In the 1980's President Reagan, in an attempt to reduce nonmilitary federal spending, tried to reduce or cancel federal matching dollar programs with the states, but the states resisted.[39]

The Trump Administration, The Biden Administration and Federal Funding in California

When asked in interviews about California becoming a sanctuary state (limiting cooperation with federal immigration authorities in identifying undocumented immigrants for potential deportation), President Trump responded accordingly, *"California is in many ways out of control. We give them a hell of a lot of money."* When pressed on potentially defunding the state, the President suggested, *"It's a weapon. If they're going to have sanctuary cities, we may have to do that."*[40] However, most of the $367 billion the federal government annually spends in California applies to Social Security, Medicare, and Medi-Cal; and a 1987 U.S. Supreme Court decision allowing the federal government to withhold highway funds from states that did not change their drinking age to 21 clearly stipulated a link exist between the state policy in question and the withholding of the federal dollars.[41]

What realistically could have been defunded in California by the Trump administration involved federal law enforcement grants given to the states, such as the Justice Assistance Grant Program (JAG). JAG money is used for corrections and victim programs but is also applied to the purchasing of lethal weapons, drones, and riot gear for state and local law enforcement in the Golden State. Another federal funding program for law enforcement is the State Criminal Alien Assistance Program (SCAAP). SCAAP offers federal reimbursements to local jails that detain undocumented immigrants who have been convicted of a felony or at least two misdemeanors. In return, local law enforcement will inform federal immigration officials they have someone eligible for possible deportation.[42] In excess of $50 million was distributed to California county sheriffs in federal SCAAP money in 2016. In response to President Trump's threats to curtail funding for law enforcement grants, California's Attorney General, Xavier Becerra, announced in August 2017 that the state had filed yet another lawsuit against the Trump administration, this one challenging the constitutionality of withholding federal funding for state and local law enforcement.

Four years later, in 2021, things have changed, and California is posed to receive billions from the Federal Government's $1.9 trillion COVID-19 relief bill President Joe Biden made a top priority to get through Congress. The gigantic spending package includes for California $15 billion for K-12 school re-openings, $4.6 billion for transit systems, nearly $1 billion for airports, and billions for vaccine distribution and coronavirus testing and tracing; to name a few things in the estimated $150 billion ticketed for the Golden State from the Federal Government.[43] They say elections have consequences. They are right.

THE COMPLEXITIES OF ADOPTING THE CALIFORNIA BUDGET

While the California Legislature has endured poor public approval ratings for their handling of the budget over the years, the system they operate under makes budget solutions difficult to achieve. Increasing taxes to generate more revenue requires a two-thirds vote of both the State Assembly and State Senate. Funding programs beyond what the Governor is willing to accept can be wiped out through the Line-Item Veto. Cutting education, the biggest part of the budget, is not feasible because the law requires 40% of the budget must go to public education. Slashing other programs can lead to the loss of federal matching funds. In poor economic times, with shrinking revenues, these structural roadblocks make the approved budgets passing the Legislature half baked solutions that kick the can down the road but do little to ensure future financial solvency for the state.

To be sure, there has been some progress made with the creation of a reserve fund and making it easier for the Legislature to approve the budget. However, depending on a tax system in which a tiny minority of wealthy earners provide the lion's share of income tax revenue is risky, especially when a recession hits (like the one in 2008) and the stock market takes a dive and property values drop. It also remains an open question if the economy will make a full recovery from the pandemic by the end of 2021.

Politicians on both sides of the aisle don't seem interested in compromising. Partisan districts (that skew heavily Republican or Democratic) discourage lawmakers from negotiating with the other party on the budget, and as both sides dig in, the ability to reach a deal diminishes. The 2011/2012 budget was an example of this. Anti-tax groups demanded that Republican lawmakers not give in to any tax extensions or increases. Public union groups expected Democrats to maintain protections of pension and health care benefits for state and local government employees. The end-product was a budget that gambled on more revenues materializing in future years, which fortunately occurred. When lawmakers refuse to compromise, the voters are asked to make budget policy through the previous discussed propositions.

California's $200 billion budget is also critically important for California's local governments that depend on funding from the state for many of their functions. California's 58 counties and 480 cities, along with all the school and special districts throughout the state, are the bodies of government that administer most of the services to Californians. The complexity of the state budget makes it extremely difficult for these local government entities to adopt their own budgets given the year-to-year uncertainty of the California state budget. Let us now examine how these local governments operate in California.

CALIFORNIA COUNTY GOVERNMENT

California has 58 counties, and county borders are set by the State Legislature. In 1850, the year California became a state, the State Legislature adopted 27 counties. The 58th county, Imperial County, was created in 1907, and the state has added no new counties since then. California's counties provide numerous services such as:

- Providing police and fire protection
- Maintaining roads and bridges
- Administering the welfare programs
- Conducting all elections
- Tax collection
- Maintaining county records (deeds, wills, licenses, etc.)
- Administers the operation of California's Superior Courts

Californians that live in **unincorporated areas of the state (areas which are under no city jurisdiction)** rely on the counties to provide services to them.

General Law Counties

Most of California's counties are known as **General Law Counties (counties that operate according to general laws passed by the State Legislature).** These general laws include the elected officers of the county, the structure of county government, what county services must be provided, and how taxes can be levied.

Charter Counties

An amendment to California's Constitution in 1911 (known as the Home Rule Amendment) allowed for the creation of **Charter Counties (counties that are granted more flexibility in the governing structure of their county).** These charters act like mini constitutions for the county. While flexibility is allowed in setting up the government in a charter county, the state requires all charter counties provide for an elected County Board of Supervisors and an elected Sheriff.

County Board of Supervisors

The governing body for each county is the **County Board of Supervisors.** These elected county officials adopt the county budget (determining how much money will be spent on the services the county provides). In addition, the County Board Supervisors sets the land use policies for property under their jurisdiction. Five members are elected to serve on the County Board of Supervisors in all of California's counties except **San Francisco**. In San Francisco, which is the only combined county and city government in the state, 11 Board of Supervisors are elected by San Francisco voters. An attempt was undertaken in 2017 to add two seats to the Los Angeles County Board of Supervisors and create an elected county executive. State Senator Tony Mendoza proposed the change, attempting to convince the Legislature to place it on the 2018 ballot as a state constitutional amendment for the voters to decide, something that did not fly.[44] But one has to wonder why a resident of Humboldt County should vote on the composition of government in Los Angeles County.

CALIFORNIA MUNICIPAL GOVERNMENT

Similar to counties, municipal governments provide such services as:

- Law Enforcement
- Fire Protection
- Water Service
- Sewer Maintenance
- Leaf Pickup
- Recreation Service

There are 480 cities operating in California, and if a community wants to become a city they must go through the process of **Incorporation (the method provided by the State Legislature for California communities to become a legal city).** Citizens in a California community seeking incorporation must submit a petition to **LAFCO (The Local Agency Formation Commission established by the State Legislature in 1963).** Each county has its own LAFCO agency consisting of 5 members (2 County Board of Supervisors, 2 representatives of incorporated cities within the county, and a public member selected by the other LAFCO officials). If LAFCO approves the incorporation request, the citizens in the proposed community will vote on whether or not to incorporate and become a legal city. Like county governments, municipal governments are either **General Law Cities or Charter Cities**.

General Law Cities

A majority of cities in California are **General Law Cities (operating based on general laws created by the State Legislature).** Incorporated cities with populations under 3500 must begin their existence as general law cities. All general law cities are required to maintain a **General Plan (a document that guides**

the city's future physical development in such areas as land use, expansion, infrastructure goals, and environmental preservation).

Charter Cities

Slightly over 100 California cities have become **Charter Cities (cities that are granted more flexibility in organizing their government).** A city can become a charter city by having the city council or a specially elected board draft a charter. The proposed charter is submitted to the city voters, and a majority vote approves the charter.

Council/Manager System

Smaller populated California cities adopt a **Council/Manager System of government.** In this system, the City Council is part time and they hire a City Manager and other professionally trained staffers to run the day to day operations of the city. A Mayor is chosen among the City Council members, but the position is mostly ceremonial, and the Mayor has no more authority than the other City Council members.

Mayor/Council System

Most heavily populated California cities have adopted the **Mayor/Council System of government.** Under this system the Mayor is elected separate from the City Council. Some of these Mayors have veto authority over the City Council, separate budget authority, and the ability to appoint city government officials. In larger populated cities, both the Mayor and the City Council are full time positions.

Municipal Governing

California City Councils are the governing body for their cities with the Mayor in some larger cities also possessing governing authority. The City Council adopts the budget, approves the General Plan, and makes land use decisions on property within the city's jurisdiction.

SPECIAL DISTRICTS

California has approximately 4000 **Special Districts (local government bodies created to provide a specific service in such areas as recreation, water, sewer, garbage collection, and education).** In California, some 1000 public school districts exist in addition to the 4000 special districts providing services in other areas. Special district board members are either governed by the County Board of Supervisors or elected by the voters living within the special district's jurisdiction.[45] Funding for many of these special districts comes from tax assessments levied on property owners living within the jurisdiction of the special district.

FINAL THOUGHTS ON CALIFORNIA IN THE AMERICAN SYSTEM

Politics, the process by which decisions get made, can be extremely frustrating to the American public concerning the laws, policies, and regulations developed by the federal government, and the state and local governments. This book has examined how California government operates and co-exists under the system of Federalism crafted by the U.S. Constitution. There are distinct differences between how California and the federal government exercise power and authority over the people they govern, and how democracy works in both systems.

As the Golden State grapples with pressing issues like immigration, affordable housing, health care, the environment, education, pension debt for state workers, and reviving the economy in the COVID-19 era, an ongoing debate rages-on about the proper purpose of government. Such debates are healthy in a democracy, and a free press (sometimes referred to as the fourth branch of government) is instrumental in fostering the public dialogue. Yet, the growth of **Fake News, Internet hoaxes or intentionally made-up stories offered as news and intended to sway public opinion**, is both a political and economic opportunity to subvert democratic institutions (such as elections and free speech), especially through online services (like Google, Facebook, and Twitter) that have come under public scrutiny for providing a medium that profligates fake news.

The problem with these online providers is that their algorithms (computer driven) are crafted to favor stories and posts that attract the most shares and comments, increasing advertising revenue for the Internet companies.[46] The computer is programmed for profit, not to determine if the story or post is accurate. In 2021, Google, Facebook, and Twitter have faced growing demands to delete posted material spreading misinformation about vaccines. Twelve state attorneys general have warned the online companies such misinformation compromises efforts to halt the pandemic and reopen the economy.[47] Congress has considered legislation amending section 230 of the Communications Decency Act, which grants these tech giants immunity from lawsuits for much of what their users post. However, Congresswoman Anna Eshoo (D – California) wants to do more, introducing a bill ending immunity for the bigger online platforms if their algorithms display content that results in violence. A co-sponsor of Eshoo's bill, Representative Tom Malinowski (D – New Jersey), said Facebook, Google, and Twitter, "Want us to focus on putting out fires and not on the fact that their product is flammable."[48] There may be bi-partisan support to end legal immunity for these social media behemoths. Republicans in Congress have alleged Facebook, Google, and Twitter have demonstrated bias against conservatives, and with former President Donald Trump having been banned by Facebook, Google, and Twitter in the wake of the January 6 insurrection, Republicans view these internet companies as hostile to conservative speech. But the reality is, the damage has already been done, and a growing number of Americans are accessing false information on a regular basis. According to a Pew Research Center survey, over two-thirds of Americans claim they get at least a portion of their news from social media.

In response to the growing number of Americans, especially younger aged ones, utilizing social media to access news, legislation was introduced in 2017 in the California Legislature requiring curriculum guidelines be developed by a consortium of educators, librarians, parents, students, and media experts to assist students in distinguishing between actual news and fake news.[49] But like so many other proposed laws and policies discussed in this book, not everyone is on board, including Republican State Senator Andy Vidak, who opposed the law, arguing teachers should not waste their time on such curriculum when education standards in the state are waning. Vidak's chief of staff, Jim Kjol, added, *"Now we're going to ask teachers to start monitoring political speech on social media? Teachers should not serve as "thought police."*[50]

Perhaps Senator Vidak and his chief of staff are correct, yet politics has become extremely tribal in the 21st century, not only nationwide, but in California as well. Those who practice tribalism, whatever side of the political spectrum they occupy, usually are not interested in considering opposing points of view. Growing numbers of politicians are finding it more difficult to govern (which means compromising from time to time) in such an environment. This may explain why Congress has failed to adequately address such important issues as immigration, health care, Social Security, the environment, repairing the nation's infrastructure, criminal justice reform, and gun violence. Even as Democrats control both houses of Congress and the White House after the 2020 election, they have a modest majority in the House and a one vote majority in the U.S. Senate. President Biden remains optimistic he can get big things done in his first term, buoyed by the passage of the $1.9 trillion COVID-19 relief bill in March 2021 and achieving over 200 million administered vaccinations within the first 100 days of his presidency. We shall see.

In California, with the Democrats operating with a two-thirds majority in both houses of the State Legislature and Governor Gavin Newsom in office, the state has not been able deal with the massive health care and pension debt of state employees that continues to grow or the lack of affordable housing in the Golden State. After over a year of lockdowns, school closings, and high unemployment rates the state is attempting to move forward from COVID-19, but the numbers of cases (3.7 million) and deaths (over 61,000) at the end of April 2021 led the nation. Governor Newsom and the Legislature have provided economic relief packages to open schools back up and help those unemployed with financial assistance and eviction protections. At the end of April 2021 over 29 million vaccines had been administered to Californians and 26% of Golden Staters were fully vaccinated.

As cited in Chapter 3, voter turnout in the country for the 2020 election was impressive with 160 million Americans casting ballots, some 18 million of them in California. With Californians facing a gubernatorial Recall election in the Fall of 2021, it will be interesting to see how many turn out to judge the job Governor Newsom has done in navigating the state through the pandemic. COVID-19 provides an insight into the tribal politics of our time. In the worst pandemic in 100 years, we can't seem to agree on wearing a mask or getting a vaccination. At the end of April 2021 health officials fear we are reaching a point where the supply of vaccine is greater than the demand.

Americans have a cultural habit of maintaining a fierce independence, valuing freedom. That is why so many Americans bristle when the government (at any level) attempts to enforce laws and policies that restrict freedom. There is no doubt Governor Newsom's executive actions to close swaths of the state's economy, issue stay at home orders, and threaten to withhold state funding from cities that did not comply with his directives helped feed the Recall movement against him. Governing is not easy in normal times given our political differences, but the challenges are magnified when dealing with a 100-year pandemic, persistent drought conditions and some of the worst wildfires in the history of the Golden State. Regardless of how one feels about government, it is a necessity as English philosopher Thomas Hobbes articulated the concept that without order, there would be chaos. Government provides order, but it also is entrusted with preserving freedom and guaranteeing equality in the United States. Today, based on one's political point of view, government is either the problem or the solution. What do you think?

NOTES

CHAPTER ONE

[1] Best states for business California forbes.com/places/ca/?sh=59b10cc83fef

[2] Real Value Added To The Gross Domestic Product (GDP) of California In 2019 By Industry statista.com/statistics/304869/California-real-gdp-by-industry/

[3] David G. Lawrence, *California The Politics Of Diversity* (Wadsworth, 2010) pg. 233

[4] ballotpedia.org/wiki/index.php/California_Proposition_30_Sales_and_Income_Tax_Increase_(2012)

[5] Margot Roosevelt, "State's job losses this winter were worse than expected", *Sacramento Bee*, March 16, 2021, pg. 6A

[6] State of California, Department of Industrial Relations, Minimum Wage dir.ca.gov/dlse/faq-minimumwage.htm

[7] Lawrence G. Giventer, *Governing California*, (McGraw Hill, 2008), pages 6–7

[8] The U.S. Department of Housing and Urban Development, The 2016 Annual Homeless Assessment Report To Congress, Nov. 2016, www.hudexchange.info/resources/documents/2016-AHAR-Part-1-pdf

[9] Angela Hart, "Housing crisis has roots in slow building pace", *Sacramento Bee*, August 21, 2017, pg. 1A

[10] Ibid, 7A

[11] Ibid, 7A

[12] Ray Pearl, "We must address crisis of high housing costs", *Sacramento Bee*, January 29, 2017, pg. 5E

[13] Department of Numbers, California Residential Rent and Rental Statistics deptofnumbers.com/rent/California/

[14] Dan Walters, "Feel-good efforts won't solve California housing crisis", *Sacramento Bee*, January 23, 2017 pg. 2B

[15] Ibid., 2B

[16] Andrew Sheeler, "How state's new eviction moratorium will work", *Sacramento Bee*, January 31, 2021 pg. 12A

[17] Mackenzie Hawkins, "State has six months to turn hotels into housing for homeless", *Sacramento Bee*, July 2, 2020, pg. 8A

[18] Ibid, 8A

[19] Mona Field, *California Government And Politics Today*, (Longman, 2011), pages 12–13

[20] Lawrence G. Giventer, *Governing California*, (McGraw Hill, 2008), pg. 4

[21] Steven Magagnini and Phillip Reese, "Fewer Whites Reside In State," *Sacramento Bee*, May 16, 2011, pg. A1

[22] Ibid, A14

[23] Dom Difurio, "Musk's move to Texas follows 687,000 other Californians in the last decade", *Sacramento Bee*, Dec. 11, 2020, pages 1A and 9A

[24] Cal Matters California migration: The story of 40 million calmatters.org/explainers/California-population-migration-census-demographics-immigration/?

[25] Jim Miller, "Voters continue to shun party ties", *Sacramento Bee*, March 23, 2017, pg. 6A

[26] Anita Creamer and Phillip Reese, "Seniors To Skew State's Balance", *Sacramento Bee*, June 23, 2014, pg. A14

[27] Matt Weiser and David Siders, "Unprecedented Cuts", *Sacramento Bee*, April 5, 2015, pages A1 and A10

[28] Tim Hearden, "Governor Brown declares drought over, issues conservation orders, *Capital Press*, April 7, 2017, www.capitalpresss.com/Water/20170407/gov-brown-declares-drought-over-issues-conservation-orders

[29] Seth Bornstein, "Wind and drought worsen fires, not bad management scientists say", *Sacramento Bee*, November 13, 2018, pg. 5A

[30]Ibid, 5A

[31]Paul Rogers, "Survey: Sierra snowpack down; drought looms for California this summer", *Sacramento Bee*, March 3, 2021, pg. 7A

[32]Dale Kasler, "Cities, farms get grim warning on water supply, *Sacramento Bee*, March 24, 2021, pg. 1A

[33]Bernard L. Hyink and David H. Provost, *Politics And Government In California*, (Longman, 2004) pg. 198

[34]California State Water Project Overview; www.water.ca.gov/swp

[35]David G. Lawrence, *California The Politics Of Diversity*, (Wadsworth, 2010), pg. 254

[36]Bernard L. Hyink and David H. Provost, *Politics And Government In California*, (Longman, 2004), pg. 196

[37]Dan Reidel "100 Days Of Dam Drama," *Chico Enterprise Record*, May 18, 2017, A4

[38]Don Nottoli and Darrell Fong, "Delta Plan Threatens Water Rights," *Sacramento Bee*, December 4, 2012, pg. A19

[39]*Sacramento Bee*, "Brown Needs To Answer EPA On Impact Of Delta Tunnels", Sept. 7, 2014, pg. E6

[40]Matt Weiser, "EPA Warns On Tunnels Plan," *Sacramento Bee*, August 29, 2014, pg. A2

[41]Adam Beam, "Governor restarts giant tunnel project", *Chico Enterprise Record*, January 17, 2020, pg. 3A

[42]Jim Miller, "In 2014, Remodel Not So Simple", *Sacramento Bee*, Dec. 11, 2013, pg. A1

[43]Mariel Garza, "Desalination Comes Of Age," *Sacramento Bee*, October 19, 2014, pg. E1

[44]Larry N. Gerston and Terry Christensen, *California Politics & Government*, (Wadsworth, 2009), pg. 9

[45]David. G. Lawrence, *California The Politics Of Diversity*, (Wadsworth, 2010), pg. 12

[46]Mark Grossi, "Farmers Tell Of Drought Impact", *Fresno Bee*, March 20, 2014, pg. A1

[47]Mariel Garza, "Proposed Water Sale Is Appalling", *Sacramento Bee*, May 25, 2014, pg. E1

[48]Ellen Le, "Heat Still Plagues Farmworkers", *Sacramento Bee*, July 7, 2013, pg. A4

[49]www.allgov.com/usa/ca/news/controversies/settlement-pushes-cal-osha-to-enforce-2005-heat-protection-for-Farmworkers-150612

[50]Kim Bojorquez, "Berkeley study looks at COVID-19 impact on farmworkers", *Sacramento Bee*, December 11, 2020, pg. 7A

[51] Ibid, pg. 7A

[52]Erin Rode, "Growers ask judge to block hero pay for farmworkers", *The Desert Sun*, March 15, 2021, pg. 6A

[53]Ibid, pg. 1A

[54]David Siders and Jeremy B. White, "Governor signs bill for farmworker OT," *Sacramento Bee*, Sept. 13, 2017, pg. 1A

[55]Mary Clare Jalonick, "Budget Cuts, Negotiations Worry Farmers," *Chico Enterprise Record*, July 18, 2011. Pg. 9A

[56]www.reuters.com/2015/us-usa-agriculture-fapri-idUSKBNO

[57]*Chico Enterprise Record*, "Room For Reform On Farm Subsidies," July 19, 2011, pg. A8

[58]California State Profile and Energy Estimates, Profile Analysis, February 18, 2021 eia.gov/state/analysis.php?sid=CA

[59]California Energy Commission; energyalmanac.ca.gov/naturalgas/index.html

[60]California State Profile and Energy Estimates, Profile Analysis, February 18, 2021 eia.gov/state/analysis.php?sid=CA

[61]Ibid.

[62]Ibid

[63]Bernard L. Hyink and David H. Provost, *Politics And Government In California*, (Longman, 2004) pg. 194

[64]David G. Lawrence, *California The Politics Of Diversity*, (Wadsworth, 2010) pg. 61

[65]Bernard L Hyink and David H. Provost, *Politics And Government In California*, (Longman, 2004) pg. 194

[66]California Energy Commission, ca.gov, Foreign Sources of Marine Crude Oil Imports to California 2019

[67]Lara Korte and Sophia Bollag, "Sales of gas-powered cars to be phased out", *Sacramento Bee*, September 24, 2020, pg. 1A

[68]Jude Clemente, "California's Oil Industry Collapses Despite Shale Boom", April 3, 2019, rigzone.com/news/california's_oil_industry_collapses_despite_shale_boom-03-apr-2019-158514-

[69]California Energy Commission; http://energyalmanac.ca.gov/renewables/index.html

[70]California State Profile and Energy Estimates, Profile Analysis, February 18, 2021 Eia.gov/state/analysis.php?sid=CA

[71]Craig Lewis, "Time to level the playing field for clean energy," *Sacramento Bee*, March 7, 2017 pg. 5B

[72]Trevor Nace, "California Goes All In - 100% Renewable Energy By 2045," www.forbes.com/sites/trevornace/2017/08/01california-goes-all-in-100-percent-renewable-energy-by-2045

[73]Dale Kasler, "Newsom's climate change fight could be costly", *Sacramento Bee*, September 21, 2020, pg. 7A

[74]AJ Willingham, Commuters waste an average of 54 hours a year stalled in traffic study says, CNN, August 22, 2019 cnn.com/2019/08/22/us/traffic-commute-gridlock-transportation-study-trnd

[75]Tony Bizjak, "Game Changer", *Sacramento Bee*, October 14, 2020, pg. 8A

[76]David G. Lawrence, *California The Politics Of Diversity*, (Wadsworth, 2010) pg. 260

[77]Bernard L. Hyink and David H. Provost, *Politics And Government In California*, (Longman, 2004) pg. 207

[78]www.metroactive.com/metro/04.12.06/ MEASURE A REPLAY

[79]www.vta.org/bart/funding.html

[80]Marybeth Luczak, Bart Silicon Valley Project Enters Phase 2, Railway Age, September 28, 2020 Railwayage.com/passenger/rapid-transit/bart-silicon-valley-project-enters-phase-2/

[81]Daniel Krause, "LAO On Wrong Track With Criticism Of High-Speed Rail," *Sacramento Bee*, May 25, 2011 pg. A17

[82]Michael Doyle, "House Targets High Speed Rail," *Sacramento Bee*, June 11, 2014, pg. A3

[83]"Against All Odds, the California Bullet Train Barrels Forward, Los Angeles Magazine, www.com/driver/odds-california-bullet-train-barrels-forward

[84]Kathleen Ronayne, "California pushes back high-speed rail construction deadline", *Chico Enterprise Record*, February 7, 2021, pg. 5A

[85]Dan Walters, "Fixing Roads Relies On Tax Conundrum," *Sacramento Bee*, January 19, 2015, pg. A3

[86]Christopher Cadelgo, "Governor to sign gas tax hikes for road repairs," *Sacramento Bee*, April 8, 2017 pg. 1A

[87]George Runner, "California Needs A Simpler Gas Tax, Not A Higher One," *Sacramento Bee*, Feb. 22, 2015 pg. E5

[88]Bernard L. Hyink and David H. Provost, *Politics And Government In California*, (Longman, 2004) pg. 201

[89]David G. Lawrence. *California The Politics Of Diversity*, (Wadsworth, 2010) pg. 262

[90]California Environmental Protection Agency; mhtml:file//C:\arb40thhistory.mht; History Of Air Resources Board

[91]Emily Guerin, "Take A Deep Breath And Read About How Bad LA Smog Really Is", LAist, October 3, 2018 laist.com/2018/10/03/take_a_deep_breath_and_read_about_how_bad_la_smog_really_is,php

[92]Matthew Brown, "Study: Wildfires produced up to half of pollution in US West", *Chico Enterprise Record*, January 12, 2021, pg. 2A

[93] Bill Gallegos, "State Can Still Lead On Climate Without Cap-And-Trade Farce", *Sacramento Bee*, July 2, 2011, pg. A11

[94]Ben Boychuk, "Should California Go Back To The Drawing Board With AB32?" *Sacramento Bee*, May 25, 2011 pg. A17

[95]Alexei Koseff, "Arnold Schwarzenegger teams with Jerry Brown on climate change bill," July 25, 2017 www.sacbee.com/news/politics/-government/capitol.alert/article

[96]Bernard L. Hyink and David H. Provost, *Politics And Government In California*, (Longman, 2004) pg. 201

[97]Jim Steinberg, "Federal court signs off on Eagle Mountain settlement, preserving valuable habitat," *San Bernardino Sun*, January 3, 2015, www.sbsun.com/2015/01/03/federal-

court-signs-off-on-eagle-mountain-settlement-preserving- valuable-habitat

[98]Rick Daysog, "Less Buying Eases Trash Burden," *Sacramento Bee*, June 9, 2011, pg. A11

[99]Annie Sciacca and Rachel Spacek, "Californians are recycling bottles less and less. Here's what's going on," July 4, 2017, www.latimes.com/business/la-fi-recycling-rates-down-20170704-story

[100]Jared Blumenfeld, "Brown needs to rescue California's recycling programs," *Sacramento Bee*, May 16, 2017, pg. 5B

[101]Katie Pyzyk, What's next for California container recycling after rePlanet's closure?, August 28, 2019 wastedive.com/news/whats-next-for-california-container-recycling-after-replants-closure/560916/

[102]Ibid.

[103]Developing A Health Benefit Exchange To Make It Easier To Shop For And Buy Insurance; www.healthcare.ca.gov/Priorities/HealthBenefitExchanges.aspx.2010

[104]Ibid

[105]Jim Sanders, "Power Over Rate Hikes Stirs Feverish Lobbying," *Sacramento Bee*, July 4, 2011 pg. A12

[106]Ibid., A12

[107]James G. Hinsdale, "AB 52 Would Harm Our Medical Care," *Sacramento Bee*, July 2, 2011, pg. A10

[108]California Secretary Of State Voter Guide, November 4, 2014, pg. 25

[109]CHCF, Facts and Figures on the ACA in California: What We've Gained and What We Stand to lose, November, 2016, wwwchef.org/publications/2016/11/facts-figures-aca-ca

[110]Kristof Stremikis, Ever-Rising Health Costs Worsen California's Coronavirus Threat, March 5, 2020, California Health Care Foundation chcf.org/blog/ever-rising-helath-costs-worsen-californias-coronavirus-threat/

[111]Christopher Cadelago and Taryn Luna, "Why universal health care died," *Sacramento Bee*, June 28, 2017, pg. 1B

[112]Andres Oppenheimer, "Americans are dying of despair, and Biden must address it", *Sacramento Bee*, March 3, 2021 pg. 11A

[113]Diana Lambert and Phillip Reese, "Funds Fall, Scores Rise," *Sacramento Bee*, July 2, 2011, pg. A8

[114]Ibid., A8

[115]California Prepares For Common Core Standards, Sharon Noguchi; www.mercurynews.com/education/ci.24489847/11/09/2013

[116]Adam McCann, States with the Best & Worst School Systems, WalletHub, July 27, 2020 wallethub.com/edu/e/states-with-the-best-schools/5335

[117]Thomas Elias, "Speeding CSU graduations must not dumb down degrees," *Chico Enterprise Record*, August 30, 2017, pg. A5

[118]Diana Lambert, "State's Plan Conflicts With Budgets, Contracts," *Sacramento Bee*, Feb. 5, 2014, pg. A1

[119]Heather Stringer, Zoom school's mental health toll on kids, American Psychological Association, October 13, 2020 apa.org/news/apa/2020/10/online-learning-mental-health

[120]Jocelyn Gecker, "SF sues own school district to reopen", *Chico Enterprise Record*, February 4, 2021, pg. 2A

[121]Sharon Martin, "Parent group launches effort to recall 4 board members", *Chico Enterprise Record*, March 4, 2021 pg. 5A

[122]Lara Korte, "Newsom's school bill funds extra programs", *Sacramento Bee*, March 11, 2021, pg. 6A

[123]Edward Ring, California's K-12 spending exceeds $20,000 per pupil, California Policy Center, March 3, 2020 Californiapolicycenter.org/californias-k-12-spending-exceeds-20,000-per-pupil/

[124]Sophia Bollag, Lara Korte and Hannah Wiley, "Newsom's budget proposal flush with spending on COVID-19 Relief, schools, *Sacramento Bee*, January 10, 2021, pg. 4A

[125]Jim Miller, "Prop 98 Makes Schools The Budget Winners," *Sacramento Bee*, May 16, 2015, pg. 2B

[126]California Community Colleges Chancellor's Office, Board Of Governors; www.ccco.edu/ChancellorsOffice/BoardofGovernors

[127]The California State University, Board Of Trustees, Overviews; www.calstate.edu/bot/overview

[128]Major Features Of The California Master Plan For Higher Education; www.ucop.edu/acadinit/mastplan/mpssummary

[129]www.californiacommunitycolleges.eccco.edu/PolicyInAction/KeyFacts.aspx

[130]Laurel Rosenhall, "Tuition Strains Middle Class," *Sacramento Bee*, July 12, 2011, pages A1 and A14

[131]Ibid., A14

[132]Larry Mitchell, "Chico State Tuition To Rise 12 Percent, "*Chico Enterprise Record*, July 13, 2011, pg. 1A

[133]Kevin Yamamura, "State Wants The Option To Borrow From UC, CSU," *Sacramento Bee*, July 12, 2011, pg. A4

[134]Danta Acosta, "UC budget scandal should not be swept under the rug," *Sacramento Bee*, May 10, 2017, pg. 5B

[135]Sacramento Bee Editorial Board, "CSU hid a $1.5 billion surplus while raising tuition. Where is the accountability?", *Sacramento Bee*, June 24, 2019, pg. 9A

[136]Ibid, pg. 9A

[137]Alexei Koseff, "CSU Success Fees Are Dragged Into Budget Debate," *Sacramento Bee*, May 30, 2014, pg. A14

[138]Ashley A. Smith, Students sue California universities over fees lost amid pandemic, EdSource, April 28, 2020 Edsource.org/2020/students-sue-california-universities-over-fees-lost-amid-pandemic/630377

[139]Ibid.

[140] Alexei Koseff, "Out-Of-State Interest Drives UC Applications To Record High," *Sacramento Bee*, January 15, 2015, pg. A3

[141]Abigail Johnson Hess, What's still up for debate when it comes to student debt forgiveness, CNBC, April 6, 2021 Cnbc.com/2021/04/06/what-the-student-debt-forgiveness-debate-is-about.html

[142]Alexei Koseff, "Free College is a new rallying cry in California," *Sacramento Bee*, September 5, 2017, pg. 9A

[143]Mikhail Zinshteyn, California's new 'free college' law for community colleges covers more than tuition, EdSource, February 14, 2019 edsource,org/2019/californias-new-free-college-law-for-community-colleges-covers-more-than-tuition/608612

[144]Alexei Koseff, "Free College is a new rallying cry in California, *Sacramento Bee*, September 5, 2017, pg. 9A

CHAPTER TWO

[1]Andrew F. Rolle, *California A History* (AHM Publishing, 1978), pg. 68

[2]Ibid., 121

[3]Ibid., 188–189

[4]George Brown Tindall and David E. Shi, *America* (Norton, 1993), pg. 391

[5]Andrew F. Rolle, *California A History* (AHM Publishing, 1978), pg. 221

[6]Ibid., 195–197

[7]The American Experience, *The Iron Road*, (film, 1990)

[8]Oscar Lewis, *The Big Four*, (Knopf, 1974) pg. 61

[9]Ibid., 62

[10]Norman E. Tutorow, *The Governor: The Life and Legacy of Leland Stanford* (Arthur H. Clark co., 2004), pg. 227

[11]Oscar Lewis, *The Big Four*, (Knopf, 1974) pg. 35

[12]The American Experience, *The Iron Road* (film, 1990)

[13]Ibid.

[14]George Brown Tindall and David E. Shi, *America* (Norton, 1993), pg. 475

[15]Oscar Lewis, *The Big Four*, (Knopf, 1974), pg. 264

[16]Ibid., 275

[17]Andrew F. Rolle, *California A History* (AHM Publishing, 1978), pg. 409

[18]Oscar Lewis, *The Big Four*, (Knopf, 1974) pp 284–287

[19]Andrew F. Rolle, *California A History* (AHM Publishing, 1978), pp 371–372

[20]Ibid.

[21]Ibid., 374

[22]Ibid.

[23]Ibid., 375

[24]Ashley Wong, "More than 1,600 Asians reported hate-related incidents in California", *Sacramento Bee*, March 18, 2021, pg. 6A

[25]Marcos Breton, "She's been in Yolo County for years. Then COVID hit – and anti-Asian racism began", *Sacramento Bee*, February 26, 2021, pg. 3A

[26]Bernard L. Hyink and David H. Provost, *Politics And Government In California* (Longman, 2004) pg. 22

[27]Jeremy B. White and Kevin Yamamura, "California lawmakers remain sidelined as pandemic crisis deepens", Politico, December 14, 2020 politico.com/news/2020/12/14/California-lawmakers-sidelined-during-pandemic-445370

[28]Charles G. Bell and Charles M. Price, *California Government Today*, (Brooks/Cole Publishing, 1992) pg. 47

[29]Ibid., 50

[30]Bryan Anderson, "Legislature won't have power over PG&E rates", *Sacramento Bee*, May 19, 2019, pg. 4A

[31]Dan Walters, "PUC must provide more than just promises," *Sacramento Bee*, August 27, 2017, pg. 3D

[32]Michael Hiltzik, "PG&E, our indifferent regulators, and the 8 dead of San Bruno, July 30, 2014, www.latimes.com/business/hiltzik/la-fi-mh-pge-the-puc-20140730-column.html

[33]The Associate Press, "Utilities to spend billions to cut wildfire risk", *Chico Enterprise Record*, February 7, 2022

[34]Dan Walters, "PUC must provide more than just promises," *Sacramento Bee*, August 27, 2017, pg. 3D

[35]Charles G. Bell and Charles M. Price, *California Government Today,* (Brooks/Cole Publishing, 1992) pg. 48

[36]David G. Lawrence, *California The Politics of Diversity*, (Wadsworth, 2010) pg. 80

[37]Lara Korte, "Gov. Newsom recall effort gets boost from deadline extension", *Sacramento Bee*, March 15, 2021, pg. 1A

[38] Procedure for Recalling State and Local Officials, California Secretary of State, www.sos.ca.gov/elections/recalls/procedure-recalling-state-and-local-officials

[39]Jim Miller and Taryn Luna, "Democrats push rules to avoid recall of senator," *Sacramento Bee*, June 13, 2017, pg. 5A

[40]CISION PR Newswire, $7 Signatures Block Citizen Access to Ballot Initiative Process, E-Signatures Can Restore It, Says New Report, September 25, 2020 prnewswire.com/news-releases/7-signatures-block-citizen-access-to-ballot-initiative-process-e-signatures-can-restore-it-says-new-report-301138313.html

[41]Charles G. Bell and Charles M. Price, *California Government Today*, (Brooks/Cole Publishing, 1992) pg. 50

[42]Ryan Menezes, Maloy Moore and Phi Do, Billions have been spent on California's ballot measure battles. But this year is unlike any other, Los Angeles Times, November 13, 2020, latimes,com/projects/props-california-2020-election-money/

CHAPTER THREE

[1]Rick Silva, "Senator LaMalfa Speaks In Paradise," www.chicoer.com/fromthenewspaper,ci August 8, 2011

[2]Charles G. Bell and Charles M. Price, *California Government Today*, (Brooks/Cole Publishing, 1992), pg. 55

[3]Mike Rose, "California Decline-To-State Voters At All Time High," www.sspr/news.2010/04/23

[4]Brian P. Janiskee and Ken Maugi, *Democracy In California*, (Rowman & Littlefield, 2011), pg. 53

[5]Ibid., 57

[6]Anagnoson, Bonetto, Buck, Deleon, Emrey, Kelleher, and Koch, *Governing California*, (W.W. Norton Co., 2015), pg. 93

[7]Bryan Anderson, "Anti-Trump fervor likely fueled state's huge voter turnout", *Sacramento Bee*, December 1, 2018, pg. 7A

[8]Ibid., pg. 7A

[9]Julia Zebley, "California Governor Signs Law Awarding All Of State's Electoral Votes To Popular Vote Winner," jurist.org.paperchase/2011/10/08

[10]Kenneth Janda, Jeffrey M. Berry, Jerry Goldman, and Kevin Hula, *The Challenge of Democracy*, (Wadsworth, 2008), pg. 276

[11]Map of General-Election Campaign Events and TV Spending by 2020 Presidential

Candidates, National Popular Vote, nationalpopularvote.com/map-general-election-campaign-events-and-tv-ad-spending-2020-presidential-candidates

[12]Edward Greenberg and Benjamin I Page, *The Struggle For Democracy* (Longman, 2011), pg. 346

[13]Barbara A. Bardes, Mack C. Shelly and Steffen W. Schmidt, *American Government And Politics Today*, (Wadsworth, 2008), pg. 348

[14]Supreme Court Ruling On Texas Redistricting Cheers Democrats, CBS Dallas/Fort Worth, April 4, 2016. dfw.cbslocal.com/2016/04/04/supreme-court-ruling-on-texas-redistricting-cheers-democrats

[15]David G. Savage and David Lauter, "1-Man, 1-Vote In Legal Battle," *Sacramento Bee*, May 27, 2015, pg. 2A

[16]Ibid.

[17]Bernard L. Hyink and David H. Provost, *Politics And Government In California*, (Longman, 2004), pg. 102

[18]David G. Lawrence, *California The Politics of Diversity*, (Wadsworth, 2010), pg. 138

[19]Ibid., 138–139

[20]*Los Angeles Times*, "Celebrating New Voting Districts," articles.latimes.com/2011.aug/18

[21]Assembly Passes Budget, July 17, 2001, www.recordnet.com/apps/pbcs.d11/article

[22]Jim Sanders, "Lawmaker Assails Spending Data," *Sacramento Bee*, August 30, 2011, pp. A3-A4

[23]Smart Voter Proposition 11 Redistricting State Of California, www.smartvoter.org/2008/11/04/ca/state/prop/11/

[24]California Proposition 27, Elimination Of Citizen Redistricting Commission 2010, www.ballotpedia.org

[25]Torey Van Oot, "Change Brought Tighter Races," *Sacramento Bee*, November 12, 2012, pg. A10

[26]Ibid., pg. A10

[27]California's district maps are generally fair, increase competitiveness, Public Policy Institute of California, March 5, 2018, ppic.org/press-release/californias-district-maps-are-generally-fair-increase-competitiveness/

[28]Anagnoson, Bonetto, Buck, Deleon, Emrey, Kelleher, and Koch, *Governing California*, (W.W. Norton Co., 2015), pp. 99–100

[29]Brian P. Janiskee and Ken Masugi, *Democracy In California*, (Rowman & Littlefield, 2015), pg. 56

[30]Sophia Bollag, "State voter turnout sets midterm record", *Sacramento Bee*, November 17, 2018, pg. 6A

[31]Phillip Reese and Lewis Griswold, Why California saw a record number of ballots cast in the 2020 election, Desert Sun, desertsun.com/story/news/2020/12/11/why-california-saw-record-number-ballots-cast-2020-election/

[32]Sam Stanton, "Issa sues Newsom over mail-in voting", *Sacramento Bee*, May 24, 2020, pg. 17A

[33]Porter Wells, RNC Concedes Suit Is Moot Over California's Vote-by-Mail Order, Bloomberg Law, July 10, 2020 news.bloomberglaw.com/coronavirus/rnc-concedes-suit-is-moot-over-californias-vote-by-mail-order

[34]Kevin B. Smith, *State And Local Government*, (Sage Publications 2019), pg. 17

[35]Michael R. Blood and Stephen Ohlemacher, "Democratic sweep in California raises GOP suspicion", *Enterprise Record*, December 1, 2018, pg. 2A

[36]Ibid., pg. 2A

CHAPTER FOUR

[1]www.sacwilpf.org/2011/03/pay-state-workers-minimum-wage.

[2]Madeleine Joung, Trump Has Now Had More Cabinet Turnover Than Reagan, Obama, and the Two Bushes, Time Time.com/5625699/trump-cabinet-acosta/

[3]Renee B. Van Vechten, *California Politics A Primer* (CQ Press, 2010) pg. 49

[4]Jack C. Plano and Milton Greenberg, *The American Political Dictionary* (HBJ Publishers, 1993) pp 184–185

[5]John Gabriel, "Arpaio Is No Conservative And No Hero," *USA Today*, August. 28, 2017, pg. 7A

[6]Trudy Rubin, "Blackwater pardons endanger US troops, undermine rule of law", *Sacramento Bee*, December 31, 2020 pg. 10A

[7]Eric Tucker, After pardon, Blackwater guard defiant: 'I acted correctly', Military Times, January 3, 2021 military times.com/news/pentagon-congress/2021/01/03/after-pardon-blackwater-guard-defiant-i-acted-correctly/

[8]Laurel Rosenhall, "Governor sets record for pardons," *San Jose Mercury News*, January 1, 2017, pg. A1

[9]*Sacramento Bee,* "Victim's Parents Angered As Nunez Blasts Son's Sentence", July 12, 2011 pg. A3

[10]John Gramlich, Trump used his clemency power sparingly despite a raft of late pardons and commutations, Pew Research Center, January 22. 2021 pewresearch.org/fact-tank/2021/01/22/trump-used-his-clemency-power-sparingly-despite-a-raft-of-late-pardons-and-commutations/

[11]"Governor Davis Denies Clemency Request of Manuel Babbitt", www.ca.gov/s/governor/043099.

[12]www.sanfranciscosentinl.com. Sept. 27, 2010

[13]"Supreme Court Blocks Execution of San Quentin Man, Schwarzenegger Decries Decision", http://sfappeal.com/news/2010/09.

[14]Sophia Bollag, "Newsom to halt death penalty; 737 get reprieve, *Sacramento Bee*, March 13, 2021 pp 1A and 6A

[15]David G. Lawrence, *California The Politics of Diversity* (Wadsworth, 2010) pg. 165

[16]David Siders, "Jerry Brown's Parole Reversal Rate Holds Steady," www.sacbee.com, Feb. 20, 2015

[17]Bill Barton, California's New "Progressive" Governor Seeks to Halt Parole for Some Murderers and "Serious" Offenders, Prison Legal News, April 1, 2020 prison/legal.news.org/news/2020/apr/1/californias-new-proregressive-governor-seeks-halt-parole-some-murderers-and-serious-offenders/

[18]Ibid.

[19]Jack C. Plano and Milton Greenberg, *The American Political Dictionary* (HBJ Publishers, 1993) pg. 262

[20]Sophia Bollag, "As recall looms, Newsom defends coronavirus record in State of the State speech", *Sacramento Bee*, March 11, 2021, pg. 6A

[21]Lara Korte, "Recall organizers respond to Newsom's State of the State address", *Sacramento Bee*, March 11, 2021 pg. 6A

[22]Jack C. Plano and Milton Greenberg, *The American Political Dictionary* (HBJ Publishers, 1993) pg. 375

[23]Office of The Secretary of The Senate US Government Printing Office, 1992, "Presidential Vetoes 1791–1991"

[24]Jim Miller, "State Legislature Poised For Historic Veto Override", www.pe.com/localnews/politics/stories. Sept. 9, 2009

[25]California Land Title Association, "Governor Schwarzenegger Vetoes Record Number of Bills", www.clta.org/e-news/oct2008/sacramentoReport.

[26]*Sacramento Bee*, "Governor Gets It Mostly Right On Bill Signings," Oct. 15, 2013, pg. A8

[27]David G. Lawrence, *California The Politics of Diversity* (Wadsworth, 2010) pg. 162

[28]Gov. Gavin Newsom decides final fate of 2020 legislative bills, League of California Cities, October 21, 2020 cacities.org/Top/News/News-Articles/2020/Gov-Gavin-Newsom-decides-final-fate-of-2020-legis

[29]Jim Miller, "Brown inks $167B budget; no cuts," *Sacramento Bee*, June 28, 2016, pg. 6A

[30]Steffen W. Schmidt, Mack C. Shelley and Barbara A. Bardes, *American Government and Politics Today* (Wadsworth, 2001) pages 424–425

[31]Jack C. Plano and Milton Greenberg, *The American Political Dictionary* (HBJ Publishers, 1993) pg. 161

[32]Bernard L. Hyink and David H. Provost, *Politics And Government In California* (Longman, 2004) pg. 124

[33]David G. Lawrence, *California The Politics of Diversity* (Wadsworth, 2010) pg. 165

[34]Bernard L. Hyink and David H. Provost, *Politics And Government In California* (Longman, 2004) pg. 124

[35]David Siders, "The Past Has A Future," *Sacramento Bee*, July 2, 2015 pp 1B-2B

[36]Ben Adler, "First Family Moves Into California Governor's Mansion," Capitol Public Radio, Dec. 17, 2015, www.capradio.org/articles/2015/12/17/first-family-moves-into-california-governors-mansion

[37]Sophia Bollag, "Newsoms moving to house in Fair Oaks worth $3.7M", *Sacramento Bee*, January 18, 2019 pg. 1A

[38]David G. Lawrence, *California The Politics of Diversity* (Wadsworth, 2010) pg. 166

[39]Tom LoBianco, Ted Barrett and Eugene Scott, "Betsy DeVos confirmed as education secretary; vice president casts historic tie-breaking vote," February 7, 2017, www.cnn.com/2017/02/07/politics/betsy-devos-senate-vote

[40]Lara Korte, "State files 100th lawsuit against Trump administration", *Sacramento Bee*, August 30, 2020, pg. 11A

[41]David G. Lawrence, *California The Politics of Diversity* (Wadsworth, 2010) pg. 167

[42]Anne C. Mulkern, "Lower Bar To Get On 2016 Ballot Predicted To Spur Loopy Initiatives," Mar. 31, 2015, www.eenews.net

[43]David G. Lawrence, *California The Politics of Diversity* (Wadsworth, 2010) pg. 167

[44]Barbara A. Bardes, Mack C. Shelley and Steffen W. Schmidt *American Government and Politics Today* (Wadsworth, 2008) pg. 158

[45]Bernard L. Hyink and David H. Provost, *Politics And Government In California* (Longman, 2004) pg. 132

[46]Jack C. Plano and Milton Greenberg, *The American Political Dictionary* (HBJ Publishers, 1993) pg. 499

[47]Ann O'M. Bowman and Richard C. Kearney, *State And Local Government* (Houghton Mifflin Company, 2008) pg. 410

[48]Renee B. Van Vechten, *California Politics A Primer* (CQ Press, 2010) pg. 53

[49]The National Association of Insurance Commissioners, "About The NAIC", www.naic.org/index-about.htm.

[50]Charles G. Bell and Charles M. Price, *California Government Today* (Brooks/Cole Publishing, 1992) pg. 225

[51]Ibid.

[52]California State Treasurer, Fiona Ma treasurer.ca.gov

[53]Jack C. Plano and Milton Greenberg, *The American Political Dictionary* (HBJ Publishers, 1993) pg. 393

[54]John L. Korey, *California Government* (Wadsworth, 2009) pg. 75

[55]California State Controller, Betty Yee sco.gov/eo-about-resp.html

[56]www.boe.ca.gov

[57]Adam Ashton, "Lawmakers move to blow up tax board," *Sacramento Bee*, June 13, 2017, pg. 1A

[58]Ibid., pg. 1A

[59]Chuck McFadden, Brown dismantles 'powerful but obscure' Board of Equalization, Capitol Weekly, June 27, 2017, capitolweekly.net/decline-board-of-equalization-powerful-obscure

[60]Ibid

CHAPTER FIVE

[1]The Free Library, "The Unsinkable Willie Brown," www.thefreelibrary.com March 1, 1995

[2]Ibid.

[3]Charles G. Bell and Charles M. Price, *California Government Today* (Brooks/Cole Publishing, 1992) pg. 182

[4]Steffen W. Schmidt, Mack C. Shelley and Barbara A. Bardes, *American Government and Politics Today* (Wadsworth, 2001) pg. 388

[5]Brian P. Janiskee and Ken Masugi, *Democracy In California*, (Rowman and Littlefield, 2011) pg. 63

[6]Jim Sanders, "Harris Asked To Weigh in On Pay," *Sacramento Bee*, June 29, 2011 pg. A3

[7]Alexei Koseff, "Getting rid of California lawmakers' cars actually did save money, *Sacramento Bee*, August 7, 2017, pg. 1A

[8]Brigid Callahan Harrison, Jean Wahl Harris, Susan J. Tolchin and Gary M. Halter, *American Democracy Now* (McGraw Hill, 2009) pg. 39 Steffen W. Schmidt, Mack C. Shelley and Barbara A. Bardes, *American Government and Politics Today* (Wadsworth, 2001) pages 54–55

[9]Steffen W. Schmidt, Mack C. Shelley and Barbara A Bardes, *American Government and Politics Today* (Wadsworth, 2001) pp 55–56

[10]Robert Longley, "Salaries and Benefits of US Congress Members: The Truth, ThoughtCo, September 7, 2017, www.thoughtco.com/salaries-and-benefits-of-congress-members

[11]Charles G. Bell and Charles M. Price, *California Government Today* (Brooks Cole Publishing, 1992) pg. 196

[12]Bernard L. Hyink and David H. Provost, *Politics And Government In California* (Longman, 2004) pg. 109

[13]David G. Lawrence, *California The Politics of Diversity* (Wadsworth, 2010) pg. 168

[14]Larry N. Gerston and Terry Christensen, *California Politics and Government* (Wadsworth, 2009) pg. 69

[15]Malcolm MacLachlan land Alisen Boada, "Late Amends Leave Advocates Punched In The Gut," *Capital Weekly* www.capitolweekly.net/article.Sept. 15, 2011

[16]Don Thompson, "California Legislature's Gut-And-Amend Bills Avoid Scrutiny," www.mercurynews.com/california. /Sept. 17, 2011

[17]Nannette Miranda, "Gut-And-Amend Controversial In CA Legislature," Aug. 23, 2012, abc7.com

[18]Dan Walters, "Sneakiness Takes Over In Last Days," *Sacramento Bee*, Aug. 19, 2014, pg. A3

[19]Nannette Miranda, "Gut-And-Amend Controversial In CA Legislature," Aug. 23, 2012, abc7.com

[20]California General Election Voter Guide, Secretary of State's Office, November 8, 2016, pg. 38

[21]William Kolkey, In EDC.com, Placerville News Wire, Sept. 5, 2017, inedc.com/14/assembly-calls-back-bills-passed-violation-prop-54

[22]Tony Butka, The Democratic 'Gut and Amend' Supermajority Morphs into One Party…No Voters Needed, City Watch, October 3, 2019 citywatchla.com/index.php/2016-01-01-13-17-00/los-angeles/ 18567-the-democratic-gut-and-amend-supermajority-morphs-into-one-party-no-voters-needed

[23]Kenneth Janda, Jeffrey M. Berry, Jerry Goldman and Kevin Hula, *The Challenge of Democracy* (Longman, 2008) pg. 348

[24]Michael Doyle, "Despite End Of Filibuster, Tactics For Obstruction Remain," *Sacramento Bee*, November 23, 2013, pp A1 and A14

[25]Alex Tausanovitch and Sam Berger, The Impact of the Filibuster on Federal Policymaking, Center for American Progress, December 5, 2019, americanprogress.org/issues/democracy/reports/2019/12/05/478199/impact-filibuster-federal-policymaking/

[26]"Yee's UC, CSU Transparency Act Sent To Governor," www.dist08.casen.govoffice.com/index.asp. August 18, 2011

[27]Ibid.

[28]David Lightman, "Audit looks at how state missed massive unemployment fraud," *Sacramento Bee*, January 29, 2021, pg. 8A

[29]Renee B. Van Vechten, *California Politics A Primer* (CQ Press, 2010) pages 41–42

[30]Jeremy B. White, "California's New Legislature Inexperienced But Has More Time To Adjust," November 9, 2014, www.sacbee.com/news/politics-government/election

[31]California State Legislature, "Oversight And Review," www.legislature.ca.gov/the_state_legislature/oversight

[32]Laurel Rosenhall, "De Leon Eliminates Government Oversight Office," Dec. 12, 2014, www.sacbee.com/news/politics-government.capital-alert/article

[33]Jack C. Plano and Milton Greenberg, *The American Political Dictionary* (HBJ Publishers, 1993) pg.165

[34]David M. Herszenhorn, "House Benghazi Report Finds No New Evidence of Wrongdoing by Hillary Clinton, June 28, 2016, www.nytimes.com/2016/06/29/us/politics/hillary-clinton-benghazi

[35]The Mueller Report, Volume II, Melville House Printing, April 2019, pg. 330

[36]Lauren Lantry, Former President Donald Trump acquitted in 2nd impeachment trial, ABC News, February 13, 2021 abcnews.go.com/politics/president-donald-trump-acquitted/story?id=75853994

[37]Renee B. Van Vechten, *California Politics A Primer* (CQ Press, 2010) pg. 107

[38]Karl Evers-Hillstrom, State of Money in Politics: The price of victory is steep, Open Secrets.org, February 19, 2019, opensecrets.org/news/2019/02/state-of-money-in-politics-the-price-of-victory-is-steep/

[39]John L. Korey, *California Government*, (Wadsworth, 2009) pg. 58

[40]David G. Lawrence, *California The Politics of Diversity* (Wadsworth, 2010) pg. 142

[41]Patrick McGreevy, California Assembly Republicans elect Escondido's Marie Waldron new leader, The San Diego Union Tribune, Nov. 8, 2018 sandiegounion.com/news/politics/sd-me-marie-waldon-assembly-republican-leader-20181108-story.html

[42]Bernard L. Hyink and David H. Provost, *Politics And Government In California* (Longman, 2004) pg. 238

[43]Thomas E. Patterson, *We The People* (McGraw Hill, 2011) pg. 382

[44]Steffen W. Schmidt, Mack C. Shelley and Barbara A. Bardes, *American Government and Politics Today* (Wadsworth, 2001), pg. 399

[45]Sophia Bollag, "Recall rules give Newsom 'huge cash advantage', *Sacramento Bee*, March 22, 2021, pg. 1A

[46]Ibid., pg. 6A

[47]www.nationaljournal.com/congress/disgraced-congressman-randy-duke-cunningham-is-a-free-man-again, July 10, 2014

[48]inyourfaceradio.net/ex-felon-rep-randy-duke-cunningham-get-a-full-pension

[49]Alexei Koseff, "Yee Pleads Guilty To Racketeering," *Sacramento Bee*, July 2, 2015, pp 1A and 15A

[50]Josh Gerstein, "Dennis Hastert Before The Fall," 6/11/15; www.politico.com/story/2015/06/denis-hastert-before-the-fall

[51]Benjamin Weiser, "Prosecutors Want Anthony Weiner to Serve About 2 Years In Prison," New York Times, September 20, 2017, www.nytimes.com/2017/09/20/nyregion/prosecutors-want-anthony-weiner-to-serve-about-2-years-in-prison

[52]Jeremy B. White and Jim Miller, "Ride Service Ends For State Senators," *Sacramento Bee*, June 6, 2015, pg. 1A

[53]Ken Stone, Ex-Congressman Duncan Hunter Gets 11 Months in Prison for Spending Crimes, Times of San Diego, March 17, 2020 timesofsandiego.com/politics/2020/03/17/ex-congressman-duncan-hunter-gets-11-months-in-prison-for-spending-crimes/

CHAPTER 6

[1]Sam Stanton, Michael Doyle and Kevin Yamamura, "State Must Slash Prison Population", *Sacramento Bee,* May 24, 2011 pages A1 and A8

[2]Ibid.

[3]John L. Korey, *California Government*, (Wadsworth, 2009) pg. 91 From *The Federalist Papers*

[4]John L. Korey, *California Government*, (Wadsworth, 1999) pg. 98

[5]Jack C. Plano and Milton Greenberg, *The American Political Dictionary* (HBJ Publishers, 1993) pg. 247

[6]Brian P. Janiskee and Ken Masugi, *Democracy In California* (Rowman and Littlefield, 2011) pg. 86

[7]Brian P. Janiskee and Ken Masugi, *Democracy In California* (Rowman and Littlefield, 2015). Pg. 85

[8]Larry N. Gerston and Terry Christensen, *California Politics and Government* (Wadsworth, 2009) pg. 76

[9]Ibid., 79

[10]Maura Dolan, "What's the California Supreme Court thinking? One justice gives us a clue," LA Times, March 31, 2016, www.latimes.com/local/california/la-me-supreme-court-dissents-20160331-story

[11]California Courts Newsroom, "A Year in Review at the Supreme Court of California," November 10, 2016, newsroom.courts.ca.gov/news/supreme-court-year-in-review

[12]National Conference of State Legislatures, "Same-Sex Marriage, Civil Unions and Domestic Partnerships", www.ncsl.org/default.aspx. July 14, 2011

[13]Hannah Wiley, "Newsom appoints Jenkins to state Supreme Court," *Sacramento Bee*, October 6, 2020, pg. 1A

[14]Charles G. Bell and Charles M. Price, *California Government Today* (Brooks/Cole Publishing, 1992) pg. 265

[15]Ibid., 266

[16]Renee B. Van Vechten, *California Politics A Primer* (CQ Press, 2010) pg. 62

[17]National Conference of State Legislatures, "Same-Sex Marriage, Civil Unions and Domestic Partnerships", www.ncsl.org/default.aspx. July 14, 2011

[18]A Brief History of Civil Rights in the United States, Proposition 8, Georgetown Law Library, guides.ll.georgetwon.edu/c.php?g=592919&p=4182204

[19]Ibid.

[20]Jack C. Plano and Milton Greenberg, *The American Political Dictionary* (HBJ Publishers, 1993) pages 254–255

[21]Thomas E. Patterson, *We The People* (McGraw Hill, 2011) pg. 494

[22]Brigid Harrison and Jean Wahl Harris, *A More Perfect Union* (McGraw Hill, 2011) pg. 516

[23]Steffen W. Schmidt, Mack C. Shelley and Barbara A. Bardes, *American Government and Politics Today* (Wadsworth, 2001) pg. 488

[24]Library Of Congress, Federal Impeachment, Samuel B. Kent, guides.loc.gov/federal-impeachment/samuel-kent

[25]Census Of State And Local Law Enforcement Agencies, 2008, July, 2011, www.bjs.gov/content,pub/pdf/cslleq08.pdf;Census

[26]Rachel Treisman, Darnella Frazier, Teen Who Filmed Floyd's Murder, Praised For Making Verdict Possible, NPR, April 21, 2021 npr.org/sections/trial-over-killing-of-george-floyd-2021/04/21/989480867/darnella-frazier-teen-who-filmed-floyds-murder-praised-for-making-verdict-possible

[27]Diana Kendall, *Social Problems In A Diverse Society*, (Pearson, 2013), pg. 213

[28]www.nytimes.com/2014/12/21/nyregional/two-police-officers-shot-in-their-patrol-car-in-brooklyn.html

[29]NPR, Was Anything Accomplished By Racial Justice Protests In The Pacific-Northwest?, November 19, 2020 npr.org/2020/11/19/936567267/was-anything-accomplished-by-racial-justice-protests-in-pacific-northwest

[30]Ibid.,

[31]Christopher Mims, "What Happens When Police Officers Wear Body Cameras," *The Wall Street Journal*, Aug. 18, 2014, www.wsj.com/articles/what-happens-when-police-officers-wear-body-cameras

[32]Steve Zansberg, American Bar Association, Public Access to Police Body-Worn Camera Recordings (Status Report 2020), January 22, 2021 americanbar.org/groups/communications_law/publications/communication_lawyer/fall/2020/public-access-police-body-worn-camera-recordings-status-report-2020/

[33]Natasha Chen, Gregory Lemos and Eric Levenson, Attorney for Andrew Brown Jr.'s family says video of fatal police shooting shows 'execution,' CNN April 26, 2021 cnn.com/2021/04/26/us/Andrew-brown-elizabeth-city-shooting/inex.html

[34]Anita Chabria, "Capital's cop videos affecting morale," *Sacramento Bee*, May 19, 2017, pg. 1A

[35]Ibid., pg. 1A

[36]Tami Abdollah, "California DOJ Unveils Website With Law Enforcement Data," *Chico Enterprise Record*, September 3, 2015, pg. A3

[37]Michael Balsamo, "157 People Killed by Police in California in 2016," U.S. News And World Report, August 17, 2017, www.usnews.com/news/best-states/california/articles/2017-08-17/157-people-killed-by-police-in-california-in-2016

[38]Ibid.

[39]Laurel Rosenhall, California's attempt to reduce police shooting, explained, Cal Matters, July 18, 2019, calmatters.org/explainers/California-police-shootings-deadly-force-new-law-explained

[40]Lars T. Reed, "Governor Newsom Signs Police Use-of-Force Bill AB 392, California Public Agency Labor and Employment Blog,

August 19, 2019 calpublicagencylaboremploy-
mentblod.com/uncategorized/governor-new-
som-signs-police-use-of-force-bill-ab-392/
[41]Don Thompson, "Police groups back requiring college classes for recruits", *Chico Enterprise Record*, November 20, 2020 pg. 5A
[42]Ibid., pg. 5A
[43]Chandelis Duster, 'We compromise, we
die': Rep. Cori Bush says she won't support qualified immunity compromise in policing bill talks, CNN April 25, 2021, cnn.
com/2021/04/25/politics/qualified-immuni-
ty-police-reform-bill-bush-capito-cnntv/index.
html
[44]David M. Greenwald, "Governor Signs
Bills Banning Use Of Grand Juries In Police
Shooting And Allowing Citizen Recording Of
Police Officers," *The People's Vanguard Of
Davis*, August 12, 2015, www.davisvanguard.
ord/2015/08/governor-signs-bills-banning-
use-of-grand-juries-in-police-shootings-and-
allowing-citizen-recording-of-police-officers/
[45]Hannah Wiley, "California tax filers could
get jury duty under new bill", *Sacramento Bee*,
February 15, 2020 pg. 1A
[46]Sfpublicdefender.org
[47]Curtis Skinner, "ACLU Sues California
County Over Public Defender System," *Re-
uters*, July 15, 2015, www.reuters.com/arti-
cle/2015/07/15/us-usa-california-defender
[48]Governor's Budget Summary 2020/2021 E:/
SummaryCharts%202020-2021.pdf
[49]Judges can refuse to cut 'three strike' sentences, *Chico Enterprise Record*, July 5, 2017,
pg. 6A
[50]California radically revamping prison system,
San Francisco Chronicle, March 15, 2016,
www.sfchronicle.com/opinion/editorials/ar-
ticle/california-radically-revamping-prison-
system
[51]Magnus Lofstrom and Brandon Martin,
Crime Trends in California, Public Policy Institute of California, February 2021, ppic.org/
publication/crime-trends-in-california/

CHAPTER 7

[1]David G. Lawrence, *California The Politics of
Diversity* (Wadsworth, 2010) pg. 225
[2]Kevin Yamamura, "Governor's Budget Clears
A Hurdle", *Sacramento Bee,* January 15, 2013
pg. A3
[3]Dan Walters, "Growing retirement costs are
hitting new state budget hard," *Sacramento
Bee*, May 28, 2017, pg. 3A
4Rahhika Mehlotra and Patrick Murphy, Public Pensions in California, Public Policy Institute of California, March 2019 ppic.org/publi-
cation/public-pensions-in-california/
[5]Lawrence L. Giventer, *Governing California*,
(McGraw Hill, 2008), pg. 104
[6]Ibid., pg. 104
[7]Ibid., pg. 105
[8]David G. Lawrence, *California The Politics of
Diversity* (Wadsworth, 2010) pg. 205
[9]Kevin Yamamura, "Governor Gets Aggressive
Against State's Many Debts", *Sacramento Bee,*
May 23, 2011 pg. A4
[10]Dale Kasler, "Urban Renewal Plans In Jeop-
ardy", *Sacramento Bee*, June 30, 2011 pg. A14
[11]Robert Lewis "A Scramble To Save Projects",
Sacramento Bee, March 11, 2011 pg. A1
[12]Kevin Yamamura, "Court To Review Budget
Fix", *Sacramento Bee,* Aug. 12, 2011 pg. A3
[13]David G. Lawrence, *California The Politics
of Diversity* (Wadsworth, 2010) pg. 228
[14]Sophia Bollag, "State tax revenue surges
$14.3B above expectations, freeing money for
relief," *Sacramento Bee*, March 23, 2021, pg.
5A
[15]Melanie Mason and John Myers, "With a
deadline looming, there's a deal between Gov.
Jerry Brown and lawmakers on a new state
budget," *LA Times*, June 13, 2017, www.la-
times.com/politics/la-pol-sac-california-bud-
get-agreement
[16]Jim Miller, "Governors rarely leave budget
intact, *Sacramento Bee*, July 1, 2017, pg. 3B

[17]John R. Wood, *Taking Sides*, (McGraw Hill, 2011) pg. 13

[18]Josephine Djuhana, "Trailer Bills Seek To Expand CA Water Board Authority," June 17, 2014; CalWatchdog.org

[19]Bitter or sweet, trailer bills let California lawmakers slip new policies into the budget, Daily News, June 24, 2017, www.dailynews.com/2017/06/24/bitter-or-sweet--trailer-bills-let-california-lawmakers-slip-new-policies-into-budget

[20]Governor's Budget Summary – 2021-22 E:/Calif%20Budget%202021-2022.pdf

[21]Larry Mitchell, "Local Legislators Claim Strategic Victory Over Budget", *Chico Enterprise Record,* June 30, 2011 pg. 5C

[22]Katy Sweeny, "Sales Tax Decrease Friday Stalls June Car Sales", *Chico Enterprise Record, June* 30, 2011 pg. 5A

[23]Ramona Giwargis, "Higher sales tax on the horizon," *San Jose Mercury News*, January 1, 2017, pg. 1B

[24]Dan Walters, "Sales Tax Obsolete, Needs Fix," *Sacramento Bee*, May 24, 2015, pg. 3A

[25]Steve Westly, "Pandemic provides opportunity for state to reform tax system," *Sacramento Bee*, February 7, 2021

[26]Dale Kasler, "Amazon To Shift Online Tax Fight To The Ballot Box", *Sacramento Bee,* July 12, 2011 pg. A3

[27]Dale Kasler, "Brown, Dems Reach A Deal", *Sacramento Bee,* June 28, 2011 pg. A7

[28]Sophia Bollag, New California law requires Amazon to collect sales tax for small online retailers, The Sacramento Bee, April 25, 2019 sacbee.com/article229699444.html

[29]Kevin Yamamura, "Experts: GOP Won Tax Fight, Little Else", *Sacramento Bee,* July 6, 2011 pg. A1

[30]Sophia Bollag, "Newsom signs California COVID-19 stimulus bills," *Sacramento Bee*, February 24, 2021, pg. 1A

[31]David G. Lawrence, *California The Politics of Diversity* (Wadsworth, 2010) pg. 239

[32]Cynthia Hubert, "Poor Just Got Poorer", *Sacramento Bee,* July 1, 2011 pg. A1

[33]Sydney Kurle, Health proposals in Governor Newsom's 2021-22 budget, State of Reform, January 8, 2021, stateofreform.com/featured/2021/01/health-proposals-in-governor-newsom's-2021-22-budget/

[34]Sam Stanton, Michael Doyle, and Kevin Yamamura, "State Must Slash Prison Population", *Sacramento Bee,* May 24, 2011 pg. A1

[35]California Prison Closings Could Save More Than $1 Billion, KPBS, November 20, 2020, kpbs.org/news/2020/nov/20/California-prison-closings-could-save-1-billion/

[36]California Secretary of State, Voter Guide, November 2014, pg. 16

[37]Public Policy Institute of California, California's State Budget: The Enacted 2017-18 Budget, www.ppic.org/publications/california-state-budget

[38]Barb Rosewicz, Justin Theal, and Joe Fleming, COVID-19 Prompts States To Start Tapping Financial Reserves, PEW, October 13, 2020, pewtrusts.org/en/research-and-analysis/articles/2020/10/13/covid-19-prompts-states-to-start-tapping-financial-reserves

[39]Jack C. Plano and Milton Greenberg, *The American Political Dictionary* (HBJ Publishers, 1993) pg. 393

[40]Thomas Elias, "Trump's threat about defunding California an empty one," *Chico Enterprise Record*, February 15, 2017, pg. A5

[41]Ibid., pg. A5

[42]Lee Fang and Ali Winston, "Trump Threatens Funding for California Cops over 'Sanctuary State' Bill. Maybe That's a Good Thing," The Intercept, August 22, 2017, theintercept.com/2017/08/22/federal-funding-local-police-sanctuary-city-sb54-california

[43]Emily Hoeven, As California racks up huge surplus, billions set to flow in from feds, Cal Matters, March 8, 2021 calmatters.org/newsletters/whatmatters/2021/03/california-federal-stimulus-package/

[44]Joel Bellman, "Does Los Angeles County need more politicians?" *Sacramento Bee*, May 21, 2017, pg. 3D

[45]Mona Field, *California Government and Politics Today* (Longman, 2011) pg. 123

[46]David Pierson, "Facebook and Google pledged to stop fake news. So why did they promote Las Vegas-shooting hoaxes?" *LA*

Times, www.latimes.com/business/la-fi-tn-ve-
gas-faxk-news-20171002-story

[47]Shannon Bond, Facebook, Twitter, Google CEOs Testify Before Congress: 4
Things To Know, NPR, March 25, 2021 npr.
org/2021/03/25/980510388/facebook-twitter-
google-ceos-testify-before-congress-4-things-
to-know

[48]Ibid.

[49]Carolyn Jones, "Bill would help California
schools teach about fake news', media literacy,"
EdSource, May 24, 2017, edsource.org/2017/
bill-would-help-calfornia-schools-teach-about-
fake-news-media-literacy

[50]Ibid.